# PENSION PLANS AND EMPLOYEE PERFORMANCE

# Pension Plans and Employee Performance

EVIDENCE, ANALYSIS, AND POLICY

## Richard A. Ippolito

The University of Chicago Press
Chicago and London

Richard A. Ippolito is chief economist for the Pension Benefit Guaranty Corporation and was formerly director of the
Office of Policy and Research, Pension and Welfare Benefits
Programs of the U.S. Department of Labor. He is the author
of four books, including *Pensions, Economics, and Public
Policy* and *An Economic Appraisal of Pension Tax Policy in
the United States.*

The University of Chicago Press, Chicago 60637
The University of Chicago Press, Ltd., London
Published 1997
Printed in the United States of America

06 05 04 03 02 01 00 99 98 97    1 2 3 4 5

ISBN: 0-226-38455-1 (cloth)

Library of Congress Cataloging-in-Publication Data

Ippolito, Richard A.
    Pension plans and employee performance : evidence,
analysis, and policy / Richard A. Ippolito
        p.  cm.
    Includes bibliographical references and index.
    ISBN 0-226-38455-1
    1. Pension trusts—United States.  2. Labor productiv-
ity—United States.  3. Labor turnover—United States.
I. Title.
HD7105.45.U6I6153     1997
658.3'253—dc21                              97-16796
                                               CIP

♾ The paper used in this publication meets the minimum
requirements of the American National Standard for Information Sciences—Permanence of Paper for Printed Library
Materials, ANSI Z39.48-1984.

*For my great-aunt Rose, with deep appreciation*
ROSE WILLETTE, 1893–1995

# CONTENTS

# FIGURES

# TABLES

# *Part One*

## PENSION EFFECTS ON WORKER BEHAVIOR

## CHAPTER ONE

# Developments in the Market for Private Pensions

Pensions are an important source of private savings and retirement income in the United States. From their inception, however, pensions have been intertwined with firms. Individuals typically do not save most of their retirement income on their own; they participate in pension plans offered by their employers. Although this situation is partly explained by the tax preferences made available through firm-offered pensions, firms offered pensions before taxes became important during World War II. By 1933, private pensions covered roughly one in six workers in the economy.[1] Employers' acting as intervening agents for pension savings creates the possibility that the pension, in addition to providing retirement income, can be used by the firm to enhance labor productivity.

The role of pensions in enhancing productivity is the subject of much study, and it is the main focus of this book. I do not assess the effect of pensions on productivity by direct measurement; I approach it indirectly based on pensions' ability to influence the type of worker attracted to the job and to shape behavior while on the job. In part 1, I focus on the traditional view that pensions help employers reduce quit rates at early ages and increase retirement rates at later ages. In this view, the productive effects of pensions are exclusive to defined benefit plans. The emphasis is on the power of these plans to influence workers' behavior on the job.

In part 2 I consider a less traditional, but perhaps equally important view—that pensions sort workers based on characteristics desirable to the firm. The focus is not on pensions' ability to influence behavior, but on their ability to attract workers who have desirable behavior patterns. In this view, pensions help the firm select a high-quality workforce, motivate the best workers to stay, and encourage the worst to leave. Notably, the discussion reaches beyond the traditional notion that productivity

3

effects are exclusive to defined benefit plans. I show how 401k plans help the firm select and pay its best workers and explain how they compete with defined benefit plans to reduce quit rates in the firm. In the current chapter, I introduce some themes for the ensuing chapters in the book.

## 1.1 THE IMPLICIT PENSION CONTRACT

I start with a selected review of the professional pension literature that develops the implicit pension contract (chapter 2). The implicit pension contract theory explains why and how defined benefit plans help the firm control the composition and productivity of its workforce.

In the middle 1980s, the development of the theory represented the forefront of economic research in pensions. Now the treatment of defined benefit pension plans as implicit contracts is standard in the literature.[2] The first part of the book presents ideas and empirical work substantiating the hypothesis that defined benefit plans exert an important influence on quitting and retirement behavior and, like other deferred wages, dissuade workers from shirking or engaging in malfeasance on the job. The theory can explain, for example, why federal employees seemingly never quit (chapter 4) and why retirement ages in the economy decreased markedly after 1970 (chapter 6).

The appeal of pensions compared with other deferred wages is partly attributable to the tax advantages afforded pensions.[3] It also is attributable to the flexibility inherent in defined benefit pension formulas. In chapter 3 I show the dominant effect of pensions over "wage tilt" in affecting tenure in the firm. In chapter 5 I illustrate the wide range of incentives that can be erected by writing different provisions into the retirement formulas in defined benefit pensions. And in chapter 6 I show how the federal government has used its pension to encourage the voluntary retirement of virtually all of its older workers within a few years of their eligibility for retirement benefits.

## 1.2 THE EMERGENCE OF DEFINED CONTRIBUTION PLANS

The most important development in private pensions in the past fifteen years is the gradual shift away from defined benefit plans and toward defined contribution plans. In 1979, among workers covered by a pension plan, approximately 83 percent were primarily covered by a defined benefit plan. By 1996 this share was about 50 percent. This development has spawned a series of empirical studies to explain the trend. Defined benefit plans still dominate coverage in large firms, but among small and medium-sized firms (particularly those with fewer than one thousand employees), defined contribution plans have acquired a large market share.

In chapter 7 I show that about half of the change in defined benefit market share is attributable to the shift in employment from large, union-ized firms in the manufacturing sector—where defined benefit plans have been used most intensively—to nonunion jobs in smaller firms in ser-vice industries—where defined contribution plans traditionally dom-inate. Even after employment shifts are netted out, however, the data reveal a marked change in preferences toward defined contribution plans. The reasons for this change have been the focus of considerable debate.

### 1.2.1 Regulatory Cost and Tax Policy

One hypothesis revolves around increasing regulatory cost. During the 1980s, legislation was enacted raising the administrative costs of defined benefit plans. The data show that for large firms, the increases is administrative costs of operating a defined benefit plan during the 1980s com-pared with a 401k plan were small and thus are unlikely to have signifi-cantly influenced the choice of pension plan type. But for small plans (particularly those with fewer than one hundred employees), the regula-tory cost increases were large and could perhaps explain a substantial shift within these firms.

Tax policy also changed. Various legislative changes occurred at that time that significantly reduced the tax advantages of pensions, particu-larly defined benefit plans. In chapter 12 I show that the enactment of a new full funding limit in 1987 had a large and pervasive effect on the tax benefits of defined benefit plans that may have importantly affected the probability of choosing defined benefit coverage. But the trend toward defined contribution plans already was under way before 1987, sug-gesting that other factors also influenced the shift. One likely candidate is the introduction of 401k plans.

### 1.2.2 Introduction of 401k Plans

Legislation establishing 401k plans was enacted in 1978 and became ef-fective in 1981.[4] Arguably, 401k plans are superior to ordinary defined contribution plans. Like traditional defined contribution plans, the 401k permits an unconditional employer contribution (say, 5 percent of pay or profits) to all employees. Beyond this feature, however, 401k plans have unique characteristics. First, workers can make voluntary pretax contributions to a 401k plan, affording them more freedom to attain desired savings rates beyond the employer's contribution. Second, the firm can match workers' contributions.

In some sense the growth of 401k plans contradicts the increasing-cost hypothesis. Compared with a straightforward money purchase or profit sharing defined contribution plan, the 401k plan is more costly to administer because the voluntary contribution rates must be monitored to ensure compliance with Internal Revenue Code discrimination requirements. These laws, in some cases, restrict contributions to higher-paid workers.[5] But the introduction of a good substitute for both defined contribution and defined benefit plans, *together* with increasing tax and regulatory costs, may explain the reduction in defined benefit plan market share over the period.

The emergence of defined contribution plans—and 401k plans in particular—as prominent forms begins to question the adequacy of the implicit contract theory of pensions. If defined benefit plans are so successful in enhancing firm productivity, why have other types of pensions increased their market share with such apparent ease? To begin to answer this question, I devote two chapters to a reformulation of existing pension theory.

In chapter 8 I develop a more general model of the implicit pension contract. The new model relaxes the assumption that workers accept long-term deferred wage contracts for free. In reality, workers sacrifice some of their economic freedom in exchange for employment with a large pension payoff contingent on not quitting. To offset this cost, the firm must pay a wage increment to these workers, which I call the "indenture premium." These problems explain many characteristics of the labor market that are inexplicable in a more simplified version of the implicit contract theory.

The theory also gives prominence to the sorting effects of pensions: workers least likely to have alternative wage offers arise in midcareer are attracted to defined benefit plans; those most likely to have other offers are attracted to defined contribution plans.

In chapters 9 and 10 I develop a model in which sorting effects of pensions play an important role in the firm. I consider workers with characteristics likely to be affiliated with high-quality workers and show how pension plans of all types, particularly defined contribution plans, can effectively select workers based on productivity characteristics. When the matching feature is added, 401k plans help align wages to productivity and encourage long tenure of the firm's best workers. Within the new framework, a viable hypothesis emerges to explain why the introduction of 401k plans, together with increasing regulatory, administrative, and tax costs, reduced the market share of defined benefit plans.

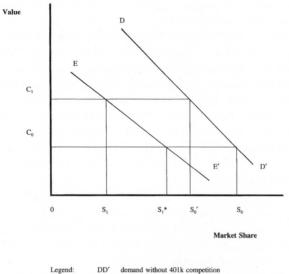

**Figure 1.1** The market for defined benefit plans.

## 1.3 IMPACT OF 401K PLANS ON DEMAND FOR DEFINED BENEFIT PLANS

The introduction of 401k plans had two effects on the demand for defined benefit plans. First, it reduced the demand. Second, it made the demand more sensitive to price. The higher price elasticity reflects the existence of viable substitutes, namely 401k plans, making defined benefit plans more vulnerable to increases in their operational costs.

Figure 1.1 demonstrates this point. We can think of the demand curve for defined benefit plans before 401k plans as the schedule labeled $DD'$. The introduction of a substitutable 401k plans shifts the demand curve to a schedule like $EE'$. The introduction of 401k plans reduces the market share of defined benefit plans from $S_0$ to $S_1^*$. But in addition to introducing a competing product, Congress enacted legislation that increased the relative cost of using defined benefit plans, in terms of both higher regulatory burden and smaller tax advantages. These cost increases are measured by the difference between $C_0$ and $C_1$ in the figure.

Had 401k plans not been introduced, the cost increases would have had a small effect on the share of defined benefit plans—see the distance between $S_0$ and $S_0'$ in the figure. But in the face of new competition, the increase in cost caused a substantial reduction in market share—measured by the distance between $S_1^*$ and $S_1$. In short, the interaction of the regulatory and tax changes *and* the availability of better substitutes combined to exert a strong reduction in market share for defined benefit plans (the difference between $S_0$ and $S_1$ in the figure).

## 1.4 INTERNAL DISCOUNT RATES AND PENSIONS

One recurring theme in the book is the role played by workers' subjective discount rates—parameters that quantify the value workers attach to future considerations compared with immediate gratification. Pensions defer compensation to some future period, perhaps twenty or thirty years in the future in the case of defined benefit plans, so the issue of discounting is important. Yet most pension literature assumes that all workers discount future benefits at the market interest rate. This characterization is perhaps appropriate for low discounters—those who attach approximately equal value to future and present consumption (apart from the normal discounting to account for the time value of money). But "high discounters"—those who attach disproportionate value to current consumption—tend to discount pensions heavily in comparison with cash wages.

Some applications of this idea are obvious. For example, pensions ought to attract low discounters and discourage high discounters from entering the firm. But as I show in chapter 9, some high discounters are bound to enter pension firms, despite the emphasis on deferred wages. In this case the calculus the firm depends on to reduce quits and encourage retirement depends on which workers are making the calculations. It is predictable, for example, that high discounters will perceive lower capital losses from quitting than low discounters and thus are more likely to impose quitting costs on the firm. They also will view the incentives to retire early more favorably than low discounters, which may affect the firm's choice of pension formula.

I also explore the idea that high and low discounters differ not only in the way they perceive pensions, but also in how they approach their responsibilities on the job. I explore the hypothesis that high discounters are lower-quality workers than low discounters. I alluded above to one possible reason for this distinction—that high discounters are more likely to impose quitting cost on a firm that prefers long-tenure workers. But the role of discount rates on productivity is fundamental.

High discounters tend to ignore the future implications of their current performance and therefore attach less value to future promotions resulting from good work (and may not heed admonitions about poor work). They may be likely to take more sick leave or other unscheduled time off (chapter 11). If high discounters are poorer-quality workers than low discounters, the role of pensions takes on additional significance for the firm.

The existence of differences in worker qualities creates a value of sorting based on desirable work characteristics. If internal discount rates are important, pensions can perform important functions for the firm by either encouraging high discounters to leave the firm early or aligning their pay and productivity *without* the firm's engaging in costly monitoring. I pursue the sorting issues in chapters 8 and 9 in particular, but I allude to them throughout the book.

Finally, I take into account the implications of discount rates for public retirement policy. High discounters create problems for a national retirement policy that depends on workers to save for their retirement. If high discounters ignore their retirement consumption, it sets up a conundrum for low discounters: Do they assume responsibility for high discounters who become old and impoverished? If so, what are the long-term implications for the economy's savings rate and consumption rate during retirement for low and high discounters? I show that much of the nation's pension policy, and especially its social security policy, is designed to reward workers who are inclined to neither work nor save, thereby encouraging a long-term deterioration of incentives to be industrious and parsimonious.

## CHAPTER TWO

# Defined Benefit Plans
# as Implicit Contracts

A defined benefit pension is a contract, albeit an implicit and conditional one. Workers forgo wages in exchange for a pension. Numerous studies report evidence consistent with the idea that firms effectively return these forgone wages (plus interest), conditional on the worker's retiring during a preannounced age window.[1] If the worker leaves the firm "too early" or "too late," a portion of pension wealth is forfeited. In other words, in addition to providing a tax-preferred vehicle to save for retirement, a pension can be, and apparently is, used by the firm to enforce a long-term implicit contract with workers. This model explains substantial portions of observed mobility and retirement patterns in the United States and is the genesis for the concept of "economic" pension liabilities.[2]

It is important to clarify at the outset that unless otherwise stated, references to "pensions" in the first six chapters of this book are to the defined benefit variety. These plans promise an annuity starting at retirement, usually in proportion to service level and final wages.[3] Workers do not own pension assets as such; instead, they own the rights to a pension annuity in exchange for a lower cash wage. Although the trend has been away from defined benefit plans, they still are the primary plans for about half of covered workers in the private sector[4] and still dominate coverage in large firms in the United States (chapter 9).

## 2.1 PENSIONS AND RETIREMENT BEHAVIOR

Although pensions have existed for over one hundred years, their widespread use is primarily a post–World War II practice. Although the basic tax rules toward pensions were established in 1926, they became important when marginal income tax rates increased sharply during the 1940s. Pensions became more common during the next decade, though they did not represent significant accumulated assets and liabilities until the 1960s.[5] In this sense most pension literature is relatively new.[6] Nevertheless, it is useful to separate the literature into "old" and "new" components.

The "old" pension economics literature views pensions as savings devices. The important issues are the effect of pensions on savings rates[7] and the optimal asset allocation in pensions.[8] The "new" economics portrays pensions as labor contracts that can importantly affect productivity in the firm. The way pension wealth changes with age becomes the dominant factor in explaining retirement decisions, superseding the concept of the wage replacement rate. The concepts of "stay pensions," "quit pensions," and "pension capital losses" are introduced. Economic significance is attached to the notion of leaving the firm "too early" or "too late." And the actuarial terminology of accrued pension liabilities is replaced by a concept of "economic pension liabilities," reflecting the true nature of the economic pension contract.

The genesis of the implicit pension contract can be found in various forms in the early labor, contract, and finance literatures, but its formal development begins with Richard Burkhauser.[9] His study demonstrates that pensions are providing an economic function beyond transferring earnings from work years to retirement years. Other research had implicated pensions in the retirement decision,[10] but the rationale for this relationship went unexplored. Burkhauser redefines the central pension variable from the flow of pension benefits to the present value of pension benefits (pension wealth) and demonstrates that this variable is not independent of retirement age.

Burkhauser shows that pension wealth over a range of potential retirement ages for workers in the automobile industry forms a hill-like function. There are particular retirement ages where pension wealth is at a maximum. Retirement at other ages, especially late ages, triggers pension penalties. A pension penalty is defined as a reduction in the present value of the pension annuity from working an additional year. Subsequent research verifies the dependence of pension wealth on retirement age in other pension plans, and various statistical studies implicate the age dependent changes in pension wealth in the retirement decision.[11]

The role played by age related changes in pension wealth on retirement can be clarified by a simple example. Suppose the worker starts with the firm at age zero and the pension annuity is proportional to service level at retirement age $R$ and final wage $W_R$. The inflation rate, the real interest rate, and wage growth are zero. I also assume that the worker's subjective discount rate is zero. At the plan's "normal"[12] retirement age $R$, the lump sum value of the pension is

$$P_R = bRW_R(D - R), \tag{2.1}$$

where $D$ is the (assumed certain) age of death and $b$ is the generosity factor in the pension plan, and thus $bRW_R$ is the annuity collected during $D - R$ retirement years.

Virtually all firms penalize late retirement through the pension plan. They do this not by reducing the nominal pension annuity (this is not permitted by the 1974 Employee Retirement Income Security Act, ERISA), but by refraining from awarding offsetting increases in annuities to workers who choose to retire beyond the normal retirement age. For example, consider a simple case where the firm freezes the pension after the worker attains thirty years of service.[13] And suppose a worker with this level of service is eligible for normal retirement. If he chooses to work an extra year, he forgoes his pension annuity. In effect, the firm's cost for the worker's marginal year of employment is lower, because it pays the worker's wage but saves the amount of the pension annuity.[14]

The forgone penalty from retiring too late acts just like a tax on wages. Since the pension generosity parameter in the typical plan is approximately 1 percent, then if normal retirement in the model comes after thirty years of service, the pension penalty imposed by the firm in this example for retiring one year "late" is 30 percent.[15]

If postponing retirement results in a higher pension annuity, the penalty for continuing to work is diminished. In general, however, as long as the firm denies fair economic adjustments to workers after normal retirement age, the pension rules exert a penalty on late retirement.[16] By choosing different accrual rules, firms can exert an important influence on the ages at which workers retire.

There usually is not just one age at which workers can retire without incurring a penalty. Typically there is a range of ages over which they can leave without absorbing a notable pension loss. I discuss the economic aspects of this range in more detail in chapters 4 and 5. In general, however, if normal retirement age in the pension plan is $R$, then the firm may permit early retirement at age $E$. During the age interval $[E,R]$, the firm often adjusts the pension in a more or less economically fair way, thereby eliminating important pension penalties during these ages, though the adjustments also vary across pension plans.[17]

Taken as a whole, the "new" pension literature suggests that an implicit agreement is made between workers and firms: that the present value of pension savings (forgone wages) is returned *conditional* on the workers' retiring at particular ages. Workers who retire "too late" break the contract and forfeit a portion of their pension savings.

## 2.2 LEAVING THE FIRM TOO EARLY

If the pension penalizes workers who break the long-term contract by retiring "too late," the question arises whether it penalizes workers who retire "too early." That is to say, if pensions are used to control retirement behavior, perhaps they also are used to control quit behavior. The quit literature has developed in much the same way as the retirement literature. It has long been known that pensions are affiliated with lower worker mobility,[18] but the rationale for this relation was not well understood until recently.

A paper by Jeremy Bulow[19] was the catalyst for developments in this area.[20] Bulow recognizes the constraint implied by the compensating wage principle: pension liabilities must equal the sum of wages that workers sacrifice in exchange for a pension at retirement. If these savings (forgone wages) can be estimated, a way of calculating economic pension liabilities emerges, one that is consistent with labor market equilibrium. Bulow links the financial and labor markets by explicitly recognizing the constraint that workers must pay for their pensions.

Bulow posits a special version of labor market equilibrium. His hypothesis is simply stated: The firm can terminate the pension plan at any time. Upon termination, the firm legally is required to pay "termination" pensions. In his view, rational workers do not forgo wages in excess of the termination value of the pension.

This hypothesis, which recurs as a theme throughout much published work, is important for two reasons. First, in this model, economic pension liabilities (the sum of forgone wages) approximate pension liabilities as calculated by accountants,[21] and thus Bulow vindicates accounting reporting practices. Second, the model contradicts the notion that pensions affect worker turnover. The model conforms to a "spot" labor market: workers invest no more in the firm than they can take out if they leave. Thus there is no penalty imposed by quitting or being fired.

The alternative theory is that workers and firms agree to a long-term implicit contract. In this contract, workers and the firm effectively agree that unless unusual market exigencies arise, the firm will not exercise its legal right to terminate the pension plan. Workers forgo wages for the pension assuming that they stay with the firm until retirement; and the firm does not terminate the pension except for compelling reasons.

A central feature of this model is that workers contribute more for the pension than they receive if they quit midstream. Similarly, workers do not receive the sum of forgone wages plus interest in the form of a pension if they retire later than the preannounced normal retirement age. Put simply, in the implicit pension contract theory, early and normal retirement ages bound the set of retirement ages during which the full value of workers' pension contributions is returned.

## 2.3 A THEORY OF PENSIONS AND MOBILITY

I now formalize these ideas in a simple labor market model.[22] Consider a worker who begins working at the firm at age zero. This notation permits me to denote age and service by a single variable, say $a$. Thus the worker retires at age and service level $R$. Assume the normal retirement age in the pension is $R$; for simplicity, assume there is no early retirement age. Upon retirement, the worker is entitled to an annuity whose lump sum value $P$ equals some constant $b$, times service $R$, times wage $W_R$ at retirement:

$$P = bRW_R. \tag{2.2}$$

Suppose a worker of age and service level $a$ has a zero chance of dying before retirement, and the firm has a zero chance of failing or otherwise terminating the plan. If the worker also views the chance of quitting or being fired before retirement as zero, the present value of his pension based on $a$ years of service rendered to date is

$$P_a = baW_R e^{-i(R-a)}, \tag{2.3}$$

where $i$ is the nominal interest rate. Assume that the nominal wage is expected to grow at the rate $g$, and, for simplicity, assume that expected wage growth equals the nominal interest rate ($g = i$). Then the pension value expression in (2.3) can be rewritten as a proportional function of current wage and service:

$$P_a = baW_a. \tag{2.4}$$

Consider the value of the pension if the worker quits the firm at age and service level $a$. Without consequence, I assume that the worker vests in the pension upon joining the firm. A vested quit is entitled to a pension at retirement age $R$ that is fixed in current dollars at age $a$; that is, upon quitting, the wage in the pension formula is frozen at the nominal level prevailing at the time the worker quits. The present value of this pension is

$$P_a^* = baW_a e^{-i(R-a)}. \tag{2.5}$$

Expression (2.5) is similar to (2.4) except for a discounting term. The discounting term reflects the reality that the right to a wage indexed pension otherwise available upon successful completion of the contract is forfeited upon premature quitting, and therefore wage growth does not "offset" the discount effect.

I call $P_a^*$ the *quit pension*. I call $P_a$ the *stay pension*. The quit and stay pensions are related in the following way:

$$P_a^* = P_a e^{-i(R-a)}. \tag{2.6}$$

The difference in these pension values can be large. For example, suppose the nominal interest rate $i$ is 10 percent. In this case, a worker ten years from retirement is entitled to a quit pension that is only about one-third of the stay pension. The difference in pension values is not attributable to years of service—both are calculated based on $a$ years of service rendered to date—but solely to the difference between indexed and unindexed wages in the formula.

Thus far I have merely developed a mechanical relation between quit and stay pensions, not a theory of pensions and mobility. Economic content is introduced by specifying the amount of wages sacrificed in exchange for the pension. That is, firms do not award pensions gratis: workers must pay for them through forgone wages.[23]

The particular way these payments of sorts occur over the tenure cycle has important economic implications. If workers forgo wages in excess of the value of the pension they receive upon departure, a pension loss is absorbed upon quitting, and hence we have a theory of pensions and mobility.

### 2.3.1 The Implicit Contract Theory

Suppose the firm and the worker have a long-term implicit contract that the worker will not quit before age $R$. As a part of this agreement, the firm requires the worker of age and service level $a$ to deposit the amount $P_a$ through forgone wages during the tenure interval $[0,a]$. That is, the firm requires the worker to pay for a stay pension. In this model there is a large cost of quitting a pension firm, and hence pensions deter mobility.

To convey the essence of the pension bond without introducing cumbersome mathematics, assume that each worker has one chance to quit the firm. If he decides to stay, he stays until retirement. This assumption overstates the capital loss from quitting but not in an important way.[24] If forgone wages equal the stay pension $P_a$, the pension capital loss from quitting is the difference between the stay and quit values of the pension:

$$CL_a = P_a - P_a^*. \tag{2.7}$$

### 2.3.2 The Spot Pension Model

Suppose alternatively that the worker has no implicit agreement to stay with the firm over the long run—that the firm and worker realize the other party may terminate the contract at any time (the worker may quit or the firm may terminate the plan or lay off the worker). In this model, the worker does not forgo wages in excess of the "quit pension." He forgoes wages in the amount $P_a^*$ as of age and service level $a$, exactly the amount he receives if he quits. There is no implicit contract, and therefore no pension loss for quitting: pensions do not deter mobility.

## 2.4 EVIDENCE SUPPORTING THE IMPLICIT CONTRACT MODEL

The economic theory linking pensions and mobility is testable. First, implicit pension savings rates can be estimated. In this way it can be determined whether firms require workers to pay for "stay pensions" or "quit pensions." The implicit pension savings rate is found by differentiating expressions (2.4) and (2.5) with respect to service and netting out interest payments. If pension wealth is $P$ (see expression 2.4), the savings rate is a constant $b$; if pension wealth is $P^*$ (see expression 2.5), the savings rate increases with tenure.[25]

Evaluation of data describing wage histories for workers with or without pensions, and pension-covered workers with different pension generosity factors, supports the constant savings rate hypothesis.[26] These results are consistent with the notion that workers pay for stay pensions, and hence they are consistent with the theory that pension impose penalties on workers who quit.

Second, pensions can be related empirically to quit rates. If the pension is an implicit contract, workers forgo wages in the amount $P_a$ even though they receive $P_a^*$ if they quit. Pensions reduce quit rates because workers absorb a pension capital loss. If the pension is not a long-term implicit contract, workers forgo wages in the amount $P_a^*$, which is exactly what they receive if they leave: pensions do not reduce quit rates. The evidence supports the hypothesis that pensions reduce quit rates, which is consistent with the notion that pensions are implicit contracts.[27]

Other data are consistent with the implicit pension contract theory. For example, though not legally required to do so, many firms adjust postretirement benefits to partly offset some portion of inflation. In 1978, workers who retired with a pension in 1968 were collecting pensions that had lost only 20 percent of their original purchasing power, despite inflation in excess of 100 percent over the period.[28] In addition, as a part of the pension package, retirees typically receive supplemental health insurance policies during retirement. Since the costs of these policies have been increasing faster than the rate of inflation, it is likely that postretirement adjustment of the total pension-plus-health benefits is understated by measuring pension benefits alone.[29]

## 2.5 CONCLUDING REMARKS

Developments in the pension literature generally are consistent with a concise model of the labor contract. Workers and the firm implicitly agree that workers will pay for a real pension, one indexed to the final wage. Departure from the firm either "too early" or "too late" breaks the contract and triggers pension penalties. The pension bonds the worker's promise to stay with the firm and hence tends to attract those who anticipate staying for the long term.[30]

This theory explains why pensions are affiliated with lower quit rates and "on time" retirement. It also challenges a prevailing notion: that firms rely on "twisting" the wage profile to control workers' tenure in the firm. Pensions can work just as well and confer large tax advantages.[31] In fact, in the next chapter I show empirically that the pension mechanism is a better predictor of labor mobility than wage tilt.

More generally, the implicit contract theory is the basis for the productivity theory of pensions. By establishing a policy that returns workers' implicit pension contributions *conditional* on their fulfilling certain tenure, the firm has a tool to influence the tenure and retirement decisions of its workforce. The next several chapters describe how this tool is used by employers and how pensions influence tenure patterns in the firm and the economy.

CHAPTER THREE

# Impact of Pensions on Quit Rates

In this chapter I address the role of pensions in encouraging long tenure in the firm. I consider a firm that wants to encourage long tenure because it invests resources in training workers, or incurs substantial hiring costs, or experiences adverse effects on productivity when workers quit because production depends on teamwork, and so on. Since indenture contracts are illegal, the firm must find alternative methods to reduce the likelihood that workers will quit prematurely. This leads naturally to a search of market solutions that discourage quitting in the firm.

## 3.1 THE CONVENTIONAL SOLUTION TO REDUCING QUITS: WAGE TILT

The conventional solution often suggested in the literature is for the firm to "tilt" the wage over tenure: pay below-market wages during workers' early years with the firm and above-market wages later on. This idea is usually affiliated with models of firm-specific investment in human capital. The firm makes investments in workers that make them more productive in the firm (but that may have no carryover value to other firms) and wants to provide an incentive for workers to stay so that the value of the investment can be recouped.[1]

The idea of "twisting" the wage profile to favor older workers has been borrowed by other theories not necessarily involving specific human capital. For example, if a firm wants to use a production function that is efficient only if workers commit to the firm for the long run, the firm can artificially tilt the wage profile to attract "stayers."[2] Or the tilt can be used to dissuade workers from shirking on the job.[3] In either case, workers have incentives to refrain from quitting (and to avoid being fired) for fear of losing the opportunity to earn higher wages during older ages.

18

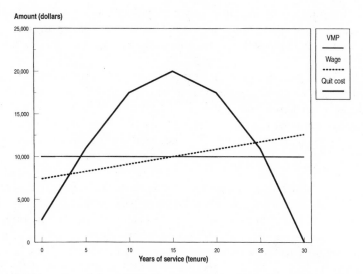

**Figure 3.1** Wage tilt and the incentive to quit. VMP is the value of marginal product.

### 3.1.1 How Wage Tilt Works

In essence, wage tilt creates a performance bond. The worker posts a bond early in the career and gradually recovers its value as he approaches retirement age. The average wage is not necessarily changed, just its distribution over the career.[4]

The magnitude and character of the quit losses imposed by wage tilt over the tenure cycle are depicted in figure 3.1. In the example, the real rate of interest is zero and the opportunity wage is $10,000 in real terms per year. The firm deliberately twists the wage-tenure profile to pay a $7,350 wage in the first year of tenure and $12,650 in real terms in the thirtieth year. This wage schedule is denoted by the dotted line in the figure.

Consider the quit cost in this compensation scheme (denoted by the bold hill-like schedule in the figure). During the first year of tenure, the worker receives a wage of $2,650 less than his alternative wage. Upon quitting, he loses the opportunity to retrieve this amount in the form of a higher wage later in tenure. The quit cost is therefore $2,650, or one-third the cash wage. At midcareer, accumulated worker deposits from "too low" wages amount to $20,000, two times the wage rate.[5] The too-low wages early in the career gradually are offset by higher wages until the entire investment is recouped in year thirty.

Although the wage-tenure profile can be measured, we cannot know a priori its economic content. For example, the wage-tenure profile depicted in figure 3.1 could simply reflect growth in general skill level gained from experience. Thus, while we may observe wages increasing with tenure, it does not tell us whether wages are increasing owing to a deliberate wage tilt.

The only way to distinguish wage tilt is through empirical test. If measured wage tilt mostly reflects the accumulation of general skills, there ought to be no statistically significant relation between wage tilt and quit rates. If an important part of observed wage tilt reflects a deliberate twisting of the wage, quit rates ought to be negatively related to wage tilt.

### 3.1.2 Problems with Wage Tilt

There are at least two problems with the wage tilt idea. First, recent studies have shown that once selection bias has been corrected, wage growth over tenure may be much smaller than previously thought.[6] Second, the same quit losses can be imposed more efficiently using a defined benefit pension plan. These pensions essentially are performance bonds, just like wage tilt, except that they have more favorable tax status. If the firm substitutes a pension for a portion of the cash wage and returns the full value of these "deposits" only if separation occurs at normal retirement ages, the firm can deter workers from quitting *and* substantially reduce workers' tax liabilities.

The tax consequences of wage tilt are unfavorable compared with those of pensions. In the wage tilt scheme, the firm may aggravate the impact of the progressive income tax by shifting taxable income from lower tax rate years early in the work life to perhaps higher tax rate years later. Pensions shift taxable income from higher tax rate work years to perhaps lower tax rate retirement years. Moreover, in the wage tilt scheme, the firm accumulates deferred wages at an after-tax rate of return. The pension trust fund is tax exempt.[7]

In addition, in the wage tilt model, the firm must find a way to close out the contract. If the firm pays "too much" during later tenure years, it must lay off older workers or reduce their wages, or try to effect a de facto mandatory retirement policy.[8] These policies, however, leave the firm vulnerable to suits under the aegis of age discrimination.[9]

The pension vehicle requires no special provisions to "close out" the long-term contract. The firm sets the retirement age in the pension plan (it could be, and often is, age 55 or 60 or 62). If the firm wishes to encourage retirement, it can do so by making the pension economically unfair, say, beyond age 65.[10] The firm can set the pension to maintain its economic value within some range of ages, allowing the worker some freedom to choose when to retire after fulfilling the contract.[11]

The relation between pensions and lower quit rates has long been known in the empirical literature.[12] Labor market models, however, are

Table 3.1 Illustrative Pension Quit Costs

| | | Divided by annual wage | | | |
|---|---|---|---|---|---|
| Age | Service | i = 10% g = 8% | i = 10% g = 10% | i = 10% g = 12% | i = 5% g = 5% |
| 35 | 0 | 0.00 | 0.00 | 0.00 | 0.00 |
| 40 | 5 | 0.39 | 0.68 | 1.15 | 0.52 |
| 45 | 10 | 0.79 | 1.27 | 1.99 | 0.95 |
| 50 | 15 | 1.15 | 1.74 | 2.52 | 1.18 |
| 55 | 20 | 1.35 | 1.89 | 2.55 | 1.17 |
| 60 | 25 | 1.11 | 1.47 | 1.85 | 0.82 |
| 65 | 30 | 0.00 | 0.00 | 0.00 | 0.00 |

*Note:* The variable *i* is the long-term nominal interest rate, and *g* is the expected growth rate in nominal wages. Pension quit costs are illustrated in chapter 2.

dominated by the wage tilt hypothesis. The implicit pension contract model challenges the presumption that wage tilt plays an important role in long-term contracts in the labor market and highlights the paucity of empirical evidence in support of the wage tilt notion. Despite a long history in the theoretical literature, there are few, if any, direct tests of the wage tilt hypothesis.

## 3.2 PENSION CAPITAL LOSSES

Recall from chapter 2 that the pension capital loss from quitting is the difference between the "stay" pension and the "quit" pension. Table 3.1 presents some calculations of these losses (as a multiple of the wage) assuming that the worker starts work at age 35 and retires at age 65. The pension generosity parameter is set so that the lump sum value of the pension benefits equals 15 percent of the final wage times years of tenure at retirement. In the first three columns, the interest rate is set to 10 percent and wage growth to 8, 10, and 12 percent. In the last column the interest and wage rates are 5 percent. The real interest rate and real wage growth are assumed to be zero.

At the 5 percent interest and wage growth rates, the maximum quit cost amounts to 1.18 times the annual wage. At the 10 percent interest rate, the cost is as high as 2.55 times the annual wage when the expected wage growth rate is 12 percent per year and 1.35 when expected wage growth is 8 percent.

Figure 3.2 shows the quit loss function when nominal wage growth and the nominal interest rate are 12 percent. The linear schedule depicts the value of the stay pension; the nonlinear dotted-line schedule depicts the quit pension. The difference in these amounts is the pension capital loss, depicted by the bold hill-like schedule.

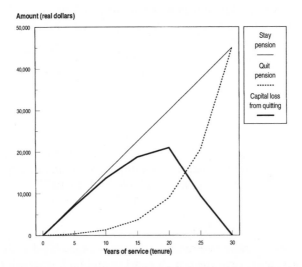

**Figure 3.2** Pension quit costs. Depicts a defined benefit plan that awards a lump sum benefit at retirement equal to .15 times wage, times service at retirement. The real wage is $10,000, and the nominal interest rate and nominal wage growth rates are both 12 percent.

Early in the career, a large portion of pension wealth is lost owing to many years of discounting between current age and retirement age. As tenure increases, the discounting effect is reduced, thus working to reduce the quit cost, but the amount of pension wealth increases, thereby working in the opposite direction. This tension produces a hill-like loss function with maximum losses occurring about midstream in the tenure cycle.

If either pensions or wage tilts deter quits, they must also deter layoffs. If the firm requires workers to pay for stay pensions, the firm itself could impose large penalties on high-tenure workers through a permanent layoff (layoffs entail payment of quit pensions). Presumably, the firm's part of the implicit pension contract is to refrain from laying off workers who stand to lose most in real pension benefits. When I refer to quits, therefore, I include permanent layoffs.[13]

## 3.3 AN EMPIRICAL MODEL OF LONG TENURE

### 3.3.1 Description of Data

In this section I test the hypothesis that wage tilt and pensions are important in affecting workers' propensity to stay with the firm.[14] The test requires data that divulge information about pensions and wage tilt. One database that satisfies these requirements is the Benefit Amounts Survey taken by the U.S. Department of Labor in 1978.

These data include information describing tenure levels at retirement and wage histories for retirees collecting pensions from a sample of private pension plans in 1978.[15] I include 109 defined benefit pension plans that have a least twenty-five workers who retired during 1970–78. The restriction on plan size ensures credible estimates of the wage tilt and pension generosity parameters for each firm. The sample size in any particular plan is limited to random selection of one hundred. Approximately 6,400 retirees are represented in the sample. Wage histories from the social security files in the data are available back to 1953.

Since quit rates are not reported in the data, tenure levels at retirement are exploited for the empirical work. If pensions and wage tilt reduce turnover, tenure at retirement age is higher.[16] This result is general as long as the age of new hires across firms is not correlated with either the pension or wage tilt parameters. If pension and high wage tilt firms tend to hire younger workers, tenure at retirement is biased upward in these firms, independent of quit rates. In fact there is some evidence that firms more likely to have delayed wage contracts are less likely to hire workers older than age 55.[17]

Since my analysis does not include workers hired beyond age 55 (see below), I am interested to know if the problem is more general; whether the average age of hire over all ages less than 55 is lower in pension and high wage tilt firms. I do not have information about hires in the firms in my sample, so I construct a test using data from the Current Population Survey. The results show that the average age of hire is not related in a statistically significant way to either pension coverage or wage tilt across three-digit industries.[18]

A similar statistical problem might also arise if I use tenure attained at retirement age. If firms use pensions to induce workers to retire early, tenure at retirement will be biased downward independent of the impact of pensions on quit rates. This factor can be accommodated by using tenure attained at age 55 (this is the earliest age of retirement for any retiree in the database). This makes it possible to measure the impact of pensions and wage tilt on quitting without contaminating the data with the separate effects these policies may have on retirement ages.

All of the firms in the database have defined benefit plans. The variation in generosity across these plans in the sample is large, providing a reliable way to measure the influence of pensions on tenure. Below I verify the results using data from the Current Population Survey, which includes data describing workers not covered by pensions.

Table 3.2  Distribution of Wage Tilt and Pension Values

| | | | Quit costs[c] | |
| Category | Pension[a] (1) | Wage growth[b] (2) | Pensions (3) | Wage tilt (4) |
|---|---|---|---|---|
| 1st Q | 6.9% | −0.40% | 0.48 | −0.22 |
| 2d Q | 9.8 | 0.74 | 0.83 | 0.44 |
| 3d Q | 12.9 | 2.81 | 1.43 | 1.54 |
| 90th P | 16.0 | 4.03 | 2.09 | 2.46 |
| Average | 10.2 | 1.10 | 1.02 | 0.60 |

*Note:* All calculations are presented in the appendix; Q, quartile; P, percentile.
[a] Pension benefits expressed as a percentage of final wage times tenure in the firm.
[b] Wages are indexed to the nonagricultural wage.
[c] Expressed in relation to annual wage during the worker's midcareer year with the firm.

Finally, I calculate the pension capital losses and wage tilt. All calculations are explained in the appendix to this chapter, but the results of the estimates are presented in table 3.2. Pension generosity is expressed as the present value of pension benefits at retirement, divided by the product of the wage rate, times tenure at retirement (column 1). Wage growth is the percentage change in the real wage per year of tenure in the firm (column 2). Pension capital losses are the difference between the quit and stay pensions, using interest rates appropriate for the period (column 3). Wage tilt losses are an estimate of the "wedge" between actual wage to midtenure and a "flat wage" alternative where the flat wage is the average over the entire career in the firm (column 4).

The median average lifetime pension benefits in the 109 plan sample are 10.2 percent of final wage times service in the firm at retirement; 25 percent of the firms had pension generosity factors less than 6.9 percent, and 25 percent had factors over 12.9 percent (see column 1). The average pension quit loss at midcareer is 102 percent of the annual wage rate.

The average potential wage tilt quit cost is .60 times annual wage, about two-thirds as high as pension losses. Roughly one worker in four in the sample has potential wage tilt losses more than 1.54 times annual wage (column 4).

### 3.3.2  The Empirical Results

The measures in table 3.2 are estimates of quit costs under the assumptions that workers pay for stay pensions, not quit pensions, and that firms deliberately twist the wage profile relative to productivity to encourage long-term commitments from workers. If wage growth reflects deliberate wage tilt—not just growth in general skill, it should be positively related

Table 3.3 Determinants of Tenure at Age 55

| Independent variable | Mean values | Individual wage growth | Firm wage growth |
|---|---|---|---|
| Wage quit costs[a] | .59 | .012 | .001 |
| | | (1.32) | (.13) |
| Pension quit costs[a] | 1.05 | .191*** | .161*** |
| | | (10.57) | (12.81) |
| Other variables[b] | | X | X |
| $R^2$ | | .168 | .140 |
| Mean dependent variable | | 2.57 | 2.57 |
| Observations | | 6,416 | 6,416 |
| Number of firms | | 109 | 109 |

Note: Dependent variable is the log of tenure at age 55; t-values in parentheses.
Source: U.S. Department of Labor, Benefit Amounts Survey, 1978 (see chapter 5). See McCarthy, Findings from the Survey, at chapter 3, note 15.
[a] Expressed as a multiple of annual wage from quitting midcareer on the assumption that all wage growth over tenure is deliberate wage tilt and workers forgo wages equal to stay pensions. Mean values differ from those in table 3.2 because numbers above are weighted by workers.
[b] An X indicates that other independent variables were included in the estimate. These include union (.057**), dummy variable denoting firm size fewer than 1,000 employees (−.00) and 1,000–10,000 employees (.148**), dummy variable equal to one for female (−.136**), nonwhite (−.00), and intercept (2.39**), and one-digit industry. Five industry dummy variables were included; four were significant at the 95 percent level of confidence in each regression. Numbers in parentheses in this note report the coefficients on these variables for the column 1 estimate, and the notation ** denotes that the coefficient is significant at the 95 percent level of confidence.
*** significant at the .01 level; **significant at the .05 level (two-tailed test).

to tenure. If pensions are used to bond workers—workers are required to forgo cash wages beyond the quit value of the pension—pension generosity should be positively correlated to tenure.

The estimates of these coefficients are shown in table 3.3, column 1.[19] The coefficient on the pension generosity variable is positive, large, and statistically significant. This result is consistent with the hypothesis that workers forgo wages in consideration of receiving stay pensions upon retirement, not quit pensions based on imminent separation from the firm. The estimated pension quit effects are large. A pension plan that imposes quit costs equal to one year's wage at midcareer results in an increase in tenure at age 55 of approximately 20 percent.

The coefficient on the wage tilt proxy is insignificantly different from zero. This result contradicts the notion that variation in wage growth across individuals and firms reflects deliberate wage tilt. Instead, it suggests that observed wage growth over tenure more likely reflects different rates of accumulation of general capital rather than deliberate twisting of the wage profile relative to productivity.

These results could be challenged owing to potential selection effects and measurement problems associated with use of individual data. In particular, measures of both types of quit costs are wholly or partly dependent on individual wage growth. If wage growth is correlated with particular workers who perform extraordinarily well in the firm, and if these workers are less likely to quit, a selection factor may bias the results. To test for this bias, I recalculate pension and wage tilt quit costs using a single wage growth parameter for all workers in each firm (the average wage growth for all workers in the firm). The results, shown in column 2 of table 3.3, essentially are the same as those reported in column 1 based on individual data.

## 3.4 IMPACT OF PENSIONS AND WAGE TILT ON QUIT RATES

Although the Benefits Amount Survey is rich in individual wage histories and firm and pension characteristics, it reports only completed tenure rather than quit rates and does not include independent variables like education or occupation. For these reasons, I checked if the results could be duplicated using other data collected during the same period.

In particular, I use the Current Population Survey (CPS), May supplement 1979, merged with the reinterview tape in March 1980.[20] Turnover rates in this sample are not reported directly. Thus I label as a separation a worker who, at the time of the reinterview, is either unemployed (only employed workers were interviewed in May 1979) or is in a different three-digit industry classification. The CPS has no information about pension plan generosity, so the pension variable is a zero-one dummy variable equal to one if the worker is covered by a pension, zero otherwise.

More particularly, the pension, wage tilt, and average wage variables are calculated for each of eighty-three three-digit industry classifications that have at least twenty observations in the sample. The pension variable is the portion of workers in the industry covered by a pension. Wage tilt is the coefficient on the log of tenure in a cross section of workers in each industry (holding constant age, education, union, race, and sex). The wage variable is the mean industry wage.

I estimate a logit model where the dependent variable equals one if the worker quit his job from May to March. The results are given in table 3.4.[21] The reported numbers are coefficients,[22] and those in parentheses are $t$-values. The results suggest the dominance of pensions in affecting mobility relative to wage tilt.

The pension coefficient is negative and statistically significant at the 99 percent level of confidence.[23] The incremental effect of pensions is −.13.[24] Pensions reduce turnover by 13 percentage points; the turnover probability in the sample is 31.5 percent. In contrast, the coefficient

## Table 3.4 Determinants of Turnover Rates

| Independent variable | Mean | Coefficients |
|---|---|---|
| Intercept | — | 2.70***<br>(5.56) |
| Industry characteristics | | |
| Wage tilt[a] | .095 | .58<br>(1.11) |
| Pension coverage[b] | .61 | −.72***<br>(3.99) |
| Hourly wage[c] | $6.61 | .008<br>(.30) |
| Other variables[d] | | |
| Mean dependent variable | | .315 |
| Observations | | 5,604 |

*Note:* Dependent variable is a dummy variable equal to unity if the worker changed industries between sample periods, zero otherwise. Reported numbers are estimated coefficients using a logit model. Point estimates for the continuous variables are derived by the expression $b_i x(1 - x)$ where $b_i$ is the coefficient on the $i$th variable and $x$ is the percentage of positive values of the dependent variable. The incremental effect on the pension variable is derived by calculated the predicted probability when the pension dummy is set alternatively to one and zero, holding all other variables at their mean values: this value is −.13.
*Source:* Current Population Survey, 1979, May supplement.
[a] Equals the coefficient on the log of tenure in a cross section regression within the worker's three-digit industry, where the dependent variable is weekly wage and the other independent variables are education, union, race, and sex.
[b] Percentage of workers covered by a pension within three-digit industry.
[c] Mean wage within three-digit industry.
[d] These variables include (coefficient in parentheses and asterisk notation denoting significance): age (−.14***), age$^2$ (.0016***), tenure (−.18***), tenure$^2$ (.005***), union coverage (−.19***), female (.23**), and black (.02). In addition, I include dummy variables denoting firm size, SMSA location, nine occupation dummy variables, and seven industry dummy variables. Three of these variables are statistically different from zero.
*** significant at the .01 level; **significant at the .05 level *(two-tailed test); $t$-values in parentheses.

on wage growth is insignificantly different from zero. The results are sensitive neither to the specification nor to the time period of the estimates.[25]

## 3.5  CONCLUDING REMARKS

Pensions are important tools to enforce long-term contracts in the firm. On average, they reduce quit rates by approximately 20 percent and increase tenure levels at older ages by over 25 percent.[26] The results offer little support for the hypothesis that wage tilt is an efficient substitute for pensions to deter quitting. In the next chapter I test this idea further by asking whether quit and retirement activity in the federal government can largely be explained by its defined benefit plan, one of the most generous in the United States.

APPENDIX: ESTIMATES OF PENSION
GENEROSITY AND WAGE TILT

A. *Pension Generosity and Wage Tilt*

To calculate pension quit costs, I need a measure of pension plan generosity. I define pension generosity as the present value of pension income during retirement, evaluated at retirement ages, as a proportion of wages at retirement (in 1978 dollars) times tenure at retirement. Pension value is approximated by the pension annuity received in 1978 times the total number of years between retirement age and expected death age, discounted back to the retirement age.[27] I assume death occurs at age 78.

The generosity parameters for the 109 pension plans in the sample ($b_1$, $b_2 \ldots b_{109}$) are estimated by the following equation:

$$\ln (\text{PENSAMT/WAGES}) = a_1 \text{J\&S} + a_2 \text{BEN} + b_1 \text{PLAN}_1$$
$$+ b_2 \text{PLAN}_2 + \ldots + b_{109} \text{PLAN}_{109} + \text{year dummies.} \quad (3.1)$$

PENSAMT is the present value of the pension at retirement, WAGES are the worker's annual earnings in the last full year of work in the firm times years of service at retirement, and $\text{PLAN}_i$ denotes a dummy variable equal to unity for all individuals in the $i$th plan, zero otherwise. A dummy variable for joint and survivor election (J&S) is included to reflect lower pensions when spouse protection is provided beyond the retiree's death.[28] A dummy variable for spouse receipt (BEN) is included to include lower pension values collected by spouse if the worker had died by 1978.[29]

Year dummies (denoting first year of pension receipt) are included to capture year effects, including, for example, less than complete inflation adjustments to benefits through 1978.[30] The coefficients on the pension dummy variables capture differential plan generosity attributable to a higher percentage of wage times service in the formula and longer retirement periods. Equation (3.1) is estimated for 6,416 workers who retired from 1970 to 1978 and are collecting pension benefits from the 109-plan sample in 1978.

To estimate the wage-tenure relation, the following equation is estimated for each individual in the sample:

$$\ln \text{WAGE}_{kj} = c_k \ln \text{TENURE}_{kj} + \text{error,} \quad (3.2)$$

where $\text{WAGE}_{kj}$ denotes real annual earnings for the $k$th worker in the $j$th year of tenure, and $\text{TENURE}_{kj}$ is the worker's tenure in year $j$. Wages are adjusted by the nonagricultural wage index.[31]

B. *Pension and Wage Tilt Quit Costs*

Pension quit cost, *PL,* is the difference between the stay, *P,* and quit, $P^*$, pensions, divided by the midcareer annual wage, $w_{t^*}$.[32] These values are expressed as follows:

$$PL = (P - P^*)/w_{t^*},$$    (3.3)

where

$$P = bTe^{(g-i)(R-a)},$$

and

$$P^* = bTe^{-i(R-a)},$$

where $g$ is nominal per annum wage growth between current age, $a$, and retirement age, $R$, $T$ is current tenure, and $b$ is pension generosity (estimated in equation 3.1).[33]

To avoid a dependence of the measure on actual tenure, the expression is solved for each individual based on the midcareer tenure for the entire sample (twelve years) and the number of years from midcareer age to retirement age for the entire sample (twelve years). I use a 5 percent interest rate, which is roughly in the range of long-term interest rates during the 1950s and 1960s when these calculations presumably were made by the worker cohorts in the sample.[34] The wage growth parameter $g$ is set to the real wage growth estimate from (3.2), plus a 4 percent inflation rate (consistent with a 5 percent long-term interest rate).

Wage tilt loss is the difference in wages earned from year zero to midterm in the career, denoted by $t^*$, and those that would have been collected had the worker been paid his average real career wage, $w_o$, over the same period, all divided by the midcareer wage:

$$WL = \left[ w_o t^* - \sum_{t=0}^{t^*} w(t) \right] \bigg/ w_{t^*}.$$    (3.4)

The wage function is given in (3.2) for each worker, and $w_{t^*}$ is implied from this function. The wage $w_o$ in the expression is the solution to this equation for each individual assuming that the same career earnings are attributable to a flat real wage $w_o$. To avoid a dependence of the measure with actual tenure, the expression is solved at the average midcareer point for all workers in the sample ($t^* =$ twelve years).

## CHAPTER FOUR

# Quits and Retirements in the Federal Government

In the previous chapter I presented evidence suggesting an important role for defined benefit pension plans in encouraging workers to stay with the firm. If pensions are important in reducing the quit rate, then one industry in which their effects ought to be particularly noticeable is the federal government. Civilian federal workers hired before 1983 are not covered by the social security system, and thus the defined benefit pension plan is extraordinarily generous by private sector standards. Owing to its size and structure, the federal pension system strongly discourages quitting and late retirement.

## 4.1 QUIT COSTS IN THE FEDERAL GOVERNMENT

Two factors explain why the pension capital loss from quitting is higher in the federal government than in firms that sponsor private pensions.[1] First, as a share of compensation, government pensions are three times larger than those in the private sector. The higher share is manifested in several ways. The pension annuity per year of service is almost 2 percent in the federal government, twice as large as in private sector firms.[2] Federal benefits are automatically indexed to the cost of living, whereas private pensions are partially indexed on an ad hoc basis.[3] Federal workers also can retire with full benefits (after thirty years of service) at age 55. Workers in the private sector more typically can retire with full benefits at age 62.[4] Early retirement is usually permissible in the private sector, but the pension is reduced to accommodate the longer period of collection. Subject to service requirements (most often fifteen years), workers who quit before age 55 in the private sector can collect their pension beginning at the early retirement age.

Second, the federal pension exacts a special penalty from quitters because it denies them the opportunity to collect a pension until age 62. Thus, if a federal worker quits with twenty-nine years of service at age 54, one year before eligibility for full benefits, he must wait eight years until age 62 to begin receiving a pension. If he waits one year to leave at age 55, he can begin receiving his full pension immediately. This provision is important because once collection starts, federal pensions have full cost of living adjustments (COLAs). By forcing age 54 quitters to wait eight more years to begin collecting their pension, not only do they miss seven years of full pension benefits, but they receive a pension at age 62 that has significantly eroded owing to inflation during the intervening years (the COLA does not apply to deferred benefits).

To demonstrate the differential cost of quitting in the federal and private sectors, I calculate capital losses for the federal government and a composite private pension firm.[5] More particularly, I calculate the pension capital loss using federal and private pension rules for a worker starting a federal or private job at age 25. The calculations assume that the worker in either sector receives an identical and constant real cash wage during the career, and that indexing for inflation after retirement is complete in *both* pensions.[6]

I assume that the nominal interest rate is 12 percent, that death occurs with certainty at age 78, and that nominal wage growth in both sectors equals the interest rate. The value of the pension capital loss is divided by current annual cash wage; hence, pension losses upon quitting are expressed as a multiple of the cash wage.

Figure 4.1 shows the cost of quitting the federal government. At age 35 with ten years of service, the private sector worker absorbs a capital loss equal to 1.2 times the current annual cash wage; a federal worker loses 2.8 times the current wage. After twenty years of service, the private worker loses 1.9 times the wage upon quitting; the federal worker loses six times the current wage. At age 54, after twenty-nine years of service, the quit penalty for the private worker is .4 times the current wage (the worker who quits can begin collecting a pension in just one year), but the federal worker who quits at this age and service length loses 7.2 times the current wage.[7]

## 4.2 CAN LARGER PENSIONS ACCOUNT FOR LOWER FEDERAL QUIT RATES?

### 4.2.1 An Estimation Model

The question I address is whether the pension quit penalties are large enough to account for the difference between federal and private sector

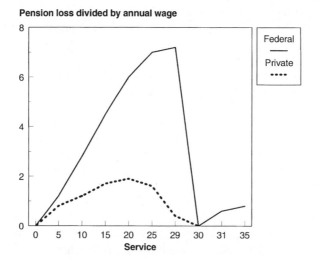

**Figure 4.1** Pension losses from quitting the federal government. Refer to text for assumptions (p. 31).

quit rates. In designing the empirical test, I assume that sorting takes place in the labor market. That is, I assume that workers do not randomly affiliate with firms but instead make long-term decisions at the time they look for a job: on average, they self-select into firms whose behavioral constraints are consistent with their own inclinations. In deciding which firm to join, workers take into account the capital loss schedules like those depicted in figure 4.1.

Individuals with the lowest quit propensities have lower expected quit losses and thus are less likely to suffer pension capital losses later in their career.[8] Workers with higher quit propensities take jobs with firms with lower quit costs. In this model, defined benefit pensions act as a self-selection device.[9] Through this selection procedure, pensions reduce the quit rate over all tenure levels and hence can be modeled by a simple dummy variable.[10]

The implicit contract model predicts that, because of the higher pension capital losses, quitting in the federal government will be lower than in private pension firms. To test this hypothesis, I need data on both private and federal workers. One database that satisfies this requirement is the May 1979 Current Population Survey (CPS) that includes the pension supplement (see chapter 3).

### 4.4.2 Empirical Results

In the May 1979 CPS, workers report their pension coverage. Some of these workers are reinterviewed the following March. These data describe

Table 4.1  Impact of Private and Federal Pensions on Separations

| Category | 1979 (1) | 1988 (2) | 1993 (3) |
|---|---|---|---|
| Average separation rate | 30 | 17 | 29 |
| Incremental effect | | | |
| Private pension | −6 | −6 | −4 |
| Federal pension | −16 | −14 | −13 |

Note: Numbers in table are incremental effects (expressed as percentages) of private and federal pensions on separation rates using CPS data. Details are provided in the chapter appendix.

separation behavior across a broad sample of workers and include a sufficient sampling of federal workers to provide a basis for the test. The data include information describing approximately 6,700 workers, including 3 percent who are federal workers.

I need to define my measure of turnover. Recall from chapter 3 that turnover in the CPS is inferred by changes in the worker's industry affiliation between the time of the survey and the subsequent reinterview. These estimates are close approximations to turnover rates measured for private and federal workers in other surveys.[11]

Also, the CPS includes quits and permanent layoffs in its separation rate. Recall from the discussion in chapters 2 and 3 that the arguments stemming from an implicit contract model apply to layoffs as well as quits; thus the turnover variable does not compromise the integrity of the implicit contract model. To exclude retirees from the turnover rate, the data are restricted to those younger than 55 for the empirical work.

I estimate a logit model where the dependent variable equals one if the worker separates from his job, zero otherwise. I include dummy variables to denote private pension coverage and federal employment. I also control for other demographic characteristics.[12]

In table 4.1, column 1, I report the estimated incremental effects for both the private pension and federal dummy variables. More detailed estimates are reported in the appendix to this chapter. All of the underlying coefficients for these variables are statistically significant at the 99 percent level of confidence.

The average separation rate in the data is 30 percent. This rate is 6 percentage points lower in firms that offer private pensions, but it is fully 16 percentage points lower in the federal government. Thus the results generally are consistent with the idea that the separation rate in the federal government is markedly lower than in private firms that offer pensions. These results are not specific to 1979. In columns 2 and 3 in the table, I show the estimates using the 1988 and 1993 CPS data for the comparable months with the pension supplements.[13]

The order of magnitude of the incremental federal effect compared with the private pension effect also is within the range expected in the implicit contract model. In particular, using the 1979 data, I estimated the comparative quit losses in the federal government pension compared with private pensions. On average, federal losses were 3.85 times higher than private quit losses.[14] When workers contemplate spending a career with the federal government, the cost of quitting during their tenure is 3.85 times the comparable quit cost from a typical private sector pension firm. It is therefore not surprising that the incremental effect of the federal pension is 2.7 times higher than the private pension effect.

## 4.3  QUIT RATES AS INDEXES OF COMPETITIVE WAGES

These results are important for three reasons. First, they reaffirm the notion that defined benefit pension plans can be effective tools to encourage long tenure. Second, they confirm that the way defined benefit plan benefit formulas are chosen importantly affects the resulting quit rate. And third, they demonstrate the peril inherent in using quit rates to determine whether a firm's wage package is competitive. Such an approach has been suggested in the literature,[15] and the government itself has occasionally embraced this notion.[16]

Consider the logic of the following proposition: *To test for noncompetitive wage levels, compare the firm's quit rate against the quit rates of competitors; if quit rates are abnormally low in the firm, reduce wages until the quit rate increases to "normal" levels.* The proposition is valid only if the firm's competitors are characterized by comparable quit costs.

Suppose a firm pays $100 cash per year (no pension); another firm pays no cash wage but contributes $100 per year into a pension. Assume a zero real interest rate and zero inflation. All workers start at these firms at age 25 and retire at age 55. Clearly, owing to the pension capital loss in the pension firm, quit rates ought to much lower than in the cash-only firm.

Suppose the pension firm does not understand the concept of pension losses and decides to reduce its wages until its quit rate matches its competitor's quit rate. For simplicity, assume that workers start in the pension firm at age 25 and retirement occurs at age 55, and that vesting does not occur until age 55; quits therefore lose their entire pension. This assumption is qualitatively similar to one that posits early vesting but significant inflation.

By assumption, the entire compensation in the pension firm ($100) is in the form of a pension. If the level of compensation is reduced to $75, most workers will not leave the firm because of the pension capital loss. If the worker quits, he receives a $25 per year higher wage in another firm for the remaining thirty minus $S$ years of his career. But he forfeits $100 in pension contributions for each of $S$ years of service he has accumulated to date (that is, each worker has an investment in the pension equal to $100 times $S$ years of service). The worker leaves only if the higher wage stream in the new firm exceeds the lost pension value, that is, if the amount $25(30 - S)$ is greater than $100S$.

In this example, only workers with fewer than six years of service leave; the rest have too much invested in the pension to rationalize a job change. Thus the pension firm can pay less than competitive wages without generating much quit activity; it generates a short-term profit by effectively underpaying its workers. But the gain is short lived. In addition to creating a "reputation" problem in the labor market, the firm will begin to observe a deterioration in the quality of its labor force.

Beginning in the next period, lower-quality workers take these jobs, because to them $75 is a competitive wage. Like their predecessors, however, since the entire $75 is a deferred, they too exhibit extraordinarily low quit rates. Thus the firm ends up with lower-quality workers but still has a low quit rate relative to its competitor who pays a higher (all cash) wage.

This example demonstrates the difficulty in using cross section quit data to determine pay adequacy and using a policy of reducing wages to "test" whether pay levels are competitive. In a competitive market, the labor market ensures that firms or the government have competitive pay levels: the quality of labor adjusts to make any announced pay "competitive." Through pay levels, firms and the government set the quality of labor they employ. They cannot set the quality *and* the wage.

Quit rates themselves do not divulge whether the government (or any other firm with deferred compensation schemes) attracts the caliber of workers it desires. As long as large portions of pay are deferred through the pension, quit rates will be lower than in firms that award a higher portion of compensation in the form of current wages, regardless of the quality of labor attracted. In addition, a wage reduction yields little information about competitive wages: most middle to high tenure workers will not quit even though they could earn a higher level of compensation elsewhere.

In this sense, it is interesting to evaluate the implications of a pay proposal made in the mid-1980s by the Office of Personnel Management.[17] It recommended that pay rates be reduced until government quit rates equaled private quit rates. As long as the portion of wages deferred through the pension remained the same, instituting this policy would have led to a degenerating solution.

Initial pay reductions would increase quit rates only for young workers. But these workers would be replaced by lower-quality workers who exhibit the same low quit rates because they too want to collect their deferred wage. So the government presumably would react by cutting wages further, which would lead to even lower-quality workers' entering government, and so on. But as long as the pension share of compensation was not changed, the quit rates would remain abnormally low. In addition, the government, by cutting wages midterm in the career, presumably would develop a "reputation" for cutting wages after pension capital losses mounted with tenure, and as a result new entrants would anticipate future wage cuts, which would reduce the quality of workers entering even further.

If the government, or a private firm, wants to increase its quit rates, it can accomplish this by establishing a defined contribution pension. In these plans, when (vested) workers quit, they retain ownership of the balance of the fund plus accumulated earnings until retirement.[18] The government can calculate workers' accumulated real pension wealth under the old pension (see expression 2.4 in chapter 2), and contribute this amount into the new pension.

This transaction does not affect workers' pension wealth but eliminates the pension capital loss from quitting. This transaction provides a true test of whether current workers are overpaid, one that disentangles the share of wage deferred from the level of compensation. If federal workers are seriously overpaid, their quit rates will not increase markedly. If they are seriously underpaid, quit rates will increase dramatically.

## 4.4 TESTING WHETHER FEDERAL WORKERS LEAVE "ON TIME"

The pension plan that has covered federal workers (except new hires after 1983), provides a good illustration how a pension can be designed to encourage workers to leave "on time." I have already demonstrated the magnitude of the early quit costs inherent in the pension, but penalties beyond normal retirement ages are also high. The pension encourages workers to remain with the government for a long tenure but to depart before their tenure becomes "too long."

### 4.4.1 Penalties for Staying "Too Long"

To illustrate the penalties for staying "too long," I consider a worker who joins the federal government at age 25. He can retire with full benefits at age 55. For simplicity, I assume that death occurs at age 80 and the real interest rate is zero. The pension annuity is set equal to 2 percent times years of service times final wage.[19]

I assume that federal workers implicitly pay for their pensions in the form of lower cash wages. The pension for my hypothetical worker is 60 percent of the final wage at age 55 (2 percent times thirty years of service). Since the federal annuity is fully indexed to inflation, the real interest rate is zero, and death occurs at age 80, then the value of the pension accrued at age 55 is $15W$, where $W$ is the annual cash wage.

Assuming for simplicity that the worker's real annual wage is constant over his thirty years of service, his lifetime federal wages at age 55 amount to $30W$. Therefore the pension is worth one-third of compensation or, equivalently, one-half of the cash wage.[20] In other words, in exchange for the pension, the worker sacrifices the equivalent of $.5W$ during each year of work ($.5W$ times thirty years equals $15W$).

Consider the worker when he attains age 55. If he works one more year, he sacrifices a full year of pension benefits worth $.6W$; he also sacrifices his implicit pension contribution equal to $.5W$. In return, he gets an annuity higher by the amount 2 percent for one more year of service, collectible for twenty-four remaining years of life if he retires at the end of one more year: the gain is $.02$ times 24 times $W$ or $.48W$. The net cost of retiring at age 56 is thus $1.1W - .48W$, or $.62W$. If he works his fifty-sixth year, he still contributes $.5W$ in lower cash wages, but now gives up an annuity equal to $.62W$ and in return, he gets 2 percent times his additional year of service for only twenty-three years, not twenty-four. Thus the net cost of working his fifty-sixth year is $1.12W - .46W$, or $.66W$, and so on.

The penalties for retiring after age 55 for the federal worker are shown in figure 4.1. There is a unique age at which this federal worker can leave the government without penalty. Similar loss schedules can be developed for workers who begin federal employment after age 25.[21]

The economics of retirement suggest that separations from the federal government occur most frequently about the date of eligibility for full benefits. Leaving earlier results in large penalties; leaving later results in smaller penalties, though they are still high in relation to the annual wage. Viewing figure 4.1, it is reasonable to expect that older workers seldom quit before normal retirement age but tend to retire at relatively high frequencies after they attain normal retirement age.

### 4.4.2 Empirical Estimates

To determine whether this model describes reality, I use data provided to me by the Defense Manpower Data Center. The data, identified by scrambled social security number, describe the personnel records of a 10 percent sample of U.S. Air Force civilian employees in three locations in the United States. The data include matched payroll records for the same individuals on the personnel tapes as of 31 December 1986.

Table 4.2  Leaving Federal Jobs "on Time"

| Independent variable | Mean values | Coefficients | Incremental effect[a] |
|---|---|---|---|
| Intercept | — | −4.94 | — |
| | | (7.45) | |
| Eligible to retire | .40 | 2.92*** | .215 |
| | | (10.60) | |
| Other variables[b] | | X | |
| Mean dependent variable | | .47 | |
| Observations | | 3,367 | |

Note: Dependent variable is a dummy variable equal to unity if the worker separated from the federal government during calendar year 1987. The data oversample separations. Estimates are made using a weighted logit model, where the weights are the population-to-sample proportions for separations and nonseparations in the data. Numbers in parentheses are asymptotic $t$-statistics.
Source: Defense Manpower Data Center, Monterey, California.
[a]The incremental effect is the change in the probability that the dependent variable is unity when the dummy variable is set alternatively to one or zero, where other independent variables are set to their mean values. The incremental effect on the intercept is the population estimate of the probability of a separation for a white male with mean sample characteristics.
[b]Includes age, service, and dummy variables for race, sex, education, and disability.
***Significant at the .01 level of confidence.

The data also describe significant personnel actions for these individuals over the ensuing calendar year, including voluntary quits and retirements.[22] To ensure an adequate sample for study, separations are oversampled in the data.

The tapes include information for 3,367 workers 45 years old or older. I define as a separation either a quit or a voluntary retirement. The question I ask is whether the separation rate follows the pattern suggested by the pension penalties outlined in figure 4.1.

I estimate a weighted logit model where the weights are the population to sample proportions of separations and nonseparations in the data.[23] The dependent variable equals unity if the worker separates from the federal government, zero otherwise. Independent variables include age, service, dummy variables for race, sex, education level, and handicap status (though these coefficients are not reported), as well as a dummy variable equal to unity if the worker is eligible for immediate pension benefits.

The results shown in table 4.2 conform to the expected pattern. Workers over age 45 who are not yet eligible for immediate full benefits have only a 2 percent chance of separating from the government.[24] Upon attaining eligibility for full benefits, the separation rate increases to 23.5 percent per annum.[25] Thus, although workers infrequently leave before attaining pension eligibility, three out of four workers depart within five years of attaining eligibility.[26]

## 4.5 CONCLUDING REMARKS

If pension plans are used to affect the quit behavior of workers, it ought to be obvious in the federal sector. Until a new plan was installed for new hires after 1983, the federal pension system exacted large penalties for either leaving the government too early or staying too late. These penalties are an order of magnitude higher than those characterizing typical private sector plans.

The data are consistent with the hypothesis that the extraordinarily low quit rates evinced in the federal sector can be explained by the unusually large quit penalties imparted by its pension plan. And retirement tends to occur within a short period of workers' eligibility age. In the context of the implicit pension contract theory, these findings are not surprising.

When combined with a hiring policy that emphasizes particular ages of new entrants, it is apparent that defined benefit plans are effective tools to manage the age-service profile in the firm. Moreover, the significant flexibility in these plans permits the firm to craft incentives to retire at particular ages, service levels, or age-service combinations. In the next chapter I present evidence illustrating some of the variety of retirement incentives evinced in a sample of private sector defined benefit plans.

## APPENDIX: DETERMINANTS OF TURNOVER RATES

Table 4.3 presents the detailed estimates of the logit model referenced in table 4.1. The numbers in the table are estimated coefficients of the model where the dependent variable equals one if a worker in the May supplement of the CPS was affiliated with a different three-digit industry in the reinterview occurring the following March. The estimates in column 2 are based on 1979 data; those in columns 3 and 4 are based on data from 1988 and 1993.[27] The results are not markedly different across the three samples.

The results do not differ markedly if the worker's wage (and its square term) are included in the estimates. For example, in the 1979 data, the coefficients on the private pension and federal government variables change to $-.31$ and $-1.37$. I do not report the coefficients for the other control variables included in the equations (see notes to table).

## Table 4.3  Impact of Pensions on Turnover Rates

| Independent variable | Mean 1979 (1) | 1979 (2) | 1988 (3) | 1993 (4) |
|---|---|---|---|---|
| Intercept | — | 2.38*** | 2.06*** | 2.83*** |
| | | (5.63) | (4.25) | (4.40) |
| Private pensions[a] | .49 | −.36*** | −.36*** | −.21*** |
| | | (5.26) | (5.94) | (3.06) |
| Federal[b] | .029 | −1.47*** | −1.30*** | −.91*** |
| | | (5.78) | (3.74) | (4.52) |
| Age | 35.9 | −.14*** | −.12*** | −.09*** |
| | | (6.09) | (4.77) | (3.74) |
| Age$^2$ | — | .0017*** | .0014*** | .001*** |
| | | (5.18) | (4.06) | (3.01) |
| Tenure | 6.5 | −.17*** | −.12*** | −.10*** |
| | | (12.44) | (9.03) | (7.54) |
| Tenure$^2$ | — | .0045*** | .003*** | .003*** |
| | | (8.81) | (6.48) | (4.73) |
| Years of education | 14 | .017 | .006 | −.02 |
| | | (1.26) | (.46) | (1.92) |
| Union | .27 | −.13* | −.26*** | −.25 |
| | | (1.79) | (2.98) | (1.17) |
| Other variables[c] | | X | X | X |
| Mean dependent variable | | .31 | .26 | .29 |
| Observations | | 6,739 | 6,532 | 6,894 |

Note: Dependent variable is a dummy variable equal to unity if the worker changed industries between sample periods, zero otherwise. Numbers in the table are estimated coefficients using a logit model. Numbers in parentheses are asymptotic $t$-statistics. See notes to table 3.4 for more details about the data.

Source: Current Population Survey, May/April pension supplements, 1979, 1988, and 1993, and subsequent March reinterviews.

[a]Equals unity if a worker in the private sector was covered by a pension at the time of the original interview. Federal workers are coded zero.

[b]Equals unity for workers who identified themselves as employees of the federal government at the time of the original interview. Military personnel are not included in the survey.

[c]These include dummy variables denoting gender, race, firm size, SMSA and city dwellers, nine major occupational dummy variables, and seven major industry variables.

***Significant at the .01 level; **significant at the .05 level; *significant at the .10 level (two-tailed test).

CHAPTER FIVE

# Pensions and Retirement Patterns

Although defined benefit plans share broad characteristics, they can be stylized to produce a workforce with an age and tenure profile that is optimal for the firm. The discussion of the federal pension plan in chapter 4 dramatically illustrates how pensions can influence quit and retirement behavior. In this chapter I illustrate the diversity of pension plan rules in the private sector in providing incentives for retirement. I also show how small changes in the pension plan can importantly affect workers' incentives to leave the firm at particular ages.

Since the federal pension discussed in chapter 4 has no early retirement provisions, I begin by showing how retirement incentives can be inferred from the plan's early and normal retirement rules, and how these rules vary across pension plans. I then analyze the variance in retirement patterns across a sample of large pension plans.

## 5.1 THE ECONOMICS OF EARLY RETIREMENT BENEFITS

In all defined benefit pension plans, there is some age at which the worker is entitled to full pension benefits. This age might be 65. In virtually all private plans, there is some earlier age at which the worker can choose to retire and receive reduced benefits. This age might be 55. This practice is akin to the social security system, which allows retirement at 65 with full benefits or at age 62 with reduced benefits.

Once the worker reaches the age of eligibility for full benefits, a decision to work one more year usually triggers a loss of pension wealth. The loss occurs because the increased annuity from working an additional year is not sufficient to offset the pension forgone during the additional year of work. This idea is illustrated in chapter 4 for the pension covering

41

federal workers (see fig. 4.1). In private pensions, however, the age of eligibility for full benefits is often younger than 65. As a general rule, the earlier the age of eligibility for full benefits, the earlier the worker faces pension penalties for retiring later.

An important source of confusion in evaluating early retirement benefits is attributable to a difference in terminology used by actuaries and economists. Based on a given level of service, and compared with retirement at normal retirement age, an *economically equivalent* early retirement reduction gives the same present value of pension benefits in *real terms*. Thus, if pension value is economically equivalent at two ages, the pension imparts no bias about which age to choose.

In contrast, an *actuarially equivalent* reduction gives the same present value of pension benefits in *nominal* terms. I will show below that a reduced pension at an early age that reflects a full actuarial reduction gives workers a clear incentive to retire at an older age. An actuarial reduction can be made economically fair by imparting a so-called subsidy to the reduction (a "subsidized actuarial reduction").

To illustrate, suppose the plan sets an actuarially fair reduction factor for workers retiring at age 55 instead of taking full benefits at age 65. For simplicity, assume that death occurs with certainty at age 80. In making his calculation, the actuary *assumes that the worker terminates employment at the early age* and will begin taking a full pension at age 65. Thus the full pension payable at 65 is proportional to the worker's wage at age 55: the reduction factor to account for a longer retirement period is applied to this amount. The actuary does not recognize the worker's alternative to stay with the firm and take a benefit indexed to wages at 65.

Consider a worker age 55 with twenty years of service. The pension pays an annuity equal to 1 percent times years of service times wage at retirement, beginning at age 65. The plan does not make cost of living adjustments after retirement. The real interest rate is zero, so the nominal interest rate reflects expected inflation. If the worker's current salary is $30,000 and expected nominal wage growth is 8 percent, his expected wage at 65 is $66,766.[1] If the worker stays until age 65, his full benefit based on the twenty years of service accumulated by age 55 is $13,353 per year starting at age 65.[2] If the interest rate is also 8 percent, the present value of this pension evaluated at age 55 is approximately $52,400.[3]

The actuarially fair annuity at age 55 is not based on the worker's alternative to retire at a later age. The actuary's hypothetical full benefit is based on the $30,000 wage at age 55, not the projected wage of $66,766. Thus the actuary calculates the age 65 annuity of $6,000.[4] Evaluated at age 55, this annuity is worth only about $23,500, not $52,400.[5]

Clearly, the actuarially fair annuity at age 55 biases the worker to post-pone retirement until normal retirement age.

An economist determines the equivalent age 55 annuity in the following way: he solves for the annuity starting at age 55 that yields a present value in this example equal to $52,400. It turns out that this annuity is about $4,850 per annum.[6] In contrast, the actuary searches for the age 55 annuity that gives a present value of $23,500, which is about $2,180.[7]

I can now convert these calculations to the nomenclature used to calculate benefits at early retirement. In the example, the worker earns $30,000 at age 55. The full benefit based on this salary is $6,000 (1 percent times twenty years times salary). The economically fair annuity at the early age is $4,850; thus the economically fair "reduction factor" is about 2.1 percent for each year that retirement occurs before normal retirement age.[8] In contrast, actuarially fair annuity of $2,180 represents a reduction of 10.1 percent per year from the full benefit.[9]

In actuarial parlance, the economic reduction factor of 2.1 percent imparts a "subsidy" to early retirees.[10] In general, if the firm does not wish to bias workers to retiring either at the early age or at the normal age, but wishes to leave the decision to its employees, it must offer an early benefit that incorporates a substantial actuarial "subsidy."[11]

## 5.2 ACTUARIAL VERSUS ECONOMIC REDUCTION FACTORS

The difference between actuarially fair and economically fair reduction factors is somewhat different depending on the age of early retirement. Figure 5.1A demonstrates these factors for retirement ages between 55 and 62 when the interest rate is 8 percent.

The spread between the actuarially fair and economically fair reduction factors increases with the interest rate. The economically fair reduction factor falls with higher interest rates (and commensurate wage growth rates), because the early benefit is subject to more inflation erosion during the early retirement period. Thus the benefits at age 55 must be higher to match the value of staying with the firm and receiving wage increases commensurate with inflation.

In contrast, the actuary assumes that the worker's wage at age 65 is the same as at age 55. The higher his expected nominal wage growth, therefore, the more inflation erosion is imparted by the actuary's assumption of constant wages. Thus his "fair" reduction rate increases with the nominal interest rate. For example, in figure 5.1B, at a 10 percent interest rate, the actuarially fair reduction factor for a 55-year-old retiree is 11.7 percent per year, and the economically fair reduction factor is 1.6 percent.

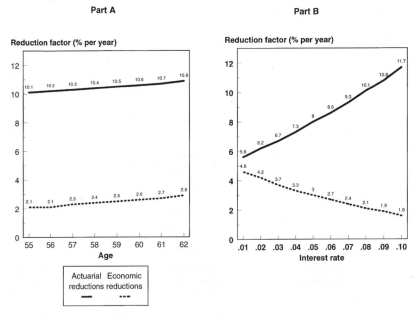

**Figure 5.1** Actuarial versus economic early reduction factors. Actuarial reductions equate the present value of pension benefits at retirement age and normal retirement age in nominal terms (based on service rendered to the time of retirement). Economic reductions equate pension values at these two ages in real terms. Both illustrations assume that death occurs at age 80, and that there are no cost of living adjustments to pension benefits after retirement. In part A the nominal interest rate is 8 percent. In part B the per annum reduction factor is for an early retirement age of 55 when normal retirement age is 65.

At a 2 percent interest rate, the economist increases his reduction factor to 4.2 while the actuary reduces his to 6.2 percent.[12]

The penalty for quitting the firm *before* early retirement age also is affected by both the subsidy rate and the plan's policy of awarding the subsidy to workers who quit the firm *before* the age of eligibility for early retirement. Some plans award the subsidy to workers retiring at the early age *and* to separated vested workers who leave at earlier ages but otherwise are eligible to collect an early benefit.[13] Other firms either apply an actuarially fair reduction to those who quit or otherwise award less generous subsidies.

Figures 5.2 and 5.3 depict the present value of pension losses as a percentage of the annual wage from leaving the firm before normal retirement age. The losses are calculated using the assumptions that underpin figure 5.1. A pension loss is the difference between the present value of the pension at the age of departure from the firm, based on service attained at

Pension loss from leaving divided by annual wage

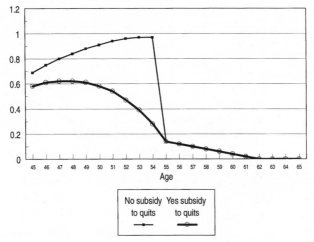

**Figure 5.2** Pension losses from early retirement, reduction factor 3 percent. Assumes that the nominal interest rate is 8 percent, service at age 45 is twenty years, the normal retirement age is 65, and death occurs at age 80.

Pension loss from leaving divided by annual wage

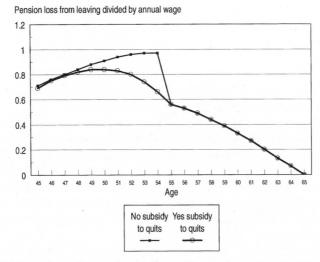

**Figure 5.3** Pension losses from early retirement, reduction factor 6 percent. Assumes that the nominal interest rate is 8 percent, service at age 45 is twenty years, the normal retirement age is 65, and death occurs at age 80.

that age, and the present value of retiring at age 65, based on the same tenure.[14]

I refer to losses attributable to leaving the firm before eligibility for early retirement as "quit losses." I refer to losses from leaving after early retirement age, but before normal retirement age, as "early retirement losses."

Figure 5.2 depicts the results for a reduction factor of 3 percent. The heavier-line schedule (open circles) assumes that the firm awards the subsidy as early as age 55 even if the worker quits between 45 and 54. The lighter-line schedule (solid boxes) assumes that the firm awards the subsidy *only* to workers who leave the firm at age 55 or older. In either case, the penalty for quitting still is relatively high before age 55 because the worker forgoes the use of the higher wage in the pension formula, but in the former case, he does not forfeit the subsidy. When the subsidy is denied, the firm provides a stronger incentive to stay with the firm.

If the pension plan awards economically fair benefits at the early age, the heavier line in the figure becomes coincident with the horizontal axis after age 55. In the example I depict, there is a 3 percent reduction factor, which is approximately economically fair for retirement ages 62 through 65; there are some losses from leaving anytime before age 62, but these losses are much higher if the worker departs before age 55.

Figure 5.3 repeats the demonstration except that it uses an early reduction factor of 6 percent per year instead of 3 percent. At the higher reduction rate, the cost of quitting earlier than the normal retirement age (65) is higher at all ages, and the relative importance of awarding the subsidy to early quitters is smaller.

It is apparent from the figures that depending on how the firm sets the early reduction factor and how it treats early quits in the subsidy formula, it markedly affects workers' incentives to quit at particular ages. A firm that wants workers to stay until age 65 sets the early retirement parameters so as to mimic figure 5.3. A firm that wants to retain its workers until age 55, but is indifferent to their departure age between ages 55 and 65, uses a low reduction factor for those who stay until age 55 but denies a subsidy to those who quit before 55, as depicted in figure 5.2 (the lighter-line (solid boxes) segment before age 55).

## 5.3 REDUCTION FACTORS FOR MEDIUM AND LARGE FIRMS, 1993

Table 5.1 presents the distribution of eligibility ages for retirement on full or reduced benefits for a large sample of private pension plans. The data are taken from the Bureau of Labor Statistics (BLS) 1993 survey of employee benefits in medium and large firms.[15] The data in column 1

Table 5.1 Eligibility for Pension Benefits

| Criterion | Full benefits | Reduced benefits |
|---|---|---|
| Age requirement[a] | | |
| 65 | 48 | — |
| 62 | 21 | 3 |
| 60 | 13 | 7 |
| 55–59 | 4 | 68 |
| 54 or earlier | — | 9 |
| Service only[b] | 5 | 5 |
| Age plus service[c] | 8 | 3 |
| Other | 1 | — |
| No early retirement | — | 5 |

Note: Numbers are percentages; columns may not add to 100 owing to rounding.
Source: U.S. Department of Labor, Employee Benefits, tables 148, 149, at chapter 2, note 5.
[a] Usually has service requirement.
[b] Usually thirty years, regardless of age.
[c] Often must total 80 or 85.

show that 69 percent of firms do not award full benefits until at least age 62.[16]

Clearly, these firms do not use their pensions to encourage workers to depart the firm at relatively young ages. The remaining firms permit retirement with full benefits at age 60 or younger. Firms permitting full benefits at age 55 generally require thirty years of service; others require a minimum combination of age plus service, often equal to 80 or 85.[17]

When a firm sets the eligibility standard for full benefits at thirty years of service at age 55 or older, or a service-plus-age eligibility of 85, a worker who starts the firm at age 25 is eligible to collect full benefits starting at age 55. A worker entering the firm at age 35 is eligible to collect full benefits starting at age 65, so the value of the pension is higher to those who start working for the firm at age 25. These firms encourage workers to join the firm early, stay for long periods, then leave when relatively young. In contrast, firms that award full benefits at age 65 do not encourage workers to leave the firm either after thirty years of service or at relatively young ages.

Table 5.1, column 2, shows the ages at which firms permit retirement at reduced benefits. Only 5 percent of firms do not permit early retirement at reduced benefits; most firms permit early retirement before age 60, often at age 55. As demonstrated above, permitting earlier retirement is not the same as encouraging earlier retirement. As long as the reduction factors are sufficiently large, workers are not encouraged to leave the firm early. In fact, the data show that reduction factors generally discourage early departure from the firm.

Table 5.2 Reduction Factors for Early Retirement

| Category | Percentage[b] |
|---|---|
| Uniform percentage[a] | |
| Less than 4.0 | 7 |
| 4.0–4.9 | 6 |
| 5.0 | 9 |
| 6.0 | 11 |
| 6.1 or more | 3 |
| Subtotal | 36 |
| Reduction varies with age or service | 64 |
| Grand total | 100 |

Source: U.S. Department of Labor, Employee Benefits, table 150, at chapter 2, note 5.
[a]Applied for each year of retirement before normal retirement age.
[b]Weighted by workers covered by defined benefit plans.

Table 5.2 presents data on early reduction factors from the 1993 BLS survey. In 1993, the ten-year U.S. Treasury bond rate was approximately 6 percent.[18] As shown in figure 5.1, when the interest rate is 6 percent, the economically fair reduction factor is approximately 3 percent—at this rate, the present value of pension benefits in real terms based on tenure at the early retirement age is the same at early and normal retirement ages. The actuarially fair reduction factor is approximately 8.5 percent.

Table 5.2 shows a distribution of reduction factors for the 36 percent of pension plans that use linear reduction factors for early retirement; most workers are in plans that use nonlinear formulas, for which the survey does not provide details.[19] The data show that one pension plan in five (weighted by participants) offers reduction factors of less than 4 percent per year. In these plans, firms offer early retirement benefits that are roughly economically fair: workers are offered a range of retirement ages over which they can choose to retire without incurring an important pension penalty.

Most plans offer pensions to early retirees that are better than actuarially fair (they are "subsidized") but less than economically fair. That is to say, most pension plans impose some penalty on those leaving before the age of eligibility for full benefits and have some bias in favor of attaining normal retirement age.

The survey also reports the availability of subsidies to deferred vested workers—workers vested in their pension benefit but who quit before early retirement age. There is a dichotomous distribution of penalties for quitting before early retirement age across medium and large firms. The survey reports that 46 percent of the pension-covered workers are in pensions that award the same subsidy to deferred vested workers as to early retirees. But fully 45 percent offer actuarially reduced benefits to workers

who depart before early retirement age (the rest of the plans adopt intermediate policies).

## 5.4 OTHER FACTORS INFLUENCING EARLY RETIREMENT INCENTIVES

### 5.4.1 High and Low Discounters

So far I have implicitly assumed that all workers discount future benefits
at the market interest rate. In reality, some workers may use a subjective
discount rate that exceeds the market interest rate. I refer to those who
discount at market rates as "low discounters" and those who discount
at substantially higher rates as "high discounters." Workers' reactions to
pension incentives depend on whether they are low discounters or high
discounters.

To make the issue concrete, I reconsider the calculations presented in
figure 5.2 for the case in which the early retirement subsidy is denied
to those leaving the firm before age 55. The reduction factor in these
calculations is 3 percent per year. For convenience, I reproduce this schedule in figure 5.4 (lighter-line schedule with solid boxes). This schedule
represents pension losses from leaving the firm from ages 45 to 64 on
the assumption that the worker discounts future benefits at the market
interest rate (8 percent in the example).

Consider a worker with the same wage, tenure, and expected mortality
who discounts future benefits at a 12 percent rate. The pension loss schedule as he perceives it is shown by the heavier-line schedule (open circles)
in figure 5.4. His perceived incentives to retire are significantly different
from those of the low discounter. The low discounter calculates a pension
loss from leaving at age 55 equal to 14 percent of his wage. The high
discounter calculates a pension *gain* from leaving at age 55 equal to 24
percent of his wage. Clearly, high discounters are more likely to take the
early retirement option than are low discounters.

This dichotomy provides an opportunity for the firm to reduce its economic pension liability. If the firm uses a reduction factor that is economically unfair, it enjoys some reduction in liability each time a worker
chooses early retirement. For example, if the interest rate is 8 percent,
the economically fair reduction factor is 2.1 percent per year (see fig. 5.1).
If the firm chooses some higher factor, like 3 percent (which is illustrated
in figure 5.4), it enjoys a 14 percent reduction in liability (based on twenty
years of tenure) if the worker retires at age 55 instead of 65.[20]

In short, even if low and high discounters are equally valued by the
firm, the distribution of subjective discount rates among workers ought

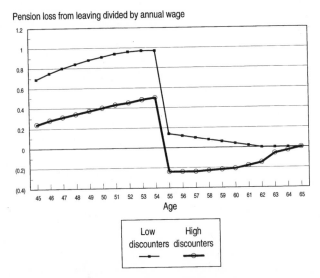

Pension loss from leaving divided by annual wage

**Figure 5.4** Pension incentives to retire: High versus low discounters. Depicts pension losses from retiring before normal retirement age using alternative discount rates (8 percent for low discounters versus 12 percent for high discounters). Assumes that the nominal interest rate is 8 percent, service at age 45 is twenty years, the normal retirement age is 65, and death occurs at age 80.

to influence the firm's optimum choice of pension rules. Even if the firm is indifferent among retirement ages between 55 and 65, it may offer a reduction factor that is unfair. As long as it employs some high discounters, this policy reduces the firm's pension liability.

### 5.4.2 No Early Retirement Option

Finally, I consider a firm that wants to encourage workers to join the firm at an early age, stay for a long period, and retire relatively young. One way to accomplish the outcome is to mimic the government pension plan described in chapter 4: set a normal retirement age based on tenure and deny an early retirement option. To be concrete, suppose the firm permits retirement with full benefits after the worker attains thirty years of tenure, but no earlier than age 55. There is no early retirement option. Workers who quit before attaining thirty years of service can retire at age 65. Using the same underlying assumptions as above,[21] I calculate the pension loss schedule under these retirement rules for a worker who starts with the firm at age 25. I depict the schedule by the heavier bold line (open circles) in figure 5.5.

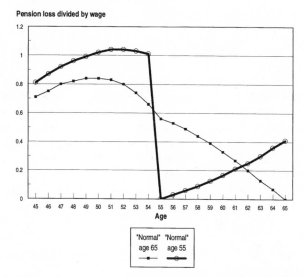

Pension loss divided by wage

**Figure 5.5** Normal retirement age and the optimal retirement age. Depicts losses from retiring at various ages on two assumptions: that full benefits ("normal" retirement) are awarded at age 65 (lighter line with solid boxes) and age 55 (darker line with open circles). Neither plan offers subsidized early retirement. The interest rate is 8 percent, and death occurs at age 80. Retirement calculations after normal retirement age are evaluated at the normal retirement age.

The schedule looks similar to the federal pension plan depicted in figure 4.1. There is a strong incentive to work until age 55; there also is a strong incentive not to work beyond age 55. In this plan, if a worker joins the firm at age 35, he can retire only at age 65 and thus collects a full pension for only 15 years of retirement instead of 25 years.[22] Assuming that the firm does not award higher cash compensation to workers hired after age 35 to compensate them for fewer years of pension benefits, the firm likely will attract young applicants (to whom lifetime compensation in this firm is highest). These workers will enjoy long careers and leave at age 55. Such a plan might work well, for example, in a firm that requires dependability of its workers and thus wants workers to retire at young ages, before significant health problems arise.

In contrast, if the firm uses a production function that is more valuable when older workers are employed, it can set normal retirement at age 65 and offer no early retirement. I depict the pension loss schedule for departing the firm as the light-line segment in figure 5.5 (solid boxes). Workers have strong incentives to refrain from departing the firm before age 65.

### 5.4.3 Cost of Living Adjustments

I have assumed throughout the discussion that the firm does not award ad hoc postretirement inflation adjustments to retirees. This assumption is consistent with prevailing practice during the 1990s. Only 10 percent of participants in 1993 were in defined benefit plans that awarded a cost of living adjustment (COLA) during the preceding five years.[23] If the firm awards ad hoc COLAs, however, this changes the calculation of economically fair reduction factors and can importantly affect the calculus of retirement. The reason is that if benefits after retirement are not indexed, but wages in the benefit formula are indexed for establishing retirement benefits, a bias is imparted to staying with the firm until a later age.

### 5.4.4 Postretirement Medical Benefits

The discussion also ignores the issue of medical insurance after retirement. Clearly, this issue is germane to the retirement incentives provided in the pension. For example, suppose a firm sets the pension so as to strongly encourage retirement at age 55. It also provides medical insurance as a fringe benefit to workers before retirement but does not offer continued medical coverage after retirement (at least until age 65, when Medicare becomes available).

In this case, workers view the incentive to leave as the difference between the pension advantages of leaving early and the cost of purchasing private medical insurance outside the firm. Since medical insurance can be expensive to older individuals outside a group, the availability of retiree medical insurance can affect the retirement calculus. It has been shown that the firm's policy on whether to extend insurance to retirees can substantially affect workers' retirement decisions.[24] I have implicitly assumed in my discussion that the firm continues medical coverage. About half of all firms that offer medical insurance to workers extend coverage to retirees; the other half do not.[25]

### 5.5 RETIREMENT AGES AND TENURE PROFILES FOR A SAMPLE OF FIRMS

It is apparent that firms can set pension parameters to generate incentives that favor particular tenure and retirement age patterns. We know from many studies, including the empirical work presented in chapters 3 and 4, that workers react to incentives embedded in the pension.[26] By implication, we can infer pension provisions, and underlying optimal age and tenure profiles, by studying actual retirement patterns across firms. I now

Table 5.3  Age Started Last Job: Sample of Retirees

| Category | Percentage | Cumulative |
|---|---|---|
| Age range | | |
| 19 or younger | 4.3 | — |
| 20–29 | 19.1 | 23.4 |
| 30–39 | 31.6 | 55.0 |
| 40–49 | 29.4 | 84.4 |
| 50–54 | 9.5 | 93.9 |
| 55 or older | 6.1 | 100.0 |
| Average, 38 years old | | |

Source: U.S. Department of Labor, Benefit Amounts Survey, 1978.

turn to an illustration of this approach using a small sample of large pension plans in the United States.

### 5.5.1 Benefit Amounts Survey

The data are from the Benefit Amounts Survey sponsored by the U.S. Department of Labor in 1978. A total of 350 pension plans participated in the survey. Information for each plan relates to retirees in pay status in 1978, including year and age of retirement, tenure at retirement, and a few additional characteristics. A limited amount of information is reported about the plan sponsors.[27] I analyze the data reported for the 57 defined benefit plans that had at least one hundred retirees over the period 1968–76.

Since the Employee Retirement Income Security Act was enacted in 1974, it is reasonable to assume that most of the data studied are unfettered by new pension rules introduced by ERISA.[28] The sample of retirees from each plan is limited to one hundred randomly chosen retirees from each firm. The plans in the sample are distributed across the following size categories: eight firms employ fewer than 1,000 workers, twenty firms employ 1,000–5,000, sixteen employ 5,000–25,000, and twelve employ more than 25,000 workers.

### 5.5.2 Age and Tenure Patterns

Table 5.3 reports the distribution of ages at which retirees in the sample start employment in the job they retire from.[29] Only 4. 3 percent of the retirees start the job they retire from before age 20. Almost one in four find their last job by age 30. More than half of the retirees in the sample joined their last jobs before their fortieth birthday; and only about 6 percent joined after age 55. Put simply, large firms that offer defined benefit pensions do not often hire older workers.[30] Workers typically have long tenure at the time of their retirement. The average worker in the sample

Table 5.4  Age of Retirement in a Sample of Fifty-seven Firms

| Category | Number of firms |
| --- | --- |
| Percentage of retirees retired by age 59 | |
| 0–10 | 24 |
| 11–32 | 25 |
| 33 or more | 8 |
| Percentage of retirees retired by age 65 | |
| 90–100 | 37 |
| 75–89 | 8 |
| 74 or less | 12 |

*Source:* U.S. Department of Labor, Benefit Amounts Survey, 1978.

joined his last firm at 38 years old; the average tenure level at retirement is twenty-four years.

Retirement ages are summarized in table 5.4. Of the fifty-seven firms in the sample, twenty-four had fewer than 10 percent of their retirees leave the firm before age 60; eight firms had at least one-third of their retirees leave before age 60. In thirty-seven firms, at least 90 percent of their retirees left by age 65. In twelve firms, at least 25 percent of retirees left after age 65.

Figures 5.6 and 5.7 present the distributions of tenure and retirement ages for the sample. Figure 5.6 presents tenure and retirement age frequencies; figure 5.7 presents cumulative distributions. Assuming that firms are successful in managing the tenure and retirement ages of their

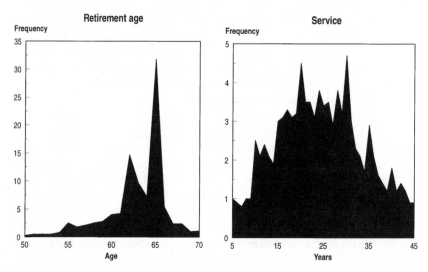

**Figure 5.6** Retirement age and tenure: Frequency distributions.

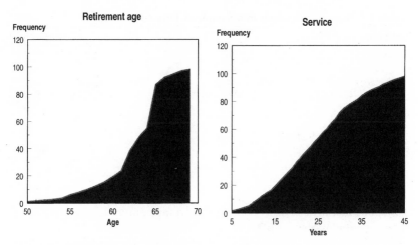

Figure 5.7 Retirement age and tenure: Cumulative distributions.

workers, it is apparent that firms are more interested in the ages at which workers retire from the firm than in their tenure level at retirement. The frequency distribution of tenure at retirement is essentially diffuse, from ten to beyond forty years. But the retirement age distribution is concentrated over a five- to ten-year age range. Few workers retire before age 50; even by age 60, only about 15 percent retire. By age 65, however, 87 percent of workers are retired from their jobs.

The data reveal a relation within the firms between age of retirement and tenure. To demonstrate, I normalize retirement patterns across firms in the sample by defining early retirees as those who leave before the median retirement age in their firm. Table 5.5 evaluates the determinants of "early" retirement as I define it. The results show that those retiring relatively early are equally likely to be earning wages above or below the median wage in the firm, but less likely to have relatively rapid wage growth over their tenure (relative to others in the firm).

The results also evince a strong relation between age of retirement and tenure. Workers with longer service at age 55 are more likely to depart the firm early than those with shorter service. For example, a worker who at age 55 has ten more years of service is likelier by 13 percentage points to leave the firm relatively early.[31] More generally, firms that hire young workers tend to have relatively young retirement ages.

I illustrate this point graphically for the entire sample in figures 5.8 and 5.9. Figure 5.8 shows two distributions: tenure at age 55 by those in the entire sample who retire between ages 55 and 60 (black), and tenure at age 55 by those who retire later than age 60. Clearly, the early retirees in the sample are those who join these firms at earlier ages.

**Table 5.5 Characteristics of Youngest Retirees in the Firm**

| Independent variable | Mean | Coefficient |
|---|---|---|
| Intercept | — | −1.24*** |
| | | (16.18) |
| Real wage growth exceeds median in firm | .50 | −.31*** |
| | | (5.26) |
| Tenure at age 55 | 17.23 | .053*** |
| | | (18.16) |
| Wage exceeds median in firm | .50 | .017 |
| | | (.30) |
| Female | .20 | .218*** |
| | | (2.87) |
| Nonwhite | .09 | −.102 |
| | | (1.06) |
| Log of likelihood | | 362.1 |
| Mean dependent variable | | .40 |
| Observations | | 5,666 |

*Note:* Dependent variable equals unity if worker retired earlier than median age in the pension plan. Estimates are made using a logit model; numbers in parentheses are *t*-statistics.
*Source:* U.S. Department of Labor, Benefit Amounts Survey, 1978.
\*\*\* significant at the .01 level (two-tailed test).

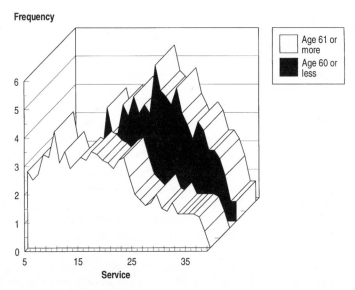

**Figure 5.8** Tenure across firms at age 55. Depicts the distribution of service levels at age 55 for two groups: those who retired at age 61 or later (white distribution), and those who retired at age 60 or earlier (black distribution).

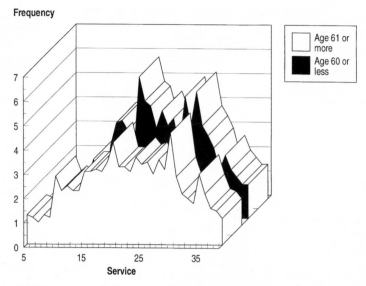

**Figure 5.9** Tenure across firms at retirement. Depicts the distribution of service levels at retirement for two groups: those who retired at age 61 or later (white distribution), and those who retired at age 60 or earlier (black distribution).

Figure 5.9 depicts tenure for these two groups at retirement age. By the time retirement occurs, the two tenure distributions are closer together: firms seemingly want workers to work at the firm over some long period, then depart.

### 5.5.3 Retirement Outcomes of Four Firms

Since firms provide different incentives for quitting and retirement, we ought to see markedly different tenure and retirement age outcomes across a sample of firms. We do. This point is made graphically in figures 5.10 and 5.11, which depict the tenure and retirement age distributions for four pension plans. Figure 5.10 depicts the data for pension plans A (solid-line schedule) and B (dotted-line schedule). In firm A, the distribution of retirement ages is fairly wide: one worker in four retires at age 59. And there is a relatively small variance in tenure at retirement: about two-thirds of retirees have from twenty to thirty years of service. The opposite pattern is evinced in firm B. No workers retire before age 60, yet all retire by age 65. But the tenure distribution at retirement is wide: only one-third of retirees have between twenty and thirty years of tenure.

Firms C and D, depicted in figure 5.11, show almost identical retirement age distributions, which are fairly typical for the sample as a whole (see figure 5.6). But their tenure distributions are dramatically different.

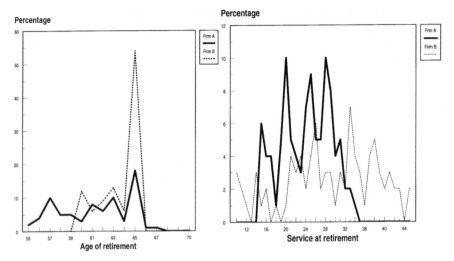

**Figure 5.10** Retirement age and tenure, firms A and B.

Neither plan had any retirees with more than thirty years of service. Approximately four in ten workers in firm D retire exactly at thirty years of service. In firm C, workers retire with no more than twenty years of service, with most retirees having service levels between ten and fifteen years.

The natural question arises how the retirement distributions vary

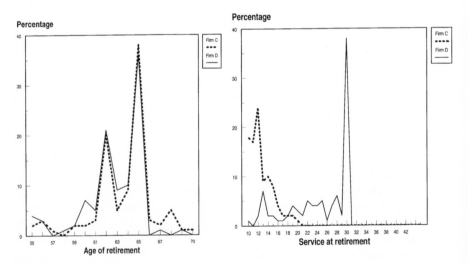

**Figure 5.11** Retirement age and tenure, firms C and D.

Table 5.6 Percentage Retired in Sample Firms by Age 59

| Independent variable | Mean | Coefficient |
|---|---|---|
| Intercept | — | .21 |
| | | (1.55) |
| Union | .28 | .089* |
| | | (1.85) |
| Median wage ($1,000) | 13.84 | −.007 |
| | | (1.24) |
| More than 1,000 workers in firm | .85 | −.143** |
| | | (2.51) |
| Median tenure at age 55 | 17.57 | .007* |
| | | (1.76) |
| Median real growth rate in wages | .06 | .07 |
| | | (.60) |
| Industry growth rate[a] 1965–70 | .22 | −.108** |
| | | (2.02) |
| Other variables[b] | | X |
| $R^2$ | | .37 |
| Observations | | 57 |

Note: Dependent variable is the percentage of retirees from the firm retired by age 59. Numbers in parentheses are t-statistics.
Source: U.S. Department of Labor, Benefit Amounts Survey, 1978.
[a] Number of employees in two-digit industry in 1970 compared with 1965, expressed as a percentage increase.
[b] Six dummy variables denoting the one-digit industry were included: none of the coefficients on these variables were statistically significant. The percentages of retirees who were females and nonwhite were included as separate variables; the coefficients on both variables were insignificantly different from zero.
** significant at the .05 level; * significant at the .10 level (two-tailed test).

across firm types. Table 5.6 reports the results of a regression relating various firm characteristics to the percentage of retirees who retired at age 59 or earlier. The results show that a larger portion of the participants in a pension plan retire at early ages if the participants are unionized, if they work in smaller firms, and if the median tenure in the firm at age 55 is relatively high. The results also suggest an industry effect. All else the same, retirement occurs at older ages in industries experiencing employment growth.

## 5.6 CONCLUDING REMARKS

It is apparent from much empirical work that pensions play an important role in influencing tenure and age profiles in the firm. The incentive structures vary markedly across firms. Accordingly, it is not surprising that patterns of tenure and ages at retirement across firms show similar variance.

Workers covered by defined benefit plans face nearly universal penalties for leaving the firm too early or too late, but there is great variation in these incentives at different ages. These differences are apparent from either studying pension plan rules and generosity levels across plans directly or evaluating the resulting retirement and tenure patterns across firms. Firms act as though particular tenure and age distributions are important to firm productivity, and they seemingly use the flexibility inherent in defined benefit plans to help them attain some of their desired labor force characteristics.

Moreover, the prevalence of particular pension benefit formulas and constraints has not been constant over time. There has been a dramatic shift toward earlier retirement ages across the United States economy. This trend, and the potential role played by pensions, is the subject of the next chapter.

CHAPTER SIX

# Role of Pensions in Earlier Retirement after 1970

In previous chapters I made the implicit assumption that pension plan rules, though widely different across firms, are static over time. In this chapter I show that since the 1960s, important changes have occurred in private pension rules affecting the age of retirement.[1] These changes, together with those in the social security system over the same period, have contributed to a substantial reduction in the average age of retirement in the United States after 1970.

During the post–World War II period, older male workers in the United States have gradually reduced their labor force participation. In 1950, 42 percent of workers aged 65 and over remained in the labor force; in 1970, 27 percent remained; and in 1985, 16 percent. Although this trend is the subject of much study,[2] little attention is given to participation rates among workers aged 55–64.[3] In many ways, the postwar evidence for this age group is more interesting and problematic.

As shown in table 6.1, from 1955 to 1970 labor force participation rates for workers aged 55 to 64 fell by only 3.4 percentage points, from 86.4 to 83 percent (column 1). In the ensuing fifteen years, however, the participation rate for this group fell by 15.1 points, to 67.9 percent in 1985. The data in column 3 show that these changes translated to parallel reductions in the average age of retirement from 66.2 years in 1970 to 64.1 in 1985.[4] This chapter addresses the likely causes of the exit of almost one in five male workers aged 55 to 64 from market work after 1970.

The relatively rapid labor market exodus of "not so old" workers tends to undermine theories tied to long-run trends in wealth, more two-earner families, and the like. I consider two institutions that have the capacity, through changes in their rules, to alter the economic calculus of the retirement decision over a short period—the social security system

Table 6.1  Retirement Statistics, 1955–85

| Year | LFPR[a] of males 55–64 (1) | Change (2) | Average retirement age of males[c] (3) | Change (4) | PIA[d] of males newly retired (5) | Percentage change (6) |
|------|------|------|------|------|------|------|
| 1955 | 86.4[b] | — | — | — | 388 | — |
| 1960 | 86.8 | 0.4 | — | — | 386 | 0.0 |
| 1965 | 84.6 | −2.2 | 66.5 | — | 358 | −7.2 |
| 1970 | 83.0 | −1.6 | 66.2 | −0.3 | 398 | 11.2 |
| 1975 | 75.6 | −7.4 | 65.1 | −1.1 | 494 | 24.1 |
| 1980 | 72.1 | −3.5 | 64.8 | −0.3 | 582 | 17.1 |
| 1985 | 67.9 | −4.2 | 64.1 | −0.7 | 580 | 0.0 |

*Sources:* U.S. Bureau of the Census, *Statistical Abstract,* various issues (col. 1); P. Rones, "Using the CPS to Track Retirement Trends among Older Men," at chapter 6, note 9 (col. 3); U.S. Social Security Administration, *Social Security Bulletin, Annual Statistical Supplement, 1987,* 120, at chapter 6, note 7 (col. 5); and *The Economic Report of the President* (1988), 298, at chapter 5, note 18 (BLS wage index).
[a] Labor force participation rate.
[b] Numbers are percentages.
[c] Average retirement age from full- and part-time work.
[d] Primary insurance amounts, adjusted to 1985 dollars using the BLS nonagricultural wage base.

and private pension plans. I show that changes in rules in these pension programs potentially can explain a large portion of the reduction in labor force participation over the period.

## 6.1  CHANGES IN THE SOCIAL SECURITY SYSTEM

Economists have devoted much study to the role played by the social security system in the decision to retire early. Particular attention has been paid to the implicit tax on work past age 65 stemming from the so-called earnings test and to lifetime "wealth effects" conferred especially on early retiree cohorts collecting social security benefits.[5] In this section I evaluate changes in this system that may explain the unusual increase in earlier retirement after 1970.

### 6.1.1  Wealth Effect

All social security system retirees—even those retiring in the 1980s— have earned an implicit rate of return on their social security taxes substantially in excess of the risk-free rate of return. That is to say, contributions made to the social security system, accumulated at risk-free market interest rates, have been less than the expected present value of benefits, and thus the system has conferred important wealth effects for a long series of retiree cohorts.

For older individuals in the workforce either when the social security system was created in 1935 or when it was greatly expanded and enhanced through the early 1950s, the wealth effects may have had a particularly dramatic impact on retirement ages. These workers may already have provided for retirement through other savings and so may have used much of the unanticipated increase in wealth to retire earlier than planned.

As subsequent cohorts progressed through the workforce, they too received benefits in excess of contributions, but the wealth effects have been progressively smaller. For example, for cohorts retiring in 1950, the real rate of return on employer and employee contributions was almost 20 percent. For those retiring fifteen years later, it was 11.6 percent.[6] As the higher benefits became more fully anticipated by subsequent cohorts, workers presumably have reduced their other savings for retirement, thereby spending part of their greater wealth in the form of higher consumption during their work life and part in the form of earlier retirement.

### 6.1.2 Re-creation of Start-up Wealth Effects

The gradual elimination of social security wealth effects for subsequent retiree cohorts, and particularly unanticipated wealth effects, suggests that though "start-up" effects could perhaps explain extraordinary movements toward earlier retirement before, say, the mid-1950s, they cannot be an important factor after 1970. This impression, however, is not supported by the data.

The data in table 6.1 portray the average monthly benefits for men collecting new awards, indexed to nonagricultural wages from 1955 to 1985 (column 5). The numbers represent "primary insurance amounts" (PIAs), which are age 65 equivalent monthly payments. Thus the numbers are not influenced by the choice of some retirees to begin collecting reduced benefits as early as age 62.

From 1955 to 1970, real average benefits remained virtually constant, reflecting the settling down of the system after numerous increases during its first twenty years of existence.[7] But from 1970 to 1980, average real benefits increased by 46.2 percent, from $398 to $582 per month (in 1985 dollars).

The increases are attributable to ad hoc adjustments enacted in 1969 and 1971 and to the 1972 Amendments, which increased benefits by 20 percent. In addition, the Amendments indexed benefits to the Consumer Price Index. Finally, owing to an error made in the 1972 Amendments (so-called double indexing), Congress set in motion a self-propelling escalation of first-year benefits beyond those explicitly enacted in the Amendments.[8] The error was corrected in the 1977 Amendments, and new rules were made effective in 1979.

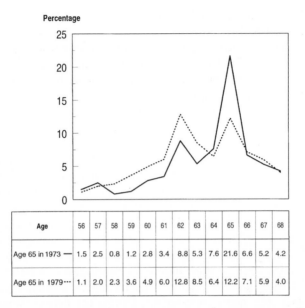

| Age | 56 | 57 | 58 | 59 | 60 | 61 | 62 | 63 | 64 | 65 | 66 | 67 | 68 |
|---|---|---|---|---|---|---|---|---|---|---|---|---|---|
| Age 65 in 1973 — | 1.5 | 2.5 | 0.8 | 1.2 | 2.8 | 3.4 | 8.8 | 5.3 | 7.6 | 21.6 | 6.6 | 5.2 | 4.2 |
| Age 65 in 1979 ··· | 1.1 | 2.0 | 2.3 | 3.6 | 4.9 | 6.0 | 12.8 | 8.5 | 6.4 | 12.2 | 7.1 | 5.9 | 4.0 |

**Figure 6.1** Retirement rates, two cohorts of men. Depicts the retirement age distribution of two cohorts, given they were still working at age 55.

Since real social security benefits were roughly constant from 1955 to 1970, it is reasonable to conclude that the increases in benefits during the 1970s were unanticipated. Older workers who planned retirement based on real benefits prevailing during the 1960s must have been surprised by their new wealth, which plausibly caused important reductions in their retirement ages.

The data in table 6.1 are consistent with this expectation. After twenty years of virtual stability, labor force participation rates for males aged 55–64 fell by 7.4 percentage points from 1970 to 1975, a period during which real social security benefits increased by 24.1 percent. From 1975 to 1979, real benefits increased by an additional 17.1 percent. By 1985, the labor participation rate among men 55 to 64 was 67.9 percent compared with 83 percent in 1970. These data suggest that increases in social security benefits during the decade 1970–80 may have had an important impact on retirement behavior.

Figure 6.1 provides graphic evidence on this point. The figure portrays distributions of retirement rates for males for two cohorts using data from the Current Population Survey.[9] Age specific retirement rates of the cohort that reached age 62 in 1970 are portrayed by the solid line. The data in the figure confirm the importance of 65 as a popular choice of retirement age during the period. Fully one in five members in the cohort retired at age 65.

The dotted line in the figure portrays the cohort reaching age 62 just six years later in 1976. During this period, which coincided with approximately a 25 percent increase in real social security benefits, the distribution shifted markedly to the left: the average retirement age for cohorts just six years apart fell by almost a full year.

### 6.1.3 Price Effects

Much attention also has been paid to price effects in the social security system. These include the "earnings test," which encouraged workers to retire no later than 65, and the "recalculation effect," which encouraged workers to postpone retirement until at least age 62. The earnings test did not change over the period of study. But the recalculation effect was altered in 1977, substantially reducing the cost of retiring before age 62.

The "tax" imposed by the social security system on work after age 65 occurs because of the combination of an earnings test, which offsets part of social security benefits against wage income, and economically unfair adjustments to benefits after age 65. During the period under study, if an individual decided to work during his sixty-fifth year, then, beyond some income threshold ($8,400 in 1988), fifty cents in social security benefits was lost for each dollar in wages earned.[10] And though the subsequent annuity was increased in real terms by approximately 3 percent, an adjustment of 8 percent would have been required to preserve the present value of social security benefits.

This combination of policies acted like an extra tax on work past age 65, and historically there has been an unusual rate of retirement specifically at this age (see fig. 6.1). In 1983 Congress legislated higher post-65 actuarial adjustments designed to eliminate the economic impact of the earnings test by the year 2005. But since these changes apply only to future cohorts of retirees, they do not explain the observed changes in labor force participation rates from 1970 to 1985.

While the earnings test discourages work past age 65, the so-called recalculation effect discourages retirement before age 62. Until 1977, social security benefits were determined by the average of lifetime earnings in *nominal* dollars. By continuing to work, workers could replace inflation-eroded earnings of the 1950s in the benefit formula with current dollar earnings. This practice generally provided an incentive for workers to postpone retirement until age 65, or at least until age 62.[11] Retirement at some earlier age, say 55, resulted in large reductions in social security benefits.

In 1977 the recalculation effect was substantially reduced because social security earnings up to age 60 were indexed to economywide wages. Thus, if an individual turned age 60 in 1980, wages earned in 1955, for example, were adjusted in the formula by the ratio of the wage index in 1980 compared with 1955. In addition, for each subsequent cohort, the number of years of wages included in the average wage formula increased by one. For those retiring at age 62 in 1970, twelve years of wages were included in the average (seventeen years of wages since 1951 minus the five lowest wage years). For those retiring at age 62 in 1977, nineteen years of wages were included. So even if workers' real wages during recent years were marginally higher than those earned in the 1950s, their impact on average wages for purposes of calculating social security benefits became progressively smaller.

### 6.1.4 Expansion of the Disability Program

Finally, it is worth considering that in 1957 social security disability payments were made available to those aged 50–64. The disability program could have enabled individuals who otherwise would have been gainfully employed to leave the workforce on disability benefits. If so, the change in eligibility age for this program is a potential avenue by which changes in the social security system could have affected labor force participation rates for men age 55–64.[12]

### 6.1.5 Potential Magnitudes of Social Security Effects

It is interesting to ask whether available data can suggest an order of magnitude for the effects of observed social security changes on retirement trends after 1970. It seems apparent that the data do not support the disability theory of earlier retirement. First, the disability program for men aged 55–64 was put in place in 1957, almost fifteen years before a substantial acceleration of exits from the labor force occurred for men in this age group.

Second, although disability awards as a percentage of all new social security awards to males increased from 11.1 percent in 1957 to 27 percent in 1976, they subsequently fell to 19.3 percent by 1986 owing to the imposition of stricter standards beginning in 1976.[13] If the dramatic increase in disability awards was an important source of the overall trend toward lower labor force participation rates until 1976, then the subsequent reduction in disability awards should have caused a parallel reversal in the rates after 1976. The data in table 6.1 show no indication of such a reversal.

This evidence does not necessarily mean that the social security disability program had no effect on labor force participation; it just means that, if it did, its influence was overwhelmed by other effects. More evidence on this point is offered below.

Since the labor force participation rate for men 55 to 64 years old fell precipitously after 1970, a more likely candidate to explain this trend is the social security wealth effect implied by the dramatic increase in real social security benefits beginning about the same time. The importance of this effect is suggested by Gary Burtless, who measured the impact of the 20 percent increase in social security benefits in 1972.[14] Based on individual data from the Retirement History Survey, conducted by the Social Security Administration. Burtless estimated that the average retirement age would have been reduced by .17 years. Ignoring nonlinearities in his model, this result suggests that a 46 percent unanticipated increase in benefits (the amount that actually occurred from 1970 to 1979) would have resulted in a reduction in retirement age of .40 years. Other estimates imply reductions in the same range.[15]

For comparison, the average age of retirement for men fell by approximately 1.4 years from 1970 to 1980. These results suggest that approximately one-third of the reduction in retirement age during this period could have been explained by the increase in social security benefits after 1970.

Implications of the new recalculation rules enacted in the 1977 Amendments are more difficult to measure. Since the new rules did not go into effect until 1979, they could not have explained the reduction in retirement age for males during the 1970s. They could, however, have contributed to the continued drift toward earlier retirements during the 1980s.

The Amendments changed the social security calculus for retirement before age 62 in an important way. To illustrate, I compute the social security benefit available at age 62 for a male worker who retired at age 55 in 1977 compared with the benefit he could have received starting at age 62 by retiring five years later at age 60. I assume that both calculations are made at age 55, so that the age 60 work alternative is a counterfactual proposition. In making the latter calculation, I assume that the 55-year-old worker expected nominal wages to grow at the rate of 6.5 percent per year until age 60 (consistent with the ten-year Treasury bond rate in 1977 of 8.4 percent) and he earns the average nonagricultural wage in the United States over his work life. Using the pre–1977 Amendment rules, the benefit of retiring at age 60 turns out to be 120 percent of the benefit available by retiring at age 55. Using the post–1977 Amendment rules, this ratio is 108 percent.[16]

The change in the recalculation effect in the 1977 Amendments has not been estimated directly in the literature. The model proposed by Alan Gustman and Thomas Steinmeier,[17] however, is easily modified to make this estimate.[18]

Their model predicts that, all else equal, the change in wage indexing in the 1977 Amendments reduced the average retirement age from full- and part-time work by .2 years. The change in the recalculation rules can therefore explain about 30 percent of the reduction in retirement age that occurred after 1980 (see table 6.1).

## 6.2 CHANGES IN THE PRIVATE PENSION SYSTEM

Although the data implicate changes in the social security system in earlier retirement ages after 1970, they can explain only part of the phenomenon. In this section I show that an important contributing factor was a changing private pension system. I refer not to the perhaps important effect of growing numbers of workers retiring with pensions, but rather to changes in the incentive effects embedded in defined benefit pensions that encourage early retirement.

Unlike social security, pensions are not pay as you go systems: they are funded during workers' tenure with the firm. Presumably, workers pay for their pensions in the form of lower cash wages during working years (see chapter 2). Thus, as a first-order approximation, important wealth effects are not expected to be part of the system. An exception may have occurred when most large defined benefit pensions were created during the 1940s and 1950s and past service credit was awarded to existing workers. But the start-up wealth effects did not generate special wealth effects after 1970 and certainly would not have conveyed unanticipated wealth effects to cohorts retiring during this period.

A more likely source of change lay in pension rules that provide incentives to retire earlier. Any particular pension plan covers only a tiny portion of the workforce, and pension incentives vary greatly across firms (see chapter 5). But approximately half of male retirees during the 1970s retired with pensions,[19] so if the pension system evinced a broad tendency to encourage earlier retirement, it could have significantly affected national retirement behavior. And though pension incentives to retire from firms do not necessarily imply exit from the workforce, as an empirical matter the two are closely related.[20]

### 6.2.1 Historical Trends

In this section I describe the changes in pension plan rules that occurred from 1960 to 1980. It is apparent that over this period there was an important and pervasive trend in private pension plans to reduce the age of eligibility for full benefits and for reduced benefits and to award more actuarial subsidies to early benefits.

I used data published by Bankers Trust Company.[21] Bankers Trust is

Table 6.2  Pension Eligibility at Age 55

| Plan type | 1960 | 1965 | 1970 | 1975 | 1980 |
|---|---|---|---|---|---|
| Pattern plans[a] | 17 | 23 | 39 | 44 | 67 |
| Conventional plans[b] | 30 | 38 | 46 | 58 | 57 |

Note: Service requirements range from five to thirty years.
Source: Bankers Trust Company, Corporate Pension Plan Study, at chapter 2, note 16.
[a]Pattern plans always cover union workers. The term "pattern" denotes that the same plan is used by more than one firm. Each plan, however, is operated independently by each plan sponsor. Thus pattern plans are not multiemployer plans.
[b]Conventional plans can cover union workers, but often do not. The plan is specific to a plan sponsor.

one of the largest custodial banks for pension plans in the United States. Every five years, from 1955 through 1980, it reported summary data for pension plan provisions among its clients. The samples typically included 250 to 350 large firms, representing roughly 25 percent of pension plan participants in private pension plans. In its 1980 edition, it provided comparable plan provision data from 1960 through 1980.

Bankers' data are separated into two types of plans, "pattern" plans and "conventional" plans. Pattern plans are union plans—the same plan covers union members in several firms. Conventional plans sometimes cover union workers but more often cover nonunion participants. There are about four times as many conventional plans in the data as pattern plans.

Data in table 6.2 show that over 1960 to 1980, the portion of plans in the database that permitted early retirement with reduced benefits as soon as age 55 roughly doubled in conventional plans and quadrupled in pattern plans. By 1980, roughly 60 percent of pension plans in Bankers' sample permitted 55-year-old workers to retire with a reduced pension.

If reduced retirement benefits were actuarially fair, these changes alone would not have increased the present value of pension benefits for individuals who otherwise "quit" at age 55 and collected benefits starting at some later eligibility age previously in place. In fact, in chapter 5 I show that actuarially fair pensions encourage workers to postpone retirement. The data in table 6.3, however, show that the practice of paying actuarially fair benefits between normal and early retirement ages virtually disappeared over the period. The trend was toward actuarially subsidized benefits at early retirement ages, which makes earlier retirement more attractive to older workers (see chapter 5).

In 1960 no conventional plans in the survey paid full benefits before age 65, and only 10 percent offered subsidies to early retirees.[22] In 1965 this situation had not changed. But by 1970, 19 percent of these plans paid a full benefit to at least some retirees younger than age 65 and paid

Table 6.3 Pension Benefits before Age 65

| Benefit payable at earliest date out | Highest benefit payable before age 65 | Percentage of pension plans | | | | |
|---|---|---|---|---|---|---|
| | | 1960 | 1965 | 1970 | 1975 | 1980 |
| Actuarial equivalent | *Actuarial equivalent* | | | | | |
| | Pattern plans[a] | n/a[b] | n/a | 19 | 7 | 6 |
| | Conventional plans | 90 | 75 | 44 | 9 | 5 |
| Greater than actuarial equivalent ("subsidized early") | *Full accrued pension or greater* | | | | | |
| | Pattern plans | n/a | n/a | 36 | 80 | 79 |
| | Conventional plans | 0 | 0 | 19 | 51 | 69 |

*Note:* Note that the column numbers within plan type do not add to 100; e.g., in 1970, 19 plus 36, or 55 percent of pattern plans, fell into the categories above. The remaining 45 percent either paid an actuarial equivalent pension at the earliest age of eligibility but offered full benefits before age 65 or offered a subsidized benefit at the earliest age of eligibility but offered full benefits only at age 65.
*Source:* Bankers Trust Company, *Corporate Pension Plan Study,* at chapter 2, note 16.
[a] Pattern and conventional plans are defined in notes to table 6.2.
[b] Data not available.

an actuarially subsidized benefit to all early retirees. By 1980 roughly 70 percent of plans permitted retirement before age 65 with full benefits. Virtually all plans offered subsidized early benefits before age 65.[23]

Data in table 6.4 from the Bureau of Labor Statistics confirm these findings. The BLS published two reports during the sample period summarizing pension plan rules in 1963 and 1983.[24] Both reports are based on large surveys of pension plans in the United States.

The surveys show that in 1963, 8 percent of pension-covered workers were in plans that permitted full benefits at age 60 or earlier; by 1983 this number was 47 percent. In 1963, 75 percent of pension-covered workers were eligible for retirement with reduced benefits before eligibility for full benefits. In 1983 this number was 97 percent. Moreover, the

Table 6.4 Ages of Eligibility for Pension Benefits

| Year | Full benefits | | Reduced benefits | |
|---|---|---|---|---|
| | Age 60 or earlier (1) | Average age (2) | At some early age (3) | Average age (4) |
| 1963 | 8% | 63.8 | 75% | 59.0 |
| 1983 | 47 | 60.2 | 97 | 55.4 |

*Note:* Eligibility carries service requirements in most cases.
*Sources:* U.S. Department of Labor, *Labor Mobility and Private Pension Plans,* at chapter 2, note 18, and U.S. Department of Labor, *Employee Benefits in Medium and Large Firms,* at chapter 2, note 3.

average ages of eligibility fell dramatically over the period. From 1963 to 1983, the average ages at which covered workers could be eligible for full or reduced benefits (provided they satisfied service requirements) each fell by approximately 3.5 years.[25]

### 6.2.2 Potential Magnitude of Pension Effects

It is instructive to gauge the potential impact caused by the widespread change in retirement eligibility rules. I assume that the main influences of the trend are felt through the availability of retirement with full benefits before age 65. I assume that the economic consequences of earlier eligibility for actuarially subsidized reduced benefits would be of second-order importance.[26] If these effects are important, my estimate of the pension effects on retirement age is understated.

I use available data to estimate the portion of the United States workforce affected by the drift toward earlier eligibility for full benefits. For example, the Bankers Trust data suggest that the portion of pensions that permitted retirement with full benefits before age 65 was 22 percent in 1970 compared with zero in 1965. The retiree data in Iams[27] suggest that approximately 40 percent of males of retirement age were covered by pensions in 1970.[28] Data from the U.S. Department of Labor suggest that approximately half of workers in plans that permitted retirement with full benefits before age 65 actually had sufficient service to qualify for the earlier eligibility.[29] The product of these numbers suggests that in 1970, approximately 3.4 percent of the male workforce of retirement age qualified for full pension benefits before age 65, compared with virtually none in 1965. By 1975 this number was 10.2 percent and by 1985, 15.0 percent.[30]

Based on data from the Retirement History Survey, Gloria Bazzoli analyzes the impact of pension eligibility on retirement rates.[31] Her estimates suggest that, compared with other workers who are covered by pensions, retirement rates at ages under 65 are almost twice as high for males eligible for retirement with full pension benefits before age 65. I adjust the age specific labor force participation data from the Current Population Survey for males in the United States beginning in 1965 to reflect the changes in retirement rates implied by these data.[32] The resulting calculations suggest that, owing to pension eligibility changes, the average retirement age for males fell by .51 years from 1965 to 1985.

On balance, the numbers suggest that the potential impact caused by changing pension rules over the period is of the same order of magnitude as that attributable to social security. Together, the data suggest that changes in the social security system and private pensions could explain roughly half of the reduction in retirement age after 1970.[33]

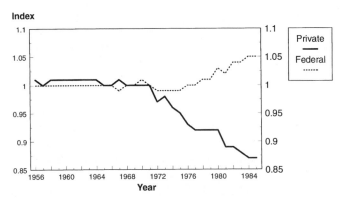

**Figure 6.2** Retirement ages, 1956–85, federal versus private. Ages divided by age of retirement in 1956 and adjusted to remove pre-1970 trend.

## 6.3 TESTING THE THEORY: RETIREMENT OF FEDERAL WORKERS

One way to test this idea is to examine retirement trends for the federal government's civilian workforce. Over the period of study, federal workers were not covered by social security, and the government's pension plan maintained relatively constant rules over the period of study. Thus, if the unusual reduction in labor force participation after 1970 could be attributable to changes in the social security system and in private pension plans, we would not expect to observe similar changes in federal retirement patterns.

Recall from chapter 4 that the federal pension plan offers retirement with full benefits after thirty years of service upon attaining age 55, at age 60 with twenty-five years of service, or at age 62 with five years of service. Reduced benefits generally are not offered, but a disability option similar to that of the social security system is available.[34]

I do not have participation rates or retirement rates for the federal workforce, but I do have average retirement age.[35] For the sake of exposition, I adjust the data for underlying trends that were apparent before 1970. Thus I calculate a simple linear trend in the federal retirement age from 1955 through 1969 and detrend the data through 1986 on the assumption that the pre-1970 trend would continue after 1969.[36] I apply the same algorithm to the time series on participation rates for males aged 55–64 in the United States workforce. Both series are indexed to their 1955 values, so that they equal unity at the beginning of the period. The question is whether, like the overall participation rate, federal data evinced inexplicably large reductions in retirement age after 1970.

It is apparent from the data in figure 6.2 that in contrast to the dramatic reduction in the overall labor force participation rate after 1970, there is no unusual reduction in retirement age after 1969 in the federal sector. In fact, beginning about 1976, there is an *increase* in retirement age.

A likely candidate to explain this increase is the application of stricter standards for disability retirement to the federal retirement system, akin to those put in place in the social security system about the same time (see above). From 1976 to 1986, the portion of federal retirements attributable to disability fell from almost 40 percent to 10 percent.

The federal results suggest that, except for other changes in the social security system and private pension rules, there would have been upward movement in labor force participation rates for older males owing to stricter application of disability eligibility rules after 1976. By implication, a similar disability effect must have occurred in the social security–covered labor force (see discussion above) but was overwhelmed by other factors over the same period, factors that were not working to affect federal retirement trends.

## 6.4 CONCLUDING REMARKS

The dramatic reduction in male participation rates since 1970, particularly for ages 55 to 64, is a labor force development that requires explanation. It seems apparent that a part of this trend is explained by the large, presumably unanticipated increase in real social security benefits from 1970 to 1980. The substantial reduction in 1977 of the so-called recalculation effect in the system is also a potential explanation for some of the drift toward earlier retirement after 1980. Pension plans also changed rules in favor of encouraging earlier retirement, which also contributed.

Since 1965, actuarially fair reductions for early retirement have been replaced by actuarially subsidized benefits, and reduced benefits have been made available to workers at earlier ages. Moreover, the age at which *full* benefits are provided also has fallen substantially, perhaps dramatically affecting the incentive to retire early. Together, changes in the social security system and in private pension plan rules could explain at least half of the reduction in retirement ages after 1970.

The question naturally arises why firms seemingly want to encourage workers to leave the firm at younger ages. Some literature indirectly implicates the entry of the baby boom generation into the labor market because of its impact on the relative wages of older versus younger men,[37] and some implicates legislation barring mandatory retirement because it may have provided incentives for firms to find other ways to encourage retirement.[38] Perhaps the answer lay in growth in jobs that favor earlier retirement.[39] Whatever the explanation, it seems clear that pension rules can

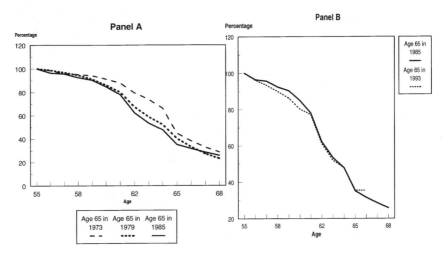

**Figure 6.3** Participation rates, four male cohorts.

dramatically affect tenure and age distributions in the firm and the economy.

Given the power of defined benefit plans to help the firm manage its workforce, it is instructive to ask why these plans have lost a significant market share since the mid-1980s. In the following chapters I propose that one reason is that defined contribution plans, properly constructed, also can help firms increase productivity at a lower cost than defined benefit plans. The increasing prominence of defined contribution plans is the subject of the next four chapters.

APPENDIX: RETIREMENT TRENDS FOR AGE 65 COHORTS AFTER 1980

It is interesting to consider developments in retirement patterns for cohorts that follow those reaching age 65 in 1979. Men in the 1979 cohort were 58 years old when the 1972 Amendments were enacted. Men in the 1985 age 65 cohort were 52 years old when the Amendments were enacted and so had additional time to make retirement decisions based on the new social security benefit levels. Figure 6.3A shows the participation rates for males who were still in the workforce at age 55 for the 1973, 1979, and 1985 age 65 cohorts.

The large reduction in participation rates in the 1979 cohort compared with the 1973 cohort noted in figure 6.1 is apparent in figure 6.3A. The data suggest that the 1985 age 65 cohort reacted more than the 1979

**Percentage**

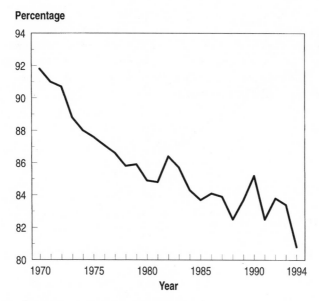

**Figure 6.4** Male participation rates at age 55, 1970–94.

cohort, but the reduction in participation rates was not large compared with the initial reactions of earlier cohorts.

Figure 6.3B compares the participation rates of the 1985 and 1993 cohorts. The participation rates are similar, suggesting that the shock to the social security system had been completed by the time the 1985 cohort retired from the labor force. Nevertheless, the data suggest that other effects, perhaps related to pensions, contribute to additional reductions in retirement ages.

More particularly, the data reveal markedly lower participation rates from ages 55 to age 60 for the 1993 cohort than for the 1985 cohort. At age 60, the participation rate of the later cohort was almost five percentage points lower than that of the earlier cohort. By age 61 participation rates converged, suggesting that, compared with the 1985 cohort, the 1993 cohort retired at faster rates in their fifties and reduced their retirement rates in their early sixties.

Even these data, however, are somewhat misleading, because the Bureau of Labor Statistics data on participation rates start at age 55, thereby making it impossible to study retirement rates before age 56. The rate at age 55, however, gives some indication of how important retirement has become in the labor force at age 55 or earlier. Figure 6.4 shows this rate for fifteen cohorts of male workers who attained age 55 from 1970 until 1974. It is apparent that the trend toward earlier retirement—particularly at very early ages—continues to move downward. The cohort reaching age 55 in 1994 had only 80.8 percent of its members still in the workforce. Future studies of retirement ages will be seriously incomplete unless retirement decisions at age 55 and younger are included. One cannot help but suspect that either pension plans rules or social security disability rules are implicated in this trend.

*Part Two*

## SORTING EFFECTS
## OF PENSIONS

## CHAPTER SEVEN

# Toward Explaining the Growth of Defined Contribution Plans

I have thus far concentrated on the productivity effects of defined benefit plans, particularly their potential impact on quit and retirement decisions. These plans traditionally have dominated pension coverage in the United States and are still the preferred primary plan in most large firms.

The most important development in private pensions over the past fifteen years is the gradual shift away from defined benefit plans and toward defined contribution plans. Historically, defined benefit plans dominated primary pension coverage. In 1979, among workers covered by a pension plan, more than 80 percent were covered by a defined benefit plan. By 1996 this share was 50 percent (see fig. 7.1).[1]

The reduction in share is primarily attributable not to replacement of existing defined benefit plans by the defined contribution variety, but rather to the predominance of new sponsors choosing defined contribution plan.[2] In addition, employment shifts in the economy have played a prominent role. Large unionized firms in the manufacturing sector—which traditionally had high rates of defined benefit coverage—lost a significant portion of their workforce to smaller, nonunion firms in the service sectors, where defined benefit plans traditionally had smaller market shares.

The key aspect to the trend, however, is that, even holding employment shares constant, the data show a widespread preference change in favor of defined contribution plans. The question is why this change occurred. One hypothesis involves federal regulation of pensions.[3] During the 1980s, the cost of administering defined benefit plans increased relative to the cost for defined contribution plans. But these increases are important only for relatively small pension plans. That is, the regulatory cost argument is capable of explaining the relatively large shift in preferences

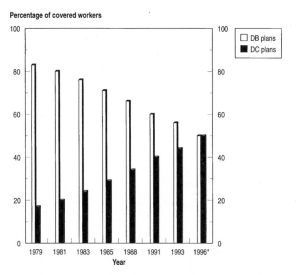

Figure 7.1 Defined benefit market share, 1979–96. *Projected based on form 5500 data and labor force trends. From U.S. Department of Labor, unpublished data.

away from defined benefit plans in small firms, but not the broad shifts across the entire market for private pensions.

Another explanation implicates changes in tax policy in 1987. In chapter 12 I show that these changes tilted tax preference in favor of defined contribution plans over defined benefit plans. Although they may have exacerbated it, however, it is apparent from figure 7.1 that the trend was well under way by 1987, suggesting that other factors also explain the growing popularity of defined contribution plans.

In this chapter I consider a different hypothesis, that the disruption in the pension market was caused by the introduction of a new kind of defined contribution plan in 1981, the so-called 401k. These plans arguably are good substitutes for both defined benefit plans and traditional defined contribution plans. By 1991, 401k plans accounted for 22 percent of all primary pension plan coverage in the private sector.[4]

## 7.1 NETTING OUT EMPLOYMENT SHIFTS

In defined contribution plans, the firm contributes some portion of wages or profits to employee accounts. Vesting usually occurs more rapidly than in defined benefit plans, and once vested, the value of the accounts belongs to workers even if they quit the firm.[5] These plans often are viewed as tax-preferred savings accounts.

In contrast, as shown in earlier chapters, defined benefit plans impose

**Table 7.1  Market Share of Defined Benefit Plans, 1979 and 1991**

| Percentage of pension-covered workers whose primary pension is defined benefit | | | Change in participant market share, 1979–91 | | |
|---|---|---|---|---|---|
| 1991 (1) | 1979 (2) | Predicted 1979 using 1991 coefficients[a] (3) | Total (4) | Explained by employment shifts (5) | Preference changes (6) |
| 66.3 | 89.6 | 79.1 | −23.3 | −12.8 | −10.5 |

*Note:* Numbers in table are percentages. The data exclude plans with fewer than one hundred participants. In addition, the sample omits firms with incomplete data; thus sample means may differ from
those characterizing the universe of pension plans.
*Source:* Form 5500 pension plan reports, 1979 and 1991.
[a]This number is the predicted percentage of active participants in defined benefit plans in 1979 using
coefficients estimated from the 1991 data (see chapter appendix).

penalties on workers who either quit the firm too early or retire too late.
Usually these plans are viewed as tools to help firms enhance productivity.[6] Presumably some firms attach more value to the attributes of defined
benefit plans, whereas others attach more value to defined contribution
plans. If firms and industries that favor defined benefit plans lose workers
to those that favor defined contribution plans, a considerable reduction
in observed participant market share for defined benefit coverage will
occur.

In the appendix to this chapter, I describe the method by which I disentangle the effects of employment and preference shifts. I study workers'
primary plan coverage, thereby ignoring secondary plan coverage.[7] I also
restrict the study to pensions with at least one hundred workers, so the
pension shares I cite are somewhat different from those shown in figure
7.1, which incorporate all plans, including those with fewer than one
hundred participants. Finally, I concentrate on the comparison of two
years of data, 1979 and 1991.[8]

Table 7.1 summarizes the empirical work. In 1979, defined benefit
plans had 89.6 percent of the market for covered participants in plans
with at least one hundred participants. By 1991, however, this share had
fallen to 66.3 percent. In a little more than a decade, defined benefit plans
lost over one-fourth of their market share to defined contribution plans
among plans with more than one hundred participants.

Of this shift, approximately 55 percent, or 12.8 percentage points, is
attributable to the falling employment levels in industries and firms that
traditionally used defined benefit plans. The remaining 45 percent, or
10.5 percentage points, is attributable to growing preference for defined
contribution plans over defined benefit plans.

Table 7.2  Change in Defined Benefit Plan Use

| | Distribution of pension-covered workers | | Percentage covered by defined benefit plans | |
| --- | --- | --- | --- | --- |
| | Actual 1979 (1) | Change 1979–91 (2) | Actual 1979 (3) | Change 1979–91 independent of employment shifts[a] (4) |
| Unionization | | | | |
| Union | 41.1 | −20.7 | 97.9 | −2.0 |
| Nonunion | 58.9 | 20.7 | 84.1 | −19.9 |
| Firm size | | | | |
| 5,000 or more | 68.8 | −12.4 | 94.6 | −9.3 |
| 2,000–4,999 | 11.3 | 1.6 | 87.6 | −19.7 |
| 1,000–1,999 | 7.8 | 2.0 | 81.4 | −25.4 |
| 500–1,000 | 6.1 | 2.0 | 72.1 | −35.5 |
| 200–500 | 5.7 | 3.3 | 63.9 | −44.4 |
| 200 or fewer | 2.2 | 1.4 | 62.0 | −36.5 |
| Major industry[b] | | | | |
| Manufacturing | 57.1 | −16.5 | 93.8 | −9.4 |
| Finance, insurance, and real estate | 10.3 | 3.3 | 84.4 | −8.4 |
| Transportation and communications | 10.8 | 0.7 | 96.1 | −6.1 |
| Services | 8.2 | 8.3 | 84.6 | −37.2 |
| Retail trade | 1.9 | 2.1 | 70.5 | −27.2 |
| Public administration | 3.9 | 0.4 | 83.5 | 1.3 |
| Wholesale trade | 7.5 | 3.7 | 75.5 | −24.0 |

Note: Numbers in table are percentages. Includes plans with at least one hundred participants.
[a] The estimated change in the defined benefit participant market share, calculated based on the 1979 distribution of pension-covered workers. It corresponds to the calculation of $U$ in expression (7.3) in the chapter appendix.
[b] Excludes industries with less than 1 percent of pension-covered participants.

The data in table 7.2 provide a finer breakdown of changing pension market shares. The data in the first column show the distribution of pension-covered workers across firm sizes, industries, and union and non-union jobs in 1979. Column 2 reports the change in these weights over the period 1979–91. Column 3 reports the defined benefit market share of pension-covered workers in 1979, and column 4 gives the change in this share between 1979 and 1991, after netting out the effects of changing employment weights.[9]

Each of the three categories in the table shows a similar pattern. Plan sponsors with the highest preferences for defined benefit plans as evinced in column 3 (union work forces; firms with at least 5,000 employees; the manufacturing sector) all experienced reductions in their share of pension-covered workers in the economy. For example, in 1979, 41.1

percent of pension-covered workers were unionized (column 1). Over the period 1979–91, this share fell by 20.7 percentage points (column 2). Similarly, in 1979, firms with at least five thousand employees had 68.8 percent of pension-covered workers in plans with at least one hundred participants. They lost 12.4 percentage points of this share over the period 1979–91.

Moreover, except for the public administration industry, the predicted probability of defined benefit coverage—independent of employment shifts—fell across all categories (column 4). The combination of the reductions in the probabilities of using defined benefit plans, plus the employment shift effects favoring firms that traditionally used defined contribution plans, generated an overall reduction in defined benefit market share over the period.

One additional result is apparent in the table. The sectors with the highest preference for defined benefit plans tend to have smaller predicted reductions in market shares after netting out employment losses. For example, pension-covered workers who were unionized had a 97.9 percent chance of defined benefit coverage in 1979 (column 3); in 1991 this probability fell by two percentage points (column 4). In contrast, nonunion workers had a smaller probability of defined benefit coverage in 1979 (84.1 percent), but this probability fell by 19.9 percentage points over the period.

This pattern is consistent with the hypothesis that either some change in cost occurred over the period or a new substitute became available. Those sectors that attached most value to defined benefit plans were not substantially affected. Those with a weaker preference for defined benefit plans evinced a larger probability of substituting the defined contribution variety.

## 7.2  TOWARD UNDERSTANDING CHANGES IN PLAN CHOICE

### 7.2.1 Regulatory Costs

During the 1980s, legislation was enacted that increased the administrative costs of defined benefit plans. Robert Clark and Ann McDermed[10] conjecture that these costs explain the drift toward defined contribution plans not otherwise explained by employment shifts. In chapter 12 I present evidence developed by the Hay-Huggins Company that offers partial support for this theory.

That is to say, their estimates show that cost increases were large for small plans, giving smaller firms progressively more incentive over the 1980s to use defined contribution plans in place of defined benefit plans.

Table 7.3 Reason for Plan Termination

| | Number of participants | | | |
|---|---|---|---|---|
| Primary reason | <25 | 25–99 | 100–499 | ≥500 |
| Government regulation | 41 | 26 | 23 | 15 |
| Plan too costly | 26 | 28 | 19 | 11 |
| Subtotal | 67 | 54 | 42 | 26 |
| Business considerations[a] | 33 | 46 | 58 | 74 |

Source: American Academy of Actuaries, *Preliminary Report*, at chapter 7, note 12.
[a]Includes categories "did not meet needs of employees or employer," "asset reversion," and "other."

But the differential administrative costs of operating a defined benefit plan compared with a 401k plan during the 1980s are small for medium and large plans, suggesting that some other factors contributed to the decline among larger firms.

The data in table 7.2 provide evidence consistent with this hypothesis. They show that the reduction in the predicted probability of defined benefit plans over the period is largest among the smallest firms (column 4), a finding consistent with the regulation hypothesis. Similar results are found across pension plan size.[11] But there is no compelling evidence that the administrative cost hypothesis explains the observed reduction in preference for defined benefit plans in plans and firms with more than five hundred workers.

This inference is supported by survey data reported in table 7.3. The data represent the responses of 1,551 enrolled actuaries to a poll conducted by the American Academy of Actuaries.[12] The survey, published in 1992, asks participants to report the reason for the most recent termination they processed for a plan sponsor. The Academy sorted the responses into categories. The two categories of interest are government regulation (which encompasses responses identifying a government regulation or tax code change) and "plan too costly" (which includes responses identifying cost reasons but not mentioning government regulation as the specific cause).

For the smallest plan terminations (fewer than twenty-five participants), government regulation or cost was the primary reason cited in two-thirds of the cases. But for plans with at least five hundred participants, these reasons were mentioned in only one in four terminations.

### 7.2.2 Introduction of 401k Plans

An alternative explanation for the change in preference away from defined benefit plans is the introduction of 401k plans. These plans were written into legislation enacted in 1979 and effective in 1981.[13] Arguably, 401k plans are superior to defined contribution plans. Like traditional defined contribution plans, the 401k permits an unconditional employer contribution (say, 5 percent of pay or profits) to all employees. Beyond this feature, however, the 401k has unique characteristics. First, workers can make voluntary pretax contributions to the plan, affording them more freedom to attain desired savings rates beyond the employer's contribution.

Second, the firm can match workers' contributions. The matching feature permits the firm to selectively pay higher wages to those who reveal themselves as savers. If these are the kinds of workers the firm wants to keep over the long run, the 401k plan provides a self-selection mechanism to identify these employees and selectively pay them higher wages. In chapter 9 I show that the 401k matching feature can encourage long tenure. The way 401k plans can help firms keep particular types of workers makes them similar to defined benefit pension plans in retention abilities. Put simply, 401k plans are more substitutable with defined benefit plans than are traditional defined contribution plans.

In some sense the growth of 401k plans contradicts the increasing cost hypothesis. The 401k plan is more costly to administer than a straightforward money purchase or profit sharing plan, because the voluntary contribution rates must be monitored to ensure compliance with Internal Revenue Code discrimination requirements, which restrict the amount contributed by higher-paid workers compared with lower-paid workers.[14] The data suggest that 401k plans have been at the core of a falling defined benefit market share during the 1980s.

### 7.2.3 Growth of 401k Plans

The growth in defined contribution plan share is almost exclusively attributable to the development of 401k plans. In 1979, traditional defined contribution plans were the primary pension plan for 10.4 percent of pension-covered workers in plans with at least one hundred participants. In 1991 this share was 12.2 percent. In contrast, starting from virtually no market share in 1979,[15] 401k plans were the sole plan for 21.7 percent of participants in plans with at least one hundred participants by 1991 (see fig. 7.2).

Table 7.4 decomposes the increase in market share for 401k plans. The estimates, derived in the appendix to this chapter, suggest that 13.7 percentage points of their market share is attributable to preference changes in favor of 401k plans. Employment changes over the period also favored the firms and industries that sponsored 401k plans, adding another 8 percentage points to their market share by 1991.

The natural question is whether the 401k market share comes from either defined benefit plans or traditional defined contribution plans. That is, if 401k plans merely replaced simpler defined contribution plans, de-

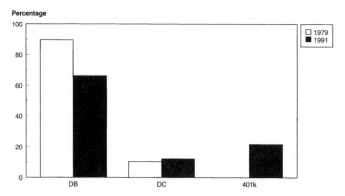

**Figure 7.2** Pension types, 1979 and 1991. Denotes the percentage of pension-covered workers in their primary pension plan. Secondary coverage is excluded. Includes only plans with more than one hundred participants.

fined benefit plan market share would have fallen over the period only because of employment shifts. Since preference changes also played a role in the decrease of defined benefit plans (see table 7.1), the natural conclusion is that some 401k growth came from firms that traditionally favored defined benefit plans.

In the appendix, I calculate the sources of 401k market share. I ask whether 401k sponsors more likely resemble firms that previously sponsored defined benefit or traditional defined contribution plans. For this purpose I consider only the 13.7 percentage points in 401k market share gained from preference changes, and thus I exclude gains attributable to employment shifts favoring 401k plan sponsors.

These calculations show that 401k plans took market share from both

**Table 7.4  Market Share of 401k Plans**

| Pension-covered workers whose primary pension is a 401k | | | Change in participant market share, 1979–91 | | |
|---|---|---|---|---|---|
| 1991 (1) | 1979 (2) | Predicted 1979 using 1991 coefficients[a] (3) | Total (4) | Explained by employment shifts (5) | Preference changes (6) |
| 21.7 | 0 | 13.7 | 21.7 | 8.0 | 13.7 |

*Note:* Numbers in table are percentages. The data exclude plans with fewer than one hundred partici-pants. In addition, the sample omits firms with incomplete data; thus sample means may differ from those characterizing the universe of pension plans.

*Source:* Form 5500 pension plan reports, 1979 and 1991.

[a] This number is the predicted percentage of participants in primary 401k plans in 1979 using coefficients estimated from the 1991 data (see table 7.1, col. 4).

Table 7.5  Sources of 401k Market Share, 1979–91

| Category | Percentage |
|---|---|
| Gain from preferences | 13.7 |
|     From defined contribution plans | 3.1 |
|     From defined benefit plans | 10.6 |

Note: See chapter appendix for calculations.

defined benefit and traditional defined contribution plans, but the primary spread of 401k coverage was in plans that had characteristics more likely affiliated with defined benefit plans, not defined contribution plans. Table 7.5 summarizes the results: approximately three-fourths of 401k coverage in 1991 came from defined benefit plans and one-fourth came from defined contribution plans.

The plan choice estimates reported in the appendix show that, except for the union sector, 401k plans have been adopted in firms across the economy. The probability of 401k coverage as a primary plan is approximately the same for all firms with employment up to two thousand workers. Beyond this size, coverage rates fall but are still relatively high. For example, firms with five thousand or more nonunion workers in the fabricated metal products industry have a 16 percent chance of being covered primarily by a 401k plan. Overall, 35 percent of primary plans with at least one hundred participants are 401k plans.[16]

Figure 7.3 gives the actual market shares for primary plans in 1979 and 1991 across six firm-size categories. The omitted category is the traditional defined contribution plan. The market shares for defined benefit (black) and 401k plans (white) in 1991 are shown by the bars. The bold line depicts the defined benefit market share in 1979. In all firm sizes, the share of defined benefit coverage has fallen, though the reduction is larger in smaller firms.

401k plans are the primary coverage for 40 percent of workers in firms with fewer than 1,000 workers, and 26 percent in firms with 2,000–5,000 workers. Defined benefit plans remain dominant only in large firms (over 5,000 workers), where they provide coverage for 79 percent of pension-covered workers in 1991.

7.3  CONCLUDING REMARKS

During the 1980s, the participant market share of defined benefit plans fell markedly. About half of the trend is explained by a reduction in the employment share in firms and industries that had relatively strong preferences for defined benefit plans. The explanation for the remaining reduction is more problematic. Increasing administrative and regulatory

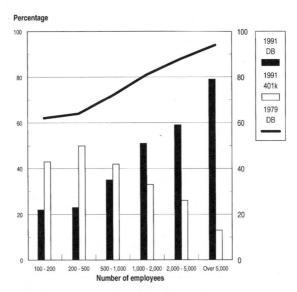

**Figure 7.3** 401k as a primary plan, by firm size. Omitted category is traditional defined contribution plans.

costs presumably helps explain the relatively large reduction in preferences among small firms (fewer than five hundred), but not the broad reductions in defined benefit use across the economy. A more plausible hypothesis is that the introduction of 401k plans in 1979 legislation provided an attractive new alternative to both defined benefit and defined contribution plans.

It is not hard to understand the popularity of 401k pensions. These plans depart from a long tradition in the Internal Revenue Code against voluntary participation and contributions to pensions within the firm. Similarly, allowing firms to match contributions is new federal tax policy. Not only do 401k plans permit more flexible savings in the pension plan, but if workers' productivity is related to their discount rates—a proposition I pursue in chapters 9 and 10—then the matching feature of 401k plans provides a mechanism for firms to pay higher wages to higher-quality workers.

The rapid rise of 401k plans challenges the paradigm that defined benefit plans are important tools for enhancing productivity, while defined contribution plans are merely tax-preferred savings accounts. If defined benefit plans are important, then why did their market share diminish so rapidly in favor of plans that supposedly have no effect on productivity? I argue, first, that the wage costs of defined benefit plans are higher than hitherto considered, making them vulnerable to cheaper substitutes (chapter 8), and second, that 401k plans are not neutral to productivity in the firm—that they can affect the composition of the firm's workforce by encouraging the early exit of lower-quality workers (chapter 9) and encouraging long tenure of higher-quality workers (chapter 10). These "sorting effects" are an important feature of the pension productivity model.

## APPENDIX: EMPLOYMENT AND PREFERENCE EFFECTS ON DEFINED BENEFIT PLANS

### A. Plan Choice Estimates

In this appendix I disentangle the employment and preference shift effects on the market share of defined benefit and defined contribution plans.[17] My data are taken from the form 5500 annual pension reports filed with the Internal Revenue Service for the years 1979 and 1991. I study plan choice for primary plan only and therefore ignore supplemental plan coverage.[18] Also, I use data describing plans with at least one hundred participants.

Table 7.6 reports the results of a logit model of pension plan choice for plans with more than one hundred participants.[19] The dependent variable in columns 2 and 4 is a zero-one dummy variable equal to unity if a primary pension plan is defined benefit in either 1979 (column 2) or 1991 (column 4). The independent variables include union status of participants covered by the plan, as well as the presence of union workers elsewhere in the firm.[20] In addition, I include variables denoting plan and firm size as well as two-digit industry affiliation. The numbers in the table are estimated coefficients; numbers in parentheses are $t$-values, and those in brackets are incremental effects: the change in the probability of defined benefit coverage when the independent variable is set alternatively to zero and one, all other variables set to zero.

The data show that the probability a pension plan with at least one hundred participants is defined benefit fell from 75.2 percent to 57.0 percent over the period. Even the intercept pension plan shows a substantial reduction in demand for defined benefit plans over the period. The intercept represents a nonunion pension plan covering workers, sponsored by a firm with over five thousand employees and no union workers in the fabricated metal products industry (SIC 34), the largest industry in the data.[21] Its estimated probability of choosing a defined benefit plan (bracketed term) is 91 percent in 1979 and 81 percent in 1991.[22]

In fact, the estimates on all firm-size dummy variables reveal a broad reduction in preference for defined benefit plans.[23] In 1979, firm size dom-

# Table 7.6 Plan Choice, 1979 and 1991

| Independent variable | DB plans 1979 Mean (1) | DB plans 1979 Coefficient (2) | DB plans 1991 Mean (3) | DB plans 1991 Coefficient (4) | 401k plans 1991 Coefficient (5) |
|---|---|---|---|---|---|
| Intercept[a] | | 2.31 | | 1.43 | −1.66 |
| | | (11.57) | | (12.96) | (13.80) |
| | | [.91] | | [.81] | [.16] |
| Union | .27 | 3.00 | .14 | 1.54 | −1.35 |
| | | (18.97) | | (29.09) | (20.87) |
| | | [.09] | | [.14] | [−.11] |
| Union and other union plan in firm | .16 | −.77 | .03 | 1.69 | −2.39 |
| | | (4.43) | | (8.88) | (6.64) |
| | | [−.09] | | [.15] | [−.14] |
| Nonunion and other union plan in firm | .10 | 1.42 | .03 | 2.11 | −1.96 |
| | | (17.40) | | (20.39) | (14.47) |
| | | [.07] | | [.16] | [−.13] |
| Firm size[b] | | | | | |
| <200 | .13 | −1.53 | .17 | −1.41 | .67 |
| | | (15.29) | | (19.36) | (9.08) |
| | | [−.22] | | [−.30] | [.11] |
| 200–500 | .21 | −1.54 | .25 | −1.54 | .92 |
| | | (16.37) | | (22.56) | (13.19) |
| | | [−.23] | | [−.33] | [.16] |
| 500–1,000 | .13 | −1.29 | .12 | −1.08 | .70 |
| | | (13.37) | | (15.27) | (9.55) |
| | | [−.17] | | [−.22] | [.12] |
| 1,000–2,000 | .10 | −1.02 | .08 | −.61 | .51 |
| | | (9.94) | | (8.33) | (6.71) |
| | | [−.13] | | [−.11] | [.08] |
| 2,000–5,000 | .08 | −.71 | .05 | −.37 | .26 |
| | | (6.52) | | (4.93) | (3.17) |
| | | [−.08] | | [−.06] | [.04] |
| Plan size[c] | | | | | |
| <200 | .46 | −.51 | .44 | −.97 | .60 |
| | | (2.62) | | (8.94) | (5.02) |
| | | [−.05] | | [−.19] | [.10] |
| 200–500 | .28 | −.37 | .28 | −.90 | .69 |
| | | (1.89) | | (8.33) | (5.76) |
| | | [−.04] | | [−.18] | [.11] |
| 500–1,000 | .12 | −.08 | .10 | −.65 | .58 |
| | | (.42) | | (5.90) | (4.70) |
| | | [−.01] | | [−.12] | [.09] |
| 1,000–2,000 | .07 | −.17 | .06 | −.47 | .41 |
| | | (.82) | | (4.06) | (3.19) |
| | | [−.01] | | [−.08] | [.06] |
| 2,000–5,000 | .04 | .20 | .04 | −.38 | .28 |
| | | (.87) | | (3.20) | (2.03) |
| | | [−.02] | | [−.07] | [.04] |
| Two-digit industry[d] dummies | | X | | X | X |
| Observations | | 21,232 | | 35,178 | 35,178 |
| Number of observations, dependent variable > 0 | | 15,972 | | 20,071 | 12,307 |
| Percentage positive | | 75.2 | | 57.0 | 34.9 |

Note: Dependent variable in columns 2 and 4 equals unity if the pension plan is defined benefit, zero otherwise. In column 5, it is equal to unity if the plan is 401k, zero otherwise. Sample includes only primary plans with at least one hundred participants. Numbers in parentheses are $t$-values. The number in brackets for the intercept is the solution to the logistics equation when all the independent variables (which are all dummy variables) are set to zero: it is the probability that a plan sponsored by a nonunion firm with more than 5,000 workers in the fabricated metal products industry is characterized by a dependent variable equal to unity. The numbers in brackets are incremental effects for the same omitted category captured by the intercept; that is, the incremental change in the probability that the dependent variable equals unity when the independent variable is set to unity (all other independent variables equal to zero).

[a] Intercept represents a pension plan sponsored by a nonunion firm with over 5,000 workers in SIC 34.
[b] Number of workers in firm.
[c] Number of active participants in plan.
[d] SIC 34 is excluded (fabricated metal products). This industry had the most observations in the data.

inates plan size as a determinant of pension plan type. Holding firm size constant, the coefficients on plan size are small and often statistically insignificant. But in 1991 plan size also figures prominently in the choice of pension plan. It is apparent that small defined benefit plans, even if sponsored by large firms, are less likely to be observed in 1991. Moreover, the mean values in columns 1 and 3 reveal a significant increase in the proportion of plans that cover either nonunion workers or workers in smaller firms, where defined benefit coverage rates are lower.

The results also show that the presence of a union in the firm is an important factor suppressing a drift toward defined contribution plans. In 1979, holding other things constant, a plan covering union workers in the omitted firm and industry was almost certainly defined benefit. In 1991 the probability still was 95 percent. And generally the results for 1979 and 1991 show that the presence of union workers in the firm increases the likelihood of observing defined benefit plans, even if the plan itself covers nonunion workers.

## B. Disentangling the Explained and Unexplained Changes

To disentangle the effects of employment shifts and preference changes, I calculate the effect of changing coefficients over the period, holding constant the values of the independent variables. That is, I multiply the 1991 coefficients in table 7.6, column 4, times the observed values of the independent variables in the 1979 data:

$$P_{DBj}^{pred} = c_0 + c_1^{91} x_{1j}^{79} + c_2^{91} x_{2j}^{79} + \ldots + c_n^{91} x_{nj}^{79}, \qquad (7.1)$$

where $P_{DBj}^{pred}$ is the predicted probability of defined benefit coverage in the $j$th plan, $c_i^{91}$ is the coefficient on the $i$th variable for 1991, as reported in table 7.6 (column 4), and $x_{ij}^{79}$ is the 1979 value of the $i$th variable in the $j$th firm. The calculation in expression (7.1) gives the predicted probability that the $j$th pension plan in 1979 is defined benefit, based on coefficients estimated from the 1991 database.

I wish to explain the *participant* market share of primary coverage. Thus I multiply $P_{DBj}^{pred}$ by the number of participants in the $j$th plan in 1979, divide by all participants in the database, and sum over all plans. The predicted participant market share for defined benefit plans in 1979 based on 1991 coefficients is

$$DB_{79}^{pred} = \Sigma_j \, P_{DBj}^{pred} \, w_j^{79}, \qquad (7.2)$$

where $w_j^{79}$ is the participant weight in the $j$th plan using 1979 participant weights. The variable $DB_{79}^{pred}$ is the predicted participant market share of defined benefit plans in 1979 using coefficients estimated on the 1991 database. Its value is 79.1 percent. That is, the estimates suggest that if employment patterns in 1991 were identical to those observed in 1979, the participant market share of defined benefit plans with at least 100 participants would have fallen by 10.5 percentage points over the decade, from 89.6 to 79.1 percent. The remaining reduction of 12.8 percentage points is attributable to changes in the employment patterns across union/nonunion jobs, large and small firms, and two-digit industries.[24]

More formally, denoting actual defined benefit market shares at the beginning and end of the period as $DB_{79}^{actual}$ and $DB_{91}^{actual}$, then the portion of the change unexplained by observed employment shifts is

$$U = DB_{79}^{actual} - DB_{79}^{pred} = 89.6 - 79.1 = 10.5. \qquad (7.3)$$

The portion that is explained by employment shifts is[25]

$$E = DB_{79}^{pred} - DB_{91}^{actual} = 79.1 - 66.3 = 12.8. \qquad (7.4)$$

Unexplained changes in market share could be attributable to changes in relative costs, the availability of new substitutes, or changes in plan sponsors' and workers' preferences for defined benefit plans.[26] For shorthand, I refer to these changes as shifts in "preferences."

### C. Sources of 401k Market Share

It is straightforward to determine whether 401k plans attained their market share at the expense of defined benefit or defined contribution plans. I first estimate a logit model using 1991 data where the dependent variable is unity if the plan is a 401k, zero otherwise. The estimates are presented in table 7.6, column 5. I then use these coefficients to calculate a 401k probability in the 1979 data. Thus, for each plan in 1979, I have a predicted probability that the plan would be a 401k plan, based on the characteristics of the plan and plan sponsor.

I then multiply the predicted probability of observing a 401k plan in the 1979 data by a zero-one dummy variable denoting whether the plan is in fact defined contribution or defined benefit in 1979. That is, the portion of the 401k plan share in 1991 estimated to come from defined contribution plans is

$$401k_{from\,DC}^{91} = \Sigma_j \, P_{401k,j}^{pred} \, DC_j^{79} \, w_j^{79}, \qquad (7.5)$$

where $P_{401k,j}^{pred}$ is the predicted probability that the $j$th plan in the 1979 data is a 401k, $DC_j^{79}$ is a zero-one dummy variable equal to unity if the $j$th plan was defined contribution in 1979, and $w_j^{79}$ is the participant weight for the $j$th plan in 1979. The variable $401k_{from\,DC}^{91}$ is therefore the portion of workers covered by a defined contribution plan in 1979 predicted to be covered by a 401k plan, had these plans been permitted in 1979.

I make the same calculation for predicted 401k coverage from defined benefit plans:

$$401k^{91}_{from\,DB} = \Sigma_j \, P^{pred}_{401k,j} \, DB^{79}_j \, w^{79}_j, \qquad (7.6)$$

where $DB^{79}_j$ is a zero-one dummy variable equal to unity if the $j$th plan was defined benefit in 1979. The variable $401k^{91}_{from\,DB}$ is the portion of workers covered by a defined benefit plan in 1979 predicted to be covered by a 401k plan, had these plans been permitted in 1979. The results of these calculations are presented in table 7.5 in the text.

## CHAPTER EIGHT

# Sorting across Plan Type

In this chapter I pursue some of the economic factors a firm must consider in choosing a pension plan for its workforce. Here I go beyond the incentives in defined benefit plans that affect quit and retirement rates and instead view the impact of pension plans on the kinds of workers attracted to the firm. I also look at the differential labor cost inherent in these plans. I continue the discussion of selection effects in the next chapter.

I consider two types of plans: defined benefit and defined contribution. The defined benefit plan defers a significant portion of compensation until the worker successfully completes long tenure. Premature quitting triggers a pension capital loss. In a simple defined contribution plan, the firm might contribute some fixed percentage of workers' wages into an account. Workers can quit at any time after vesting without incurring pension capital losses.

I ask two questions that are at the core of the firm's pension choice. What impact do these plans have on the types of workers attracted to the firm? And Is the level of required compensation the same in both alternatives?

A key assumption in the defined benefit plan model is that workers accept the capital loss structure of the pension without requiring additional compensation. Workers value their freedom to pursue other economic opportunities as they arise. If workers take a defined benefit pension job, they may forgo higher-paying jobs in other firms later in their careers. A worker may refuse a better job offer in midcareer because quitting means forfeiting part of his compensation. Because the pension capital loss restricts economic freedom, I refer to the defined benefit plan contract as an indenture.[1]

Workers do not accept an indenture for free. They require some additional wage premium to compensate them for committing themselves to one firm for the long run, thereby forgoing some attractive alternatives midway in the contract. In short, defined benefit pensions carry a cost to the firm in the form of a higher wage, which I label an "indenture premium." If the firm's productivity is sufficiently enhanced by long tenure, it will use defined benefit pensions and pay the indenture premium. Firms that do not value long tenure use defined contribution pensions and thus do not pay the premium.

The defined benefit plan has implications for the types of workers attracted to the firm. Because the plan backloads compensation, it is more attractive to those who have a lower assessment of their propensity to quit. That is to say, the plan attracts natural "stayers." In addition, because low discounters attach more value to the future pension, they perceive a higher compensation level in the firm and so are more likely to join than are high discounters.

## 8.1 A MODEL OF INDENTURE PREMIUMS

I start by adopting the common proposition that some firms enhance productivity by using production functions that depend on long-term commitments of workers. For concreteness, I assume that output depends on team production.[2] Overall productivity in the firm is higher if members of the team stay together until retirement, so the firm sets up incentives to discourage quitting.

There are two periods of work, with some possibility of better job offers arising in period 2. In period 3, workers are retired. The interest rate is zero, and there is no compensation besides cash wages and pensions. Workers take a job in some firm in period 1 and quit only if they receive a better job offer from another firm in period 2. Workers have different productive attributes but the same level of human capital.

Finally, I assume that all individuals have zero discount rates. This assumption creates the problem that all workers are covered by pensions. For the sake of developing the main implications of indenture premiums, however, uncovered workers are not required.

### 8.1.1 Lifetime Economic Opportunities

Firms that offer no deferred wages pay a period 1 wage equal to unity:

$$w_1^* = 1. \tag{8.1}$$

At the end of period 1, some shock occurs that promises wage increases for some workers. For concreteness, I assume the shock takes the form of innovations that spawn new firms. These innovations generate excess demand for workers of particular skill characteristics. The entire benefit of innovations passes to these workers in the form of a differentially higher wage, denoted by $d$. Viewed from period 1, the probability of being one of the lucky workers is $q$.[3] Thus, workers' expected period 2 wage is

$$w_2^* = 1 + qd. \tag{8.2}$$

In essence, each entrant into the labor market receives a lottery ticket at the start of the career with prize $d$ paid off in period 2 with probability $q$. The present value of expected lifetime income from working in firms with no long-term contracts is

$$w_1^* + w_2^* = 2 + qd. \tag{8.3}$$

### 8.1.2 Long-Tenure Firms

Consider a firm that wants workers to accept a long-term contract. The firm must compensate workers for forgoing some of their economic opportunities. There are several ways this compensation can be paid. The firm can match each wage offer workers receive at the end of period 1 and therefore pay some workers unity and some $1 + d$ in period 2. In general, there might be several reasons this solution is uneconomical.[4] In my model, the obvious reason is the potential for a holdup problem. If there are no penalties to quitting the firm, each team member has an incentive to threaten to quit—thereby imposing productivity losses on the firm—unless he receives the higher-tier wage.

At the other extreme, the firm could pay *all* workers the higher wage, $1 + d$, in period 2. It is easy to show, however, that a deferred wage scheme is a cheaper, yet equally effective, alternative.

Consider a firm that pays all workers the same wage and deters quitting by using a defined benefit pension. Wages in periods 1 and 2 are $w_1$ and $w_2$. A pension, $w_3$, is awarded in period 3 if the worker stays until retirement. For simplicity, I assume that if the worker quits after period 1, the pension value is zero. This specification conforms to a simplified implicit pension contract in a two-period model.[5]

The firm must pay a wage sufficient to attract workers into the indenture created by the defined benefit pension. Viewed at the time a worker takes a job in period 1, the present value of lifetime income in a firm using a defined benefit plan is

$$w_1 + w_2 + w_3 = 2 + p, \tag{8.4}$$

where $p$ is the lifetime indenture premium in the long-tenure firm. The indenture premium is found by equating the compensation schemes to workers' alternative income stream (that is, setting the right-hand side of expression 8.4 equal to the right-hand side of expression 8.3). The result

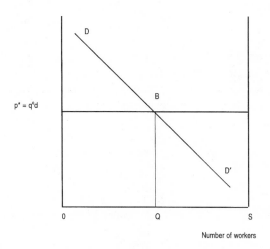

Value

D

$p^* = q^0 d$

B

D′

0             Q             S

Number of workers

**Figure 8.1** Market for long tenure.

is intuitive. The lifetime premium awarded by long-tenure firms equals the wage increases that workers expect outside these firms:

$$p = qd. \tag{8.5}$$

This result describes the indenture premium—the additional compensation that workers require to commit to the firm for long tenure. It does not describe the optimal wage structure (starting wage, ending wage, and pension amount), nor does it reveal whether the premium is effective is eliminating the incentive to quit. I address these issues in appendix A to this chapter.[6] For present purposes, I assume that the deferred wage is efficacious and instead describe the nature of equilibrium in the market when this contract is part of the wage structure.

## 8.2 EQUILIBRIUM IN THE MARKET FOR LONG TENURE

### 8.2.1 The Optimal Number of Long-Tenure Workers

Figure 8.1 depicts equilibrium in the labor market under the condition that all workers have the same chance for a better job in period 2. Thus all $S$ workers in the market are willing to take deferred wage jobs at the indenture premium denoted by $p^* = qd$. The demand for long tenure, depicted by the schedule $DD'$, arises from the underlying value that firms attach to long tenure. The demand schedule is downward slop-ing because some firms presumably attach higher value to long tenure than others.

In the solution portrayed in the figure, it is optimal for $Q$ workers to forgo their economic freedom; that is, to work in "long-tenure" firms. The remaining $S - Q$ workers are not optimally covered by deferred wage contracts and so retain their economic freedom to move to their highest alternative uses. Put differently, $Q$ workers add more value to the market by remaining in long-term contracts, compared with moving to their highest-paying job alternative during their career. The value of staying in these jobs is reflected in the higher wage they receive. In pension terms, $Q$ workers might be covered by defined benefit pensions and $S - Q$ workers by defined contribution plans.

Long-term contracts impart a total productivity increase valued by the area OQBD in the figure. The indenture premium is depicted by area OQBp*; this amount is financed by the productivity gain stemming from long tenure. In a competitive market, the remaining gain ultimately passes to consumers in the form of lower prices (area p*BD).

Figure 8.1 assumes that all workers have the same expected wage offer. More generally, the probability of finding a higher-paying job, and the size of the wage increase in another job, might differ across workers. If so, the supply of workers to long-tenure contracts is upward sloping. Workers who have lower expected alternative opportunities during their career sacrifice less by taking a job with a deferred wage; those with greater expected pay increases have a higher supply price. Figure 8.2 de-picts this equilibrium. For simplicity, I depict the same equilibrium point as in figure 8.1, with $Q$ workers covered by long-term contracts.

Under these supply conditions, workers with the lowest cost of forgo-ing their economic freedom work for firms that use deferred wages. Those with higher expected alternatives work in firms that do not defer wages (they might use defined contribution plans). In this sense, the market is efficient because it generates long tenure by those workers least likely to attain large wage increases later in their careers. I pursue some of the details of this equilibrium in appendix B.

For present purposes, however, it is interesting to consider that the marginal worker—one who has a supply price $p*$ for accepting a deferred wage—perceives no net value to working for a long-tenure firm. But for all "inframarginal" workers covered by deferred wages, the indenture premium in equilibrium exceeds the premium they would require for commuting to the firm for long tenure. Most workers covered by deferred wage contracts therefore receive total compensation that exceeds their expected alternatives outside the firm.

Value

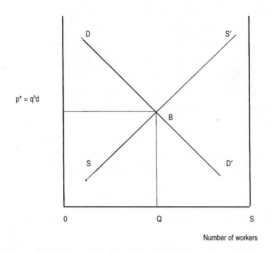

Figure 8.2 Tenure market with upward sloping supply.

## 8.2.2 Comparison with Insurance Models of Long Tenure

In an indenture model, long-tenure contracts arise from the value firms attach to continuous employment of their workers over a long period. The firm compensates workers for sacrificing some of their economic freedom.

Another approach is to view long-tenure contracts as arising from the value workers attach to job security. In the alternative model, firms accommodate workers' desire to avoid wage reductions or periods of unemployment during their work lives.[7] Workers pay for the insurance provided by job security by accepting a *lower* wage than they could obtain by working for firms with no long-term commitments.

The two models are distinguishable. In an "insurance" model, long-tenure firms pay lower wages. In an indenture model, firms pay higher wages. In fact, a positive premium can be generated *only* by a productivity-based model, because the higher productivity is the source of payment for the premium. Empirical work is consistent with an equilibrium that has a positive premium and inconsistent with one that has either a zero or a negative premium.[8]

## 8.2.3 High Discounters

If all workers in the labor market are low discounters, then all are covered by pensions because they attach value to their retirement security in the long run. Some are covered by defined benefit pensions and others by defined contribution plans, depending on whether they find the indenture premium sufficient to overcome the inherent cost of less mobility.

In reality, some workers are low discounters and some are high discounters. High discounters do not want to work in pension firms, because their preference is for immediate cash wages. Thus high discounters are expected to be affiliated with firms that do not use pensions.

In the next chapter I pursue the implications of imperfect matching. That is, even though high discounters do not seek out pension firms, they nevertheless may enter one if they cannot find a job that ideally matches their preferences. It turns out that the differences in worker discount rates, and the imperfect matches that naturally develop in the market, give rise to an economic role for defined contribution firms.

### 8.2.4  A Competing Mechanism: "Efficiency Wages"

The existence of indenture premiums explains why "efficiency wages" can compete with deferred wages to encourage long tenure. If the indenture premium is, say, 10 percent of the underlying wage, then at the same cost a firm could forgo the defined benefit pension and simply increase wages by 10 percent. This wage premium, called an "efficiency wage,"[9] discourages quitting because, by staying, workers anticipate collecting a 10 percent wage premium over their remaining tenure. In this alternative, the wage, $w^o$, in both periods is

$$w^o = 1 + p, \tag{8.6}$$

where $p$ is the equilibrium indenture premium in firms that use deferred contracts.

Figure 8.3 (dotted-line schedule) depicts the incentive to stay with a firm paying a 10 percent efficiency wage where the underlying wage, net of the indenture premium, is $10,000 per year. Assuming that a worker expects to retire after thirty years of work and that the real interest rate and the worker's internal discount rate are zero, then at the start of the contract the worker values the $1,000 per annum premium at $30,000. As tenure accumulates to, say, five years, he has collected $5,000 of the premium, leaving $25,000 still to be collected, and so on. The worker's incentive to stay is directly related to the premiums payable in future years. For comparison, the hill-like capital loss of using a defined benefit pension is reproduced from figure 3.2.

The capital loss from quitting in an efficiency wage contract is similar to that in a defined benefit pension, in that it discourages quitting. The patterns of capital losses, however, are different. The efficiency wage discourages quitting among young workers and gradually wanes with ten-

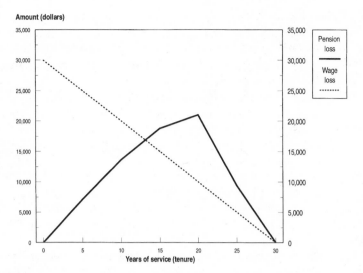

**Amount (dollars)**

Years of service (tenure)

Pension loss ——

Wage loss ········

**Figure 8.3** Pension versus efficiency wage. Assumes a wage of $10,000 per year in real terms, an indenture premium (and efficiency wage) equal to 10 percent, and a nominal interest rate and nominal wage growth equal to 12 percent per year (see figure 3.2). The losses are expressed in real dollars.

ure. The pension alternative does not discourage quitting among young workers, and it more strongly discourages quitting later in tenure.[10]

In addition, the tax treatment and sorting effects of efficiency wages and of pensions are different. Given the tax preference afforded pensions, workers are not indifferent between receiving a pension and receiving an efficiency wage. The efficiency wage does not sort exclusively for low discounters as do defined benefit plans. In the pension alternative, compensation is postponed until late in tenure, thereby discouraging the entry of high discounters. Efficiency wages are valued more highly by low discounters, because their distribution is spread over the life of the contract, but the high initial wage attracts all workers to apply for a job, including high discounters.

In chapter 10 I pursue the idea of efficiency wages in the context of pensions and show that 401k plans effectively can be used to pay efficiency wages *exclusively* to low discounters.

## 8.3 CONCLUDING REMARKS

This chapter modifies the prevailing model of the implicit pension contract by incorporating a cost of indenture. One important characteristic of the model is its consistency with a sometimes troubling finding in the empirical study of pensions—that wages seem "too high" in pension firms.[11] This finding, which shows up repeatedly in studies of compensating differentials and firm separations, cannot be explained by simple models of the implicit pension contract. Once selection effects and indenture premiums are incorporated, however, the high-wage phenomenon is a natural outgrowth of the model.

The model predicts that workers covered by defined benefit plans are disproportionately characterized by lower discount rates and lower expected future wage opportunities. This selection effect, plus the creation of the capital loss from quitting, explains why quit rates are lower in firms that offer defined benefit pension plans.

An important principle arises for the study of pensions: defined benefit pensions (and other deferred wage contracts) are more costly to use than defined contribution or 401k pensions. If defined contribution plans also provide economic benefits to the firm, a subject I take up in the next chapter, they may be attractive substitutes for defined benefit plans.

In addition, by recognizing a cost to a long-term labor contract in the form of an indenture premium, the model explains why efficiency wages themselves might be used to effect long tenure. As long as the "efficiency premium" is no higher than the prevailing indenture premium, there is no incremental cost to simply paying workers "too much" compared with deferring their wages. In the next section I show how 401k plans can perform this function, a characteristic that may help explain why 401k plans seem to have become effective substitutes for traditional defined benefit plans as vehicles for selecting and retaining high-quality workers.

### APPENDIX A: CONDITIONS FOR AN EFFECTIVE DEFERRED WAGE

The discussion in the text considers the indenture premium required to compensate the marginal worker for accepting a longterm contract. It does not consider whether the deferred wage is *effective* in preventing quitting during the work life. If the deferred wage is to be effective, the capital loss from quitting must exceed the present value of the higher wage offer, if it arises.

### A. A Sufficient Condition

Consider a firm that does not use a deferred wage. By assumption, the wage in this firm is unity. A firm offering a deferred wage pays a period 1 wage that is positive but less than unity:

$$0 \leq w_1 < 1. \tag{8.7}$$

The firm cannot ask workers to post a bond in period 1 (hence the positive wage). If the period 1 wage exceeds unity, potential quitters are better off waiting for better offers in the deferred wage firm than in firms that pay the unit wage with no deferred wage. In addition, a higher starting salary does not discourage high discounters from entering.

A necessary condition for an efficacious deferred wage is that when a worker receives an offer from some other firm in the amount $1 + d$, the wage increase, $d$, must be less than the sum of the period 2 wage and the pension:

$$w_2 + w_3 \geq 1 + d. \qquad (8.8)$$

Otherwise it is optimal for workers who receive job offers paying the wage $1 + d$ to quit. Also, recall from condition (8.5) that total wages (plus the pension) in the long-tenure firm sum to $2 + qd$.

## B. Description of the Deferred Wage

In general, condition (8.8) can be satisfied by numerous combinations of the period 2 wage and the pension. To simplify the solution, I make an assumption about the size of the pension. In particular, to mimic regulatory restrictions on pensions, I limit the pension to no more than 100 percent of the period 2 wage ($w_3 \leq w_2$).[12] Since no generality is lost from assuming the equality, I specify that the wage structure is characterized by a pension equal to the period 2 wage. I also presume that the pension is positive:

$$w_2 = w_3 > 0. \qquad (8.9)$$

An effective deferred wage might involve constant wages over the work life, or it could entail rising wages. That is, in general, the solution can be characterized by wage tilt:

$$w_1 \leq w_2. \qquad (8.10)$$

The character of the solution depends importantly on whether the deferred wage is efficacious when the indenture premium equals the expected wage increase in period 2 outside the firm ($p = qd$). It turns out that this condition prevails when the alternative job wage increase is not "too high" in relation to the probability of receiving an offer. Consider the maximum deferred wage; that is, $w_1 = 0$. If the indenture premium is set equal to the expected pay raise, $qd$, then all compensation is deferred. Thus the cost of quitting is $2 + qd$, which exceeds the alternative job offer in period 2 if[13]

$$d \leq 1/[1 - q]. \qquad (8.11)$$

## C. Wage Structure

*Pensions alone* can effect long tenure if the potential alternative job offer is relatively low in relation to the probability of receiving an offer. Suppose there is a 75 percent probability of receiving the wage increase of .67; thus $qd = .5$. The firm can pay a wage (and pension) of $0.83 per period. This solution satisfies condition (8.8). In general, a pension only solution is feasible if the alternative wage increase is small enough to satisfy the condition[14]

$$d \le 1/[3 - 2q]. \tag{8.12}$$

If the alternative wage $d$ is sufficiently high in relation to the probability of receiving the offer, so that condition (8.12) is not satisfied, then *pensions and wage tilt* are required to effect long tenure. Suppose workers have a 50 percent probability of receiving a wage increase of 1, so that $qd$ still is .5. Since this combination of $q$ and $d$ violates condition (8.12), it is apparent that wage tilt needs to be invoked to make the long-term contract binding. The deferred wage is efficacious if the firm sets the period 1 wage to .5 and the period 2 wage and the pension each to 1. The cost of quitting is therefore 1, which matches the potential wage increase from another firm: condition (8.8) is satisfied.

Finally, consider a solution where, even if deferred wages are maximized ($w_1 = 0$), an indenture premium equal to expected wage increases outside long-tenure firms does not prevent opportunistic quitting for better jobs in period 2. This problem arises if the alternative job offer is high enough in relation to the probability of receiving the better offer, so that the inequality in (8.11) is reversed. Thus we have

$$\text{if } d > 1/[1 - q], \tag{8.13}$$

then

$$p = d - 1 > qd. \tag{8.14}$$

When condition (8.13) holds, long-tenure firms must pay *efficiency wages;* that is, they must set the indenture premium *in excess* of the expected alternative wage, $qd$. In particular, the indenture premium is $d - 1$, which exceeds $qd$ when condition (8.13) is satisfied.[15] Suppose there is a 25 percent probability of receiving an alternative wage offer increase of 2. Wage tilt and the pension are maximized: $w_1 = 0$. If the indenture premium is set to $qd$, the period 2 wage and the pension are each 1.25. The deferred wage is 1.5, which is less than the potential period 2 wage increase of 2 (condition 8.8 is not satisfied): there is an incentive for workers to quit for a higher wage in period 2.

If the indenture premium $p$ is set to 1 ($= d - 1$), which is twice as high as the expected wage increase outside these firms, there is no incentive to quit.[16] The payoff from staying matches the outside wage offer. This indenture premium creates a true efficiency wage in the sense of generating a queue for long-tenure jobs.

## APPENDIX B: FURTHER EXPLORATION OF THE MODEL

The text considers the possibility that expected job offers are different across workers and thus that the supply of workers for long-tenure jobs is upward sloping. In particular, the discussion assumes that the potential higher wage premium is the same for all workers, but that the probability of receiving the higher wage differs across workers.

Consider the converse supply condition: the probability of receiving a better offer, $q$, is constant for all workers, but the value of the job offer level, $d$, is diffuse over the range zero to $d_{max}$.

When the job offer varies, the conditions to prevent opportunistic quitting are different for each worker. Even if the period 1 wage is set to zero, the $i$th worker has the incentive to quit in period 2 if *his* wage offer, $d_i$, is high in relation to the probability of receiving the offer:

$$d^i > 1/[1 - q]. \tag{8.15}$$

The interesting question is whether workers with high $d$ lottery tickets optimally decide to take jobs in a long-tenure firm—even if they would optimally quit when they receive a better offer—compared with awaiting offers in a defined contribution firm. Consider the constraining case where the deferred wage is maximized. If workers receive a better offer in period 2 and thus quit a defined benefit firm, they lose their forgone period 1 wage of \$1, which they would retain if they waited in a defined contribution firm. But if they do not receive a better job offer in period 2, they receive the indenture premium, $p$, which is not available in a defined contribution firm. Thus workers with high $d$ lottery tickets have an incentive to join a defined benefit firm with the intention of opportunistic quitting in period 2 if

$$q \, \$1 < [1 - q]p. \tag{8.16}$$

If the indenture premium is set equal to the expected wage increase of the marginal worker, $qd^o$, then (8.16) becomes

$$d^o > 1/[1 - q]. \tag{8.17}$$

This condition, which resembles (8.13), says that if the potential alternative wage offer for the marginal worker is high enough to satisfy (8.17) then *all* workers have an incentive to join a defined benefit firm, even those who will optimally quit the firm for a higher wage. In this case firms cannot select low $d$ workers into the pool, and the indenture premium is ineffective in holding workers for whom the wage offer exceeds $1 + d^o$. Thus if $q$ is .5 and the distribution of $d_i$ is diffuse between zero and four ($d_{max} = 4$), then the overall quit rate in the firm is .25, compared with the unconstrained average quit rate of .5.[17] Given this modest effect on the quit rate, it may not be optimal for the firm to offer the deferred wage contract.

In contrast, if condition (8.17) is not satisfied, then only workers for whom the indenture premium exceeds their expected wage increase enter the firm. In this case the premium is an effective deterrent to quitting in period 2 ($d_i$ in condition 8.15 is less than or equal to $1/(1 - q)$ for all workers who join long-tenure firms). A zero quit rate is attained.

These conditions give rise to some interesting equilibriums. The conditions under which defined benefit pensions are least likely to effect an efficient low quit rate are those in which the likelihood of alternative job offers is small in relation to the size of the job offers (where the values of $d$ are large in relation to $q$—see condition 8.17). In this case, defined contribution firms employ workers with relatively low probabilities of receiving high alternative job offers and thus have relatively low quit rates. Thus, depending on the nature of the supply conditions, quit rates could be low in both defined benefit plans *and* defined contribution plans.[18]

Finally, I have implicitly assumed that labor is sufficiently homogeneous so that all long-tenure firms draw from the same pool of skills. In fact, firms in some industries may draw from labor pools that are poor substitutes for workers in other industries. Therefore firms in different industries will not face the same conditions affecting the optimal long-term contract. Some groups of long-tenure firms might use only defined benefit plans. Others might use pensions and wage tilt. Still others might have pensions, wage tilt, and efficiency wages. And further, depending on the efficiency of the selection effects and the efficacy of deferred wage schemes, some defined benefit firms can have zero quitting; others may have quit rates that are positive but small.

## CHAPTER NINE

# Encouraging High Discounters
# to Quit

In previous chapters I noted that the incentive effects of pensions depend partly on workers' internal discount rates, thereby giving firms some stake in the proportion of high and low discounters in their workforce. Otherwise I assumed that high discounters and low discounters are equally productive.[1]

In this chapter I challenge the latter assumption. I consider the natural proposition that a worker's value of marginal product is importantly related to his internal discount rate. I do not refer here to productivity differences that are explicable—for instance, those due to education.[2] I consider a more subtle concept: Low discounters attach higher value to the long-term consequences of their current performance and thus are more productive than high discounters, given any level of monitoring effort by firms.

If this proposition has merit, then since internal discount rates are partly unobservable, it follows that firms will search for ways to sort workers by their internal discount rates. I pursue the idea that pensions are naturally suited to sort workers based on their internal discount rates and so can help the firm select and retain a high-quality workforce.

In this model, the value of defined benefit pensions to the firm is enhanced by their ability to attract low discounters to the firm.[3] More important, the model gives rise to a heretofore unrecognized attribute of simple defined contribution plans—their ability to encourage the early exit of high discounters who enter the firm. In chapter 10 I show how 401k versions of these plans also can play a sorting role by prodding workers to align their pay and productivity without expending the firm's monitoring resources. A productivity theory of defined contribution and 401k plans emerges that challenges the paradigm that these plans are merely tax-preferred savings accounts.

## 9.1 LOW DISCOUNTERS AS HIGH-QUALITY WORKERS

I advance the proposition that individuals with low internal discount rates are more productive and therefore command higher wages than workers with high discount rates. Just as low discounters attach more value to the long-term benefits of observable investments in education and financial assets, so do they attach more value to other investments that are more difficult to observe. The crux of the proposition is that individuals with low discount rates strongly consider the long-term implications of their current work performance.

For example, low discounters are less likely to take time off or to quit on a whim, since they appreciate the long-term implications of their reputation for reliability, which reduces the firm's expenditures on duplication and hiring. They are less likely to mistreat machines and equipment, because they recognize the long-term benefit of being labeled a "low cost" employee. They are less likely to value the short-term gains from shirking over the long-term consequences of getting caught. And they are more likely to be motivated to work hard to gain the benefits of promotions.

Presumably, if the firm expends sufficient resources, it can coax high discounters to simulate the behavior of low discounters, but high discounters' value added will be lower than low discounters' by the amount of these costs. In this sense the wedge between low and high discounters' values of marginal product is related to monitoring costs.

If each worker's internal discount rate were obvious from casual observation, then firms would set wages to reflect differences in productivity. The size of the wage effect could be measured directly by including the internal discount rate as an independent variable in a wage equation. But discount rates are not observable, and I will present evidence below suggesting that obvious proxies for discount rates (like educational attainment) cannot account for the wide variation in implied discount rates in the data.

Consider two types of workers who differ only in their internal discount rates. Low discounters have zero discount rates. High discounters have some positive discount rate, $r \gg 0$. Also assume that a worker's output is not easily determined without costly monitoring.[4] If the firm incurs a monitoring cost, $d$, per period, and receives output valued at $1 + d$, the wage is \$1. This central proposition can be stated as follows: With no monitoring, low discounters add value of $1 + d$, the same as they would with monitoring, but high discounters add value of $1 + d - y < 1$.

Market forces drive firms to find efficient ways to pay low discounters a higher wage. If firms are at least partially successful in distinguishing workers based on their discount rates, then wage differences should be correlated with workers' implied internal discount rates.

Workers' discount rates are not directly observable, so tests of discount rate models must rely on indirect evidence. My strategy is to study behavior that is naturally correlated with internal discount rates: high discounters are more likely to engage in activities that have short-term benefits and long-term costs.[5]

Suppose I denote a unit of this kind of activity as $\mu$. And suppose, for concreteness, that the utility of consuming this unit is $\eta \log(1 + \mu)$, where $\eta$ is a scaler that measures the individual's taste for this consumption. As a result of consuming $\mu$ in period zero, the individual subsequently incurs some cost, $\Delta$, in period $n$. If the individual discounts this cost at the rate $r$, then the net gain from consumption, $\pi$, is[6]

$$\pi(\mu = 1) = \eta \log(1 + \mu) - \Delta/(1 + r)^n. \tag{9.1}$$

Since high discounters attach a lower value to future costs, they are more likely to engage in such activities.

I consider two candidates for this kind of activity: taking unannounced leisure on the job (calling in sick) and consuming a product with delayed health consequences (smoking). I then consider a self-reported measure of workers' discount rates (financial planning horizon). I show that all three measures are correlated with observed wage rates.

### 9.1.1 Taking Unscheduled Time Off

Consider the calculus of calling in sick in a firm that offers paid sick leave (thus $\mu$ is a unit of unscheduled sick leave).[7] An immediate benefit is conferred: utility is derived from staying home. But there are long-term consequences from making these decisions.

Taking unscheduled time off imposes costs on the firm, and the worker builds a reputation for being undependable. These effects detract from the worker's value to the firm and thus have implications for his wage rate ($\Delta$ takes the form of future lower wages).[8]

Undependable workers have either higher preferences for unscheduled leisure (higher $\eta$s) or higher discount rates (higher $r$s). Assuming these parameters are uncorrelated, then a worker's pattern of time off ought to be a reliable, if noisy, proxy for his internal discount rate.

To test this idea, I use information reported about workers' use of sick leave in the federal government. The government awards workers thirteen days of paid sick leave per year (in addition to annual leave)[9]. Since the government cannot determine whether workers are legitimately sick, there is no effective constraint on its use. Workers can save the leave without limit for later use. Thus, even if workers have higher preferences for leisure, they can enjoy the leisure later if they do not take time off now.[10]

I have data as of October 1993 for approximately thirteen thousand civilian federal workers hired since 1983.[11] For each worker, I know the amount of sick leave accrued, $S_A$, and the amount used through current tenure, $S_U$. We can think of the portion of accrued leave that is unused, $\beta$, as a sort of savings propensity, which is inversely related to the individual's internal discount rate:

$$\beta = 1 - S_U/S_A. \tag{9.2}$$

I regress $\beta$ against the log of annual wage for workers in this sample, controlling for tenure and selected demographic variables (coefficients not reported).[12] The results are shown in table 9.1, column 1. The estimated coefficient on $\beta$ is positive and large: workers who save all their sick leave earn a wage about 15 percent higher than those who use all their sick leave. Thus we have our first result associating low discounters with higher wages.

### 9.1.2 Consumption with Delayed Health Effects

I next consider consumption of a product that confers immediate benefits but potentially imposes large costs far in the future. Victor Fuchs portrays smoking as a classic example of this kind of consumption.[13] He conjectures that smokers ought to be disproportionately high discounters. Comparing smoking habits with responses to money trade-off questions, Fuchs finds that smokers have higher implied internal discount rates than nonsmokers.[14]

A database particularly suited to a study of wages and smoking is the first wave of the Health and Retirement Survey (HRS). The HRS respondents were primarily between ages 51 and 61 in 1992[15] and were between 23 and 33 when the 1964 *Surgeon General's Report* was published. The report detailed scientific studies linking smoking to long-term health consequences.[16] Although this cohort likely made the decision to smoke before the report was issued,[17] they had ample time to assimilate the information and decide to either quit or continue smoking as adults.[18] My proxy for low discounter behavior is a dummy variable equal to unity if the worker was not smoking at age 50, zero otherwise.[19]

I restrict the sample to individuals between ages 51 and 61 who are working and not self-employed.[20] I include independent variables to control for demographic characteristics, work experience, and firm attributes. In addition, some literature suggests that smoking and wages could be correlated owing to adverse health effects while on the job.[21] I therefore include thirteen health variables that are intended to control for this prob-

Table 9.1 Wages and Low Discounter Indexes

| Independent variable | Log annual wage (1) | Log hourly wage (2) | Log hourly wage (3) | Supervisor (yes = 1) (4) |
|---|---|---|---|---|
| Sick leave balance, cumulative % (β) | .146 (16.29) | | | |
| Nonsmoker at age 50 | | .038 (2.32) | .024 (1.41) | −.007 (.67) |
| Log of planning horizon | | | .018 (2.27) | .052 (3.33) |
| Other variables | X[a] | X[b] | X[b] | X[b] |
| Observations | 13,560 | 4,868 | 4,523 | 4,566 |
| Mean dependent variable | 10.30 | 2.52 | 2.52 | .17 |
| $R^2$ | .49 | .47 | .43 | |

Note: Column headings denote the dependent variable. Estimates are made using ordinary least squares (cols. 1–3) and a logit model (col. 4). The sample in columns 2–4 comprises workers between ages 51 and 61 in 1992; the sample in column 1 comprises federal workers employed in October 1993 who were hired after 1983. The numbers in column 4 are incremental effects from setting the nonsmoker dummy variable to one and zero and the horizon equal to ten years versus six months, all other variables set to their mean values. Numbers in parentheses are $t$-values.

Source: Defense Manpower Data Center (col. 1); Health and Retirement Survey, first wave (cols. 2–4).
[a] Other variables included in the regressions (in addition to a constant term) are age, age-squared, tenure, tenure-squared, and dummy variables denoting less than high-school graduate, some college, college graduate, and graduate degree (high-school graduate omitted), disability, female, black, Hispanic, Indian, and Asian race dummy variables, and two SMSA locations different from the intercept location.
[b] These variables include a constant term, age, tenure, experience on this job, their squared terms, dummy variables denoting education level, marital status, race (black, Hispanic, Asian, and Indian), union membership, plant size, firm size; a self-reported response to a hypothetical query whether a worker would be willing to quit his job in exchange for a job that would either double his salary or reduce it by one-third; a variable (on a scale of one to ten indicating the respondent's confidence about reaching age 75), and numerous variables denoting the respondent's health status: these include dummy variables denoting whether the respondent ever had cancer, a heart attack, or a stroke, separate dummy variables denoting current affliction with diabetes, high blood pressure, or arthritis requiring medication, days spent in a hospital during the past twelve months, days missed from work during the past twelve months (with a dummy variable denoting more than ninety-five days missed), a dummy variable denoting weight 50 percent above recommended levels for reported height, and separate dummy variables denoting extreme difficulty jogging a mile, walking several blocks, or climbing a flight of stairs.

lem.[22] Finally, I include a dummy variable that denotes the respondent's self-described willingness to take risk.[23] The dependent variable is the log of the hourly wage.[24]

The smoking proxy for discount rates is correlated with observed wages in the expected direction. The estimated coefficient on the nonsmoker variable, reported in table 9.1, column 2, is positive and statistically different from zero at the 99 percent level of confidence. Workers who were not smoking at age 50 have a wage rate 3.8 percent higher than those smoking at age 50.[25]

### 9.1.3 Savings Horizon

Next I consider a direct measure of individuals' discount rates: self-reported time horizons. The Health and Retirement Survey asks respondents about the length of time they consider in financial planning, notably in making savings decisions. Permissible responses range from less than one year to more than ten years.[26]

Presumably, respondents who report the shortest horizons are the most likely candidates for high discounter status, and those reporting the longest horizons are the most likely low discounters. For simplicity, I construct a continuous variable from the discrete horizon responses[27] and use its log value as an independent variable in the wage estimates. Since the planning horizon might be influenced by expected lifetime, I include a variable describing the respondents' self-reported probability of living until age 75.[28] I also include the same independent variables as in column 2.

Table 9.1, column 3, reports the coefficients on the key independent variables. The coefficient on the planning horizon variable is positive and statistically different from zero at the 99 percent level of confidence. The estimate suggests that a worker with a financial planning horizon of ten years has a wage 5.4 percent higher than one with a six-month horizon.[29] The coefficient on the nonsmoker variable is approximately 40 percent lower when the horizon variable is included, suggesting that the worker's decision to be a smoker is correlated with his internal discount rate.[30] Other things the same, a worker who is a nonsmoker at age 50 and has a ten-year horizon has a wage rate approximately 8 percent higher than a smoker with a six-month horizon.

One way to verify the wage results is to evaluate the probability of having a supervisory job. Presumably firms select higher-quality workers to fill jobs that are more important in the firm. If so, low discounters ought to be more frequently found occupying these jobs.

Table 9.1, column 4, reports the incremental effects from estimating a logit model when the dependent variable equals one if the respondent is in a supervisory job, zero otherwise.[31] The nonsmoking variable is characterized by an incremental effect indistinguishable from zero, but the incremental effect on the financial planning horizon variable is positive, and the underlying coefficient is different from zero at the 99 percent level of confidence. The results suggest that a worker with a ten-year horizon has a 5.2 percent higher probability of having a supervisory job than one with a six-month horizon. The mean of the dependent variable is .17.

### 9.1.4 Testing the Discount Rate Indexes

I next consider other evidence that might corroborate my choice of discount rate proxies. Presumably, low discounters are more likely to forgo current consumption in exchange for higher consumption during retirement. It follows that the discount rate proxies ought to be positively correlated with pension savings.

I first consider data from the Health and Retirement Survey. Using these data, I consider whether nonsmokers and workers with longer self-reported planning horizons have a higher probability of participating in pension plans. More particularly, I estimate a logit model where the dependent variable equals one if a respondent is covered by a pension,[32] contributes to an Individual Retirement Account during the previous twelve months, or has a positive IRA balance at the time of the survey.[33] I use the same independent variables as in table 9.1, column 2, except that I exclude tenure and job experience but include the hourly wage.[34] I am interested in whether retirement savings are correlated with the low discounter variables, namely nonsmoking status and length of planning horizon.

Table 9.2, columns 1–3, reports incremental effects for these variables.[35] The results show that the nonsmoker and planning horizon variables are positively correlated with the decision to save in pension vehicles; five out of six of the underlying coefficients are statistically different from zero at the 95 percent level of confidence. The effects are large in relation to mean levels. For example, a nonsmoker at age 50 with a ten-year horizon has a probability of pension coverage approximately 11 percentage points higher than a smoker with a six-month horizon.

I also consider the federal data. I assume that the portion of accumulated sick leave unused, $\beta$, is a good proxy for the worker's internal discount rate. I test this assumption by exploiting 401k savings rates reported in the data. The 401k plan covering these workers offers a 50 percent match to voluntary contributions up to 5 percent of pay and permits an additional 5 percent savings rate with no matching.[36]

Thirty-nine percent of workers in the sample contribute up to 5 percent of pay, 32 percent make contributions beyond 5 percent (14 percent of workers contribute the maximum), and 29 percent are noncontributors.[37] The plan is not offered to workers in their first year of tenure, so I exclude them from the analysis.[38] If $\beta$ is inversely related to the internal discount rate, then high $\beta$ workers also are more likely to contribute to their 401k plan.

The dependent variable in my model is the percentage of pay contrib-

Table 9.2  Low Discounter Index and Pension Savings

| Independent variable | Mean | Pension (yes = 1) (1) | IRA contribution (yes = 1) (2) | IRA balance (positive = 1) (3) | 401k contribution (% of wage) (4) |
|---|---|---|---|---|---|
| Nonsmoker at age 50 | .67 | .046 (3.22) | .015 (1.61) | .035 (2.52) | — |
| Log planning horizon | 1.12 | .062 (3.11) | .035 (2.59) | .082 (4.72) | — |
| Sick leave balance (β) | .40 | — | — | — | .013 (12.23) |
| Wage rate[a] | 12.76 | .31 (19.78) | .01 (2.17) | .06 (7.72) | .028 (16.78) |
| Other variables | | X[b] | X[b] | X[b] | X[c] |
| Observations | | 4,544 | 4,544 | 4,544 | 13,315 |
| Mean dependent variable | | .67 | .12 | .26 | .04[d] |

*Note:* The dependent variable is a dummy variable equal to unity if a worker is covered by a pension (col. 1); a dummy variable equal to one if the worker contributed to an IRA in the previous twelve months (col. 2); a dummy variable equal to one if the respondent has a positive IRA balance at the time of the survey (col. 3); and the percentage of pay contributed to a 401k plan (col. 4). Estimates in columns 1–3 are based on a logit model; those in column 4 are based on a tobit model to accommodate truncation at zero and 10 percent. Reported numbers are incremental effects: the change in the probability that the dependent variable equals one when the independent variable is set to one versus zero, all other independent variables set to their mean values. In the case of the wage, the incremental effect is calculated by comparing the first and third quartile wages, all other independent variables set to their mean values. Numbers in parentheses are *t*-values on the underlying coefficients.

*Sources:* Health and Retirement Survey, first wave (cols. 1–3); Defense Manpower Data Center (col. 4).
[a] In columns 1–3 the wage rate is hourly (average $12.73 in 1992 dollars); in column 4 the rate is the biweekly wage rate (average $1,338 in 1993 dollars).
[b] Other variables are the same as those reported in the notes to table 9.1, column 2, except that the tenure and job experience variables are excluded, but hourly wage is included.
[c] Other variables are the same as those reported in the notes to table 9.1, column 1, except that wage and wage-squared are included as variables. The incremental effects reported in column 4 include the nonlinear effect from the wage-squared variable.
[d] 30.7 percent of the observations are zero; 14.7 percent are at the maximum value (10 percent of wage).

uted to the 401k plan. I include the independent variables reported in table 9.1, column 1, and add the worker's biweekly wage (and its square term). I use a tobit model to accommodate truncation at zero and 10 percent. The results reported in table 9.2, column 4, show the incremental effect of setting β equal to zero versus one (all other variables set to their mean values).[39] Workers who use none of their sick leave have a savings rate approximately one-third (1.3 percentage points) higher than that of those who use all their sick leave.[40] The underlying coefficient on the reliability measure is statistically different from zero at the 99 percent level of confidence.

## 9.2 INTERNAL DISCOUNT RATES AND SELECTION

### 9.2.1 Unobserved Internal Discount Rates

If low discounters are more valued workers, then competition will drive firms to identify this trait. The identification, however, is not trivially accomplished. Although firms can observe signs of job applicants' discount rates, notably education or other training, much of the variation in internal discount rates is unobserved. That is to say, I can write the individual's discount rate, $r$, as a function of a vector of education attributes, $E$:

$$r = a + bE + \epsilon, \tag{9.3}$$

where $\epsilon$ is a random error term with mean zero.[41] If $\epsilon$ is small, there is no economic function for a device that sorts for unobserved discount rates. The available evidence suggests that the error is sizable.

Consider the planning horizon variable in the Health and Retirement Survey as a measure of the internal discount rate. Table 9.3 reports the results of a regression where the dependent variable is the log of the respondent's self-reported financial horizon. The independent variables include the respondent's education level, parents' years of education, age, race, and gender. Following Fuchs, I also include dummy variables denoting various religious preferences.[42]

The results are consistent with the expectation that education, demographic characteristics, and indexes of family background are related to implied discount rates. But these observable measures explain only about 5 percent of the variation in the planning horizon. These results suggest an economic function for sorting devices that help the firm select and retain workers based on their (mostly unobserved) internal discount rates.

In pursuing this idea, it is useful to remember two axioms: First, competition ensures that low discounters receive their higher value of marginal product, minus the costs incurred by firms to identify low discounters. Second, if it expends sufficient monitoring resources, the firm can align pay and productivity across the spectrum of discount rates characterizing workers in its employ. I consider sorting devices that are efficacious in allocating high and low discounters to their best uses without imposing substantial costs on the firm. More specifically, I pursue one part of the compensation package that is naturally suited to low discounters: the pension plan.

**Table 9.3 Horizon, Education and Background**

| Independent variable | Mean | Coefficient |
|---|---|---|
| College degree | .09 | .17 |
|  |  | (3.18) |
| Graduate degree | .11 | .13 |
|  |  | (2.61) |
| Mother's education (years) | 9.44 | −.002 |
|  |  | (.27) |
| Father's education (years) | 9.03 | .009 |
|  |  | (1.54) |
| Protestant | .51 | .10 |
|  |  | (2.30) |
| Catholic | .27 | .08 |
|  |  | (1.61) |
| Jewish | .01 | .20 |
|  |  | (1.33) |
| None | .24 | −.13 |
|  |  | (1.63) |
| Black | .17 | −.34 |
|  |  | (8.31) |
| Hispanic | .08 | −.37 |
|  |  | (5.86) |
| Female | .50 | −.14 |
|  |  | (4.81) |
| Other variables[a] |  | X |
| Observations |  | 4,559 |
| $R^2$ |  | .064 |

*Note:* The dependent variable is the log of the respondent's self-reported financial planning horizon. Numbers in parentheses are *t*-values.
*Source:* Health and Retirement Survey, first wave, 1992.
[a] Besides a constant, other independent variables include dummy variables denoting grammar-school graduate, some high school, some college, age, and tenure. The omitted religion is "all other"; the omitted education category is high-school graduate.

## 9.2.2 A Selection Model

I consider the two types of workers in my central proposition. Low discounters have zero discount rates. High discounters have some positive discount rate, $r \gg 0$. Otherwise, individuals are identical. Also assume that a worker's output is not easily determined without costly monitoring.[43] The firm cannot distinguish high discounters from low discounters and thus pays the same wage to all members of a particular cohort of entering workers, but workers' value of marginal product depends on their discount rates. With no monitoring, low discounters add value of $1 + d$, the same as they would with monitoring, but high discounters add value of $1 + d - y$. I assume that $y$ is large enough that the no-monitoring value of marginal product for high discounters is less than the wage rate with monitoring:

$$1 + d - y < 1. \tag{9.4}$$

This condition merely says that monitoring firms are economical for high discounters.

There is a cost of aggregating low discounters in no-monitoring firms, but the wage rate must exceed $1; otherwise, no-monitoring solutions are uneconomical. Thus we have a condition on the wage, $w$, in a no-monitoring firm:

$$1 < w < 1 + d. \tag{9.5}$$

Assuming the firm sets aggregate wages equal to workers' aggregate value of marginal product each period, it is easy to show that, for a cohort of workers hired in period zero, the wage rate in period $t$, which I denote as $w_t$, is[44]

$$w_t = 1 + d - \alpha_t y, \tag{9.6}$$

where $\alpha_t$ is the portion of workers in this cohort who are high discounters in period $t$. The wage rate equals the value of marginal product of a low discounter, $1 + d$, minus the cost of hiring errors that persist in period $t$, $\alpha_t y$. The productivity gains over $n$ periods of a low discounter's career that derive from no-monitoring firms is the summation of the no-monitoring premiums:

$$B = \sum_{t=0}^{n} [d - \alpha_t y] \, dt. \tag{9.7}$$

The competitive process drives firms to maximize the value of $B$. In a firm where monitoring is expensive, one solution is to reduce monitoring costs to a low level and instead find a way to employ primarily low discounters.

## 9.3 SORTING OUT HIGH DISCOUNTERS

Several pension strategies are available to reduce the magnitude of the high discounter problem. For example, the firm can make a large portion of compensation payable far in the future, thereby discouraging high discounters from entering. A defined benefit pension plan characterizes this approach. Alternatively, it can accept the inevitability of high discounters' entering and instead find an economical way to accommodate them by aligning pay with discount rates. I pursue this alternative in chapter 10.

Finally, the firm can let more high discounters enter but encourage them to identify themselves and voluntarily depart early in tenure, which is the strategy I consider below.

### 9.3.1 Shortcomings of a Selection Strategy

Since defined benefit pensions skew compensation toward the end of tenure, they are suited to attract a workforce disproportionately composed of low discounters.[45] Two factors explain why defined benefit plans (or other deferred wages) may not be the most efficient sorting solution. First, deferred wages are costly. Workers covered by defined benefit plans forgo some of their economic alternatives during the life of the contract, requiring firms to pay an indenture premium (chapter 8). If firms value low discounters primarily because they are most likely to stay for the full contract (because they attach a higher value to forgone pension income from quitting), then the indenture premium may be economical. But if firms value low discounters for some other reason—for example, because they economize on monitoring costs—a defined benefit plan may be an expensive way to sort for low discounters.

Second, firms that substantially tilt compensation inadvertently hire some high discounters. As long as job search is costly and information about job alternatives is imperfect, "mismatches" will develop between workers and firms. In appendix A to this chapter, I show that the problem is exacerbated for high discounters because they attach less value to the long-term benefits of finding a good job match and often enter a firm that is not ideally suited for them.

Casual inspection of the data suggests that mismatches are common. For example, federal workers hired after 1983 are covered by a typical defined benefit pension. Yet if sick leave balances and 401k contribution rates are good indexes of workers' internal discount rates, it is hard to avoid the inference that, deferred wages notwithstanding, the federal employment pool includes at least some high discounters.[46]

Although defined benefit plans are suited to selecting low discounters, they have no natural mechanism to evict high discounters who enter inadvertently. Either the firm accepts the inefficiency of having some high discounters in its employ for longer periods, or it supplements the pension with costly monitoring to identify high discounters.

### 9.3.2 How a Defined Contribution Plan Encourages Selective Quitting

I now show how a simple defined contribution plan can effectively sort for low discounters. The firm contributes some percentage of pay, denoted by $s$, into each worker's account per period. I assume that vesting occurs after one period.[47] The balance in the account is available when the worker quits; otherwise it is inaccessible.

Compared with defined benefit plans, in defined contribution plans pension benefits are not backloaded until late in tenure, so defined contribution plans are less effective in deterring the entry of high discounters. This same provision, however, gives them an advantage in encouraging the departure of high discounters.

Consider the efficacy of a defined contribution pension in correcting hiring errors. At the end of period 1, workers decide whether to quit the firm. Presumably each worker perceived a net gain to joining the firm in the first place, or he would have chosen some other job. In appendix A I develop an expression for this gain, but for present purposes it is sufficient that the gain for the $i$th high discounter who enters the firm, $j_{Hi}$, exceeds zero. Assuming that workers have the same knowledge of the labor market as they did at the beginning of period 1, the economics of joining and staying are the same, with one important difference.

If they quit, workers obtain the lump sum $s$ after period 1; if they stay, $s$ is deferred at least until the end of period 2. For low discounters, the value of $s$ is the same whether or not it remains in the pension plan, so the gains from staying are the same as for joining.[48] For the $i$th high discounter, the perceived net gains from staying, $g_{Hi}$, are lower by the added value of obtaining the available pension amount immediately (second term):[49]

$$g_{Hi} = j_{Hi} - sr/(1 + r). \tag{9.8}$$

If the individual's discount rate is zero, the second term in (9.8) is zero, so the gains from staying are the same as for joining the firm. For individuals with large discount rates, the second term approaches $s$, so the gains from staying approach the gains from joining *minus* the full amount of the pension lump sum.

An economic function for defined contribution plans emerges. The lump sum they provide upon quitting encourages high discounters to select themselves for early departure from the firm. In effect, the plan continually sifts for high discounters, thereby improving the composition of the firm's workforce over time. High discounters with the smallest values of $j_{Hi}$ quit after period 1. But at the end of the next period, the available lump sum is $2s$, and after the third period, $3s$, and so on. Gradually, most of the high discounters find it economical to depart the firm.[50]

In appendix B I show that, under plausible assumptions, the net benefits conferred on low discounters by defined contribution plans are comparable to those conferred by defined benefit plans. That is, the efficacy of defined contribution plans in encouraging quitting can result in a workforce with higher proportions of low discounters than under defined benefit plans.

## 9.4 SOME TESTS OF QUITTING AND LUMP SUMS

### 9.4.1 Lump Sum Distributions and Rollovers

The model predicts that workers who quit firms that award lump sums upon quitting ought to reveal behavior consistent with a high internal discount rate. More particularly, the theory anticipates that quitters receiving lump sums will spend the proceeds rather than roll them over into Individual Retirement Accounts (IRAs). Behavior reported by Joseph Piacentini is consistent with this expectation.[51] Based on the May 1988 pension supplement to the Current Population Survey (CPS), Piacentini finds that approximately 90 percent of quitters who leave with preretirement pension lump sums do not roll over them over into IRAs. Instead, unless they are older than age 59½, they pay the 10 percent excise tax and take the funds as immediately taxable income.

I pursue this idea by differentiating between those who quit earlier and later in tenure. The sorting model suggests that among workers who quit with lump sums, those departing early in tenure have higher discount rates than those who quit later. Higher-tenure quits have demonstrated their ability to resist the lump sum for longer periods and thus are more likely to have lower discount rates. If so, they are more likely to roll over their lump sums into an IRA. The CPS asks respondents the size of the lump sum and the year they received it, but not their tenure at the time they quit.

I create an estimated tenure variable. As a first-order approximation, pension value is proportional to the wage rate times years of tenure times some generosity parameter. The survey reports the amount of the lump sum and the worker's current annual wage in May 1988. I also know the average generosity parameter for pensions.[52] Although I do not know the worker's wage at the time he quits, I know the wage rate on the date of the survey. By restricting the sample to workers who received lump sums in the few years before the survey date, I can use each recipient's current wage as an approximation to his wage at the time he took the lump sum.[53]

I consider workers under age 40 in May 1988 who received a lump sum from a past pension plan in 1982 or later and who had no more that six years of tenure in May 1988.[54] These criteria generate 499 observations. I estimate a logit model where the independent variable equals one if the worker rolls over at least part of the lump sum, zero otherwise.

Table 9.4  Lump Sums and Discount Rates

| Independent variables | Mean | IRA rollover (1) | Participate in a 401k (2) |
|---|---|---|---|
| Estimated tenure[a] at quit date (years) | 1.03 | .14 (3.20) | — |
| IRA rollover | .17 | — | .22 (2.15) |
| Year dummy variables | | X | |
| Other variables[b] | | X | X |
| Observations | | 499 | 202 |
| Percentage positive | | 14.6 | 42.5 |

Note: The sample used in the first column comprises workers interviewed in 1988 who are under age 40, have less than or equal to six years of tenure, and reported receiving a lump sum from a previous pension since 1982. The subset of this sample in a firm offering a 401k plan in 1988 composes the sample for the second column.

The dependent variable equals one if the respondent rolled over at least a portion of a lump sum into an IRA, zero otherwise (col. 1); contributes to his 401k plan in 1988, zero otherwise (col. 2). The coefficient on estimated tenure in column 1 is the incremental effect of quitting after five years of tenure compared with quitting after one year (all other variables set to their mean values). The coefficient on the rollover variable in column 2 is the incremental effect of setting the IRA variable to one compared with zero, all other variables set to their mean values. Numbers in parentheses are $t$-statistics on the underlying coefficients. The $t$-value in column 1 is not adjusted to account for the error embedded in the use of an estimated tenure variable.

Source: Current Population Survey, April 1988.

[a]This variable is an estimate of the tenure level when the lump sum was taken from a previous job. See text.

[b]Other variables include a constant term, age, and dummy variables denoting marital status, children under age 18 in the home, gender, race, education, and family income. Including the wage rate as an independent variable does not materially change the coefficients or significance levels.

I include estimated tenure at the time of the lump sum as an independent variable and control for age, year the lump sum was received, gender, race, marital status, education, family income, and presence of children under age 18 in the home.

The incremental effect is reported in table 9.4, column 1.[55] The incremental tenure effect compares a worker who has five years of tenure at the time of quitting with one who quits after one year (all other variables set to their mean values). This effect is fourteen percentage points, which is large in relation to the average rollover probability in the sample (14.6 percent).[56]

There is some additional information in the data that can help corroborate this finding. Of the 499 workers who took a lump sum between 1982 and 1988, 202 were working in firms in May 1988 that offer a 401k plan. If workers who rolled over their lump sums into IRAs have lower discount rates, they are more likely to contribute to their 401k plans in 1988. To test this idea, I estimate a logit model where the dependent variable equals one if the worker contributes to his 401k plan in

1988, zero otherwise. I include a dummy variable equal to one if the worker rolled over his prior lump sum, zero otherwise. I include the same independent variables as in column 1 (except that I exclude the year dummy variables).

The results, presented in column 2 of the table, show that the incremental effect of the IRA rollover variable is positive and the underlying estimated coefficient is statistically significant at the 95 percent level of confidence. Workers who rolled over their prior lump sums into an IRA have a probability of 401k participation in 1988 twenty-one percentage points higher than for those who did not roll over their prior lump sums.[57] The incremental effect is large in relation to the mean of the dependent variable (42.5 percent).

### 9.4.2 Quitting and Discount Rates in the Federal Government

Next I evaluate the relation between lump sums and quitting in the federal government. In the federal worker sample cited above, I used cross section data for 1993 for workers hired under the Federal Employee Retirement System (FERS—all workers hired after 1983). I also have a sample of workers covered by the earlier Civil Service Retirement System (CSRS). Whereas FERS is roughly comparable to pensions in the private sector, the CSRS is characterized by a defined benefit pension that is more generous than the typical private pension and therefore ought to be particularly suited to attract low discounters.[58] Yet it is unique in the sense that it awards a lump sum to any worker who quits equal to 7 percent times his career earnings (see chapter 4).[59] If the lump sum entices high discounters to quit, the testable proposition follows that quitters are primarily high discounters.

As a proxy for internal discount rates, I again use the sick leave balance variable, $\beta$, cited in expression (9.2).[60] As a percentage of sick leave accrued, low discounters ought to have more unused sick leave (higher $\beta$s) than high discounters. The 1993 data I used above are not suitable for this exercise.[61] I use another file for (civilian) federal workers employed by the U.S. Air Force in January 1987. I have a 10 percent sample of workers who did not quit during the ensuring twelve months and a 100 percent sample of civilian employees who quit the Air Force during 1987.

For the latter sample, I know the date of their departure and their sick leave balances on both 1 January and their departure dates. I recognize that workers anticipating quitting the federal government have an incentive to use their leave before quitting. I correct the data for this effect by estimating the increase in sick leave usage in the months before quitting and use these results to restate quitters' sick leave balances as of twelve months before their quit date.[62] I denote the adjusted sick leave balance variable as $\hat{\beta}$.

Table 9.5  Sick Leave Balances, Wages, and Quitting

| Independent variable | Quit CSRS (1) | Quit FERS (2) | Transfer CSRS (3) |
|---|---|---|---|
| Sick leave balance[a] cumulative % ($\hat{\beta}$) | −.021 (3.51) | −.040 (1.47) | −.0026 (.85) |
| Other variables[b] | X | X | X |
| Observations | 4,245 | 769 | 4,245 |
| Percentage positive[c] | .010 | .043 | .004 |

*Note:* The independent variable is a dummy variable equal to one if the worker quit the civilian Air Force for a job outside the federal government during 1987 (cols. 1 and 2); for a job elsewhere in the federal government (col. 3); zero otherwise. I report incremental effects: the change in the dependent variable when sick leave balance alternatively is set equal to one or zero, all other independent variables set to their mean values. The sample in columns 1 and 3 is restricted to workers covered by the Civil Service Retirement System (CSRS); the sample in column 2 is restricted to workers covered by the Federal Employee Retirement System (FERS). The samples are overweighted for quits, and thus the estimates are made using a weighted logit model where the weights are the population-to-sample proportions in the choice-based sample.
*Source:* Defense Manpower Data Center.
[a] Actual sick leave balance is corrected for extraordinary sick leave usage before quitting. See chapter 9, note 62.
[b] Other variables included in the regressions (in addition to a constant term) are age, age-squared, tenure, tenure-squared, and dummy variables denoting race (white omitted), gender (male omitted), less than high-school graduate, some college, college graduate, and graduate degree (high-school graduate omitted), and two SMSA locations different from the intercept location.
[c] These numbers are population estimates derived by calculating the predicted probability of quitting, setting the dependent variables to their mean values and using the coefficients from the weighted logit model.

To accommodate the choice-based sample, I use a weighted logit model.[63] The dependent variable equals one if the worker quit the Air Force during 1987 for a job outside the federal government, zero otherwise. I include the adjusted variable, $\hat{\beta}$, as an independent variable and control for age, tenure, education, race, and gender.[64]

Table 9.5, column 1, reports the incremental effect of a $\beta$ value equal alternatively to one or zero (other variables set to their mean values).[65] The estimate is negative, and the underlying coefficient is statistically different from zero at the 99 percent level of confidence. Workers who have lower sick leave balances quit more often. The effect is large: a worker who takes no sick leave ($\hat{\beta} = 1$) has a quit rate 2.1 percentage points lower than does a worker who uses all his sick leave ($\hat{\beta} = 0$); the population mean quit rate is 1 percent. These results are not appreciably altered by including wage rate and occupation dummy variables as independent variables.[66]

As a check on these results, I reestimate the equation including only workers hired after 31 December 1983. These workers are covered by a different pension plan (the Federal Employee Retirement System). FERS awards a lump sum to those who quit equal to approximately 2 percent of pay times years of service.[67] Given that the lump sum is only 25 percent of that available under CSRS, the $\beta$ variable should be a less important predictor of quitting. Given that the mean quit rate is different in the two samples, I compare the incremental effects with their respective mean values.

In the CSRS sample, the $\beta$ effect is two times the mean value of the quit rate. The $t$-value on the underlying coefficient is 3.51. The results for the FERS sample are reported in the second column of the table: the incremental effect for values of setting $\beta$ equal to one and zero is approximately equal to the mean probability population estimate.[68] The $t$-value on the underlying coefficient falls to 1.47.[69]

I also test whether the sick leave balance effect is specific to those who quit the federal government altogether. Workers who quit the Air Force to take a job elsewhere in the federal government do not have access to their lump sums. Thus, if the lump sum entices high discounters to opt out of the federal government, then the $\hat{\beta}$ variable ought to be less important in explaining quits that provide no access to lump sums. To test this idea, I reestimate the weighted logit model where the dependent variable equals one if the worker quit the Air Force but took a job elsewhere in the federal government, zero otherwise. The results in the third column are consistent with expectations: the estimated incremental effect of $\hat{\beta}$ is statistically indistinguishable from zero: the $t$-value on the coefficient is .85.

## 9.5 CONCLUDING REMARKS

Low discounters are more forward looking than high discounters. This attribute undoubtedly influences the attainment of human capital, but it also is reflected in unobservable investment decisions that influence an employee's value in the workplace. I postulate that a person's underlying internal discount rate is important in determining his earnings potential—that low discounters are better workers than high discounters.

Although internal discount rates are not directly observable, they imply behavior that can be observed and measured. Exploiting variables that reflect workers' long horizon, I find support for the proposition that low discounters are higher-quality workers.

This proposition implies an economic function for devices that can sort workers based on unobserved internal discount rates. Pensions plans are natural candidates. The ability of defined benefit pension plans to attract low discounters is apparent, but other kinds of pensions can also sort for workers on discount rates without causing the firm to incur monitoring costs.

Simple defined contribution plans can cheaply and efficaciously sort out high discounters early in tenure. The data suggest that quitters whose pension plans offer lump sums are predominantly high discounters.

In the next chapter I consider the efficacy of 401k plans in the context of this selection model. I show that 401k plans provide a more sophisticated sorting role by coaxing workers to select wages commensurate with their values of marginal product. The sorting functions greatly expand the productivity attributes of pensions and may help explain the dramatic growth of 401k plans since their introduction in 1981, described in chapter 7.

## APPENDIX A: THE DECISION TO JOIN A MONITORING FIRM

In this appendix I present a simple model of job search that has some high discounters taking jobs in firms with deferred wages. To set up the problem, I make the following simplifying assumptions. The interest rate is zero. Firms know the overall proportions of high and low discounters in the labor market and how to affect their composition with wage structure, but they do not know the discount rate of any particular applicant.[70] They simply hire all workers who apply for a job. Workers know their own discount rates but have imperfect information about the labor market. Importantly, I assume that this information varies directly with individuals' internal discount rates.

Job shopping is inherently an investment activity. Search costs incurred early in the career result in the long-term benefits of finding the "right" job. Low discounters should therefore invest more in the search process and have a greater likelihood of selecting a firm that values their long-term outlook.[71] High discounters presumably are less careful job shoppers and thus more frequently take jobs at firms with production functions designed for low discounters.

Workers apply for jobs randomly in period 1. They take a job after seeing the posted compensation offer. Total compensation, $w$, comprises a cash wage, $w_c$, plus a deferred wage, $w_d$.[72] Since high discounters attach less value to deferred compensation, the perceived wage, $\tilde{w}_i$, depends on the worker's internal discount rate, $r_i$. For a deferred wage payable in $n$ periods, we have

$$\tilde{w}_i = w_c + w_d/(1 + r_i)^n. \tag{9.9}$$

If the deferred wage is positive, high discounters perceive a lower wage than low discounters ($\tilde{w}_H < \tilde{w}_L$).

The perceived alternative wage available in monitoring firms is $\tilde{a}_i$, which I write as

$$\tilde{a}_j = 1 + \epsilon_j, \qquad (9.10)$$

where $\epsilon_j$ is an error term with mean zero and variance $\sigma^2(\epsilon_j)$.

Owing to different values attached to job market information, the amount of information about alternative wages depends on the individual's internal discount rate. For simplicity, I assume that low discounters know the compensation in monitoring firms is unity ($\sigma^2(\epsilon_L) = 0$) and thus always apply for jobs in no-monitoring firms.[73]

High discounters are uncertain about this wage ($\sigma^2(\epsilon_H) > 0$). The perceived advantage to joining a no-monitoring firm for an individual in the $j$th group, denoted by $j_j$, is the difference between the perceived compensation in the firm and the perceived alternative compensation. For high discounters, the calculation is negative for some and positive for others, depending on their estimate of the alternative wage:[74]

$$j_j = \tilde{w}_j - \tilde{a}_j = (w - 1) + [1/(1 + r_j)^n - 1]w_d - \epsilon_j(r_j). \quad (9.11)$$

For low discounters the last two terms are zero, and thus, since $w - 1$ is positive from expression (9.5), $j_L$ is always positive.

High discounters attach less value to the deferred wage, which decreases the advantages of joining, but they are less informed about the alternative wages and hence can have large values of $\epsilon$. High discounters enter the applicant pool if they are sufficiently pessimistic about their alternative cash wage ($\epsilon_j \ll 0$). As long as the distribution of error terms is wide enough, the efficient solution includes hiring errors: some high discounters are inadvertently hired.

## APPENDIX B: EFFICACY OF LUMP SUMS VERSUS DEFERRED PAY

Defined benefit and defined contribution firms increase the benefits to low discounters in different ways: the former plans strongly discourage entry but have weak incentives to quit. The latter plans are less effective in deterring entry of high discounters but are comparatively good at encouraging their early exit. From expression (9.7), I can write the benefits accruing to each low discounter in a cohort over $n$ periods as $B^k$ for the $k$th plan type ($k = b$ for defined benefit plans, $k = c$ for defined contribution plans):

$$B^k = n [d - \overline{\alpha}^k y], \qquad (9.12)$$

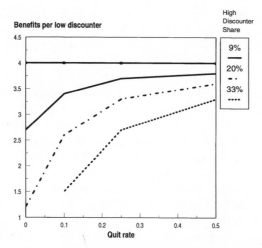

**Figure 9.1** Benefits of reducing the share of high discounters. Depicts the gain to low discounters over twenty periods as a function of the quit rate of high discounters per period. Four schedules depict the relation when the share of an entering cohort of workers is from zero to 33 percent high discounters.

where $\bar{\alpha}^k$ is the average share of high discounters for some entering cohort of workers, tracked over $n$ periods of tenure in the $k$th type of plan. For defined benefit plans, assuming a zero natural quit rate, the average share, $\bar{\alpha}^b$, is the same as the share of high discounters entering each cohort of hires:

$$\bar{\alpha}^b = \alpha_0^b. \tag{9.13}$$

In defined contribution plans, the high discounter share falls as a function of the quit rate, $q$, induced by the lump sum. If this rate is constant, then it is easily confirmed that the average share of high discounters over $n$ periods, $\bar{\alpha}^c$, is

$$\bar{\alpha}^c = \log[(1 - q + h(1 - q)^n)/(1 - q + h)]/n \log(1 - q),$$
$$h = \alpha_0^c/(1 - \alpha_0^c), \tag{9.14}$$

where $\alpha_0^c$ is the high discounter share in the defined contribution firm upon entry of the cohort.[75] Presumably, $\alpha_0^c > \alpha_0^b$.

Figure 9.1 shows the solution for expression (9.12) with either (9.13) or (9.14) substituted for $\bar{\alpha}^k$. The calculations are done for different shares of applicants who are high discounters ranging from zero to 33 percent, and for quit rate ranging from zero to 50 percent. The calculations assume that monitoring costs are $0.2, career tenure for low discounters is twenty periods ($n = 20$), and the difference in values of marginal product between low and high discounters is .5 ($y = .5$). Recall that the wage rate in a monitoring firm is $1. With perfect job matching—no high discounters entering the no-monitoring firm—the value of no-monitoring firms over twenty periods is $4 per low discounter.

The vertical distance between the schedules at a zero quit rate shows the economic effects of hiring errors in a no-monitoring firm that has no mechanism to correct the errors: the quit rate is zero. If only 9 percent of entrants in the firm are high discounters, the gains from no monitoring are reduced by one-third, from $4 to $2.70. If 20 percent of entrants are high discounters, the gains are reduced by more than two-thirds, to $1.20. But if the firm can effect a 50 percent quit rate of high discounters with lump sums, then, even if high discounters are one-third of each cohort of hires, the firm preserves over 80 percent of the gains from no monitoring—see rightmost portions of each schedule in the figure. Clearly, the lump sum scheme is a potentially efficient means to capture the gains available from congregating low discounters in no-monitoring firms.

The quit rate engendered by the lump sum payments implies a decreasing share of high discounters and thus a rising wage (see expression 9.6) over higher tenure levels. The rising wage reflects not a tenure effect, but rather the growing concentration of low discounters within the cohort over time. The wage premium reflects the simple proposition that low discounters finance the cost of the sorting process early in tenure and receive the benefits of the investment later.[76]

It is reasonable to ask whether firms that use defined contribution or defined benefit plans have workers whose discount rates are comparable to those of workers in firms that use defined benefit plans. To test this proposition, I reestimate the regression in table 9.3, where the dependent variable is the log of the respondent's financial planning horizon from the Health and Retirement Survey.

I limit the sample to workers covered by pensions (including those covered by but not participating in 401k plans).[77] I add one independent variable: a dummy variable equal to one if the worker was not covered by a defined benefit plan. The coefficient on this variable is close to zero, with a $t$-value of .17. If the self-reported horizon variable is a good index of discount rates, then based on a sample of workers in the age range 51–61, it appears that discount rates are not materially different across defined benefit and defined contribution plans.

## CHAPTER TEN

# Aligning Pay and Productivity: 401k Plans

In chapter 9 I assumed that the firm wants to encourage the exit of high discounters. In this chapter I suppose that the firm has jobs for both high and low discounters. It wishes to allocate workers to jobs based on their internal discount rates and pay low discounters more than high discounters.[1]

I show that 401k pension plans can help the firm accomplish its objective by encouraging individuals to identify their implicit discount rates, without imposing significant costs on the firm. By not taking advantage of the match provision, high discounters effectively volunteer to earn less than low discounters. In addition, the firm can use information conveyed by contribution behavior to allocate workers to their best uses. I present empirical evidence that 401k contributors are higher-quality workers than noncontributors.

## 10.1 A SORTING MODEL OF 401K PLANS

Traditional defined contribution plans often contribute some percentage of workers' pay to their pension accounts each period.[2] In 401k versions of these plans, the worker chooses some voluntary contribution rate, $v$, and the employer matches these contributions $m$ to one, where $m$ can be zero or positive. Such 401k plans also can provide for an unconditional contribution by the plan sponsor, $s$. In general, the firm's contribution to a defined contribution plan (as a percentage of pay) is

$$c = s + mv, \, s, \, m \geq 0. \tag{10.1}$$

I consider a 401k plan with matching. For simplicity, I set the unconditional contribution to zero ($s = 0$). Recall from chapter 9 that low discounters have an assumed zero internal discount rate and high discounters have some positive discount rate, $r \gg 0$. With no monitoring, low discounters add value of $1 + d$ per period, and high discounters add value of $1 + d - y$ per period. I consider the problem of paying these workers according to their underlying value when monitoring is expensive. The firm's problem is to pay the appropriate amounts to workers without having to expend monitoring resources.

One way to accomplish this outcome is to offer a 401k pension plan with matching. By choosing the appropriate match, the firm can entice workers to pay themselves according to their underlying value of marginal product.

Assume, for simplicity, that high discounters have a sufficiently high internal discount rate that they contribute nothing to the 401k plan within the relevant range of matching amounts. Low discounters make a positive contribution to the 401k plan, say $v$, and increase their contributions at higher rates of matching. In this case the optimal matching rate is easy to determine.

The firm sets compensation, net of the match amounts, equal to the high discounter's value of marginal product ($w = 1 + d - y$). It chooses the match rate, $m^*$, so that the matching amount paid to low discounters equals the differential value of marginal product between high and low discounters, $y$.[3] Inclusive of matching, compensation paid to high and low discounters is proportional to their value of marginal product:

$$w_i = 1 + d - y + m^* v = 1 + d \text{ for low discounters}$$
$$= 1 + d - y \text{ for high discounters.} \tag{10.2}$$

The results are only slightly more complex if high discounters have a positive savings rate in the face of matching.[4]

This result captures the economics of matching: workers are paid in accordance with their underlying internal discount rates, which manifest themselves in savings decisions. Contributions to 401k plans are voluntary. Presumably the firm does not ex post selectively reduce cash wages of particular workers who receive matching amounts. It also is reasonable to assume that profit maximizing firms do not award "extra" wages unrelated to workers' values of marginal product. The logical inference is that firms paying matching amounts in the 401k plan attach special value to workers who are inclined to save.

Once the firm infers workers' internal discount rates from observing 401k contributions, it can use this information to select workers for more important jobs. In this way, the implications of using the sorting device can reach beyond the wage differences established from the matching amounts. The firm also can use the 401k plan to offer efficiency wages based on workers' internal discount rates.[5] In all these ways, the firm encourages low discounters to stay with the firm.[6]

Finally, though a 401k plan can be used as an alternative to a defined benefit plan, both can be used in tandem. If the firm already has a defined benefit plan and thus pays the indenture premium, it can use the 401k matching feature to help align pay and productivity across the range of its employee discount rates, alleviating the problem posed when higher discounters inadvertently enter the firm.

## 10.2 A TEST OF MONITORING: LARGE FIRMS AND MATCHING

In the sorting theory, firms use matching to encourage workers to align their pay and productivity without incurring monitoring costs, and thus matching ought to be used in firms where such costs are higher. It is natural to assume that monitoring costs more in larger firms[7] and that they are therefore more likely to rely on sorting devices to substitute for personal knowledge of workers.[8] One test of the theory is to ask whether matching is more likely in larger firms.

To test this proposition, I use data from the 1988 Current Population Survey, May supplement, describing the behavior of workers covered by 401k pensions.[9] I construct two dummy variables reflecting firm size, one equal to unity if the worker's plant location employs more that 250 workers, and one equal to unity if the firm employs more than 1,000 workers.[10]

I also include a dummy variable denoting the worker's union status. It is well known that unions work to reduce wage dispersion within the firm,[11] so I presume that unions are more likely to oppose policies like matching that award different compensation to otherwise identical workers.

The estimates are made using a logit model, where the dependent variable equals unity if the firm offers matching contributions, zero otherwise.[12] Table 10.1 reports the estimated incremental effects.[13] The results show that workers in large plans and large firms are more likely to be offered matching. The incremental effect of setting both size variables equal to one or zero (union variable set to its mean value) is to increase the likelihood of matching by approximately thirteen percentage points.

## 10.3 EVIDENCE OF QUALITY DIFFERENCES: CONTRIBUTORS VERSUS NONCONTRIBUTORS

An alternative way to test the theory is to compare behavior on the job by 401k contributors and noncontributors. If low discounters are better workers than high discounters, then we ought to be able to find evidence

Table 10.1 Determinants of Matching

| Independent variable | Mean value | Incremental effect |
|---|---|---|
| Intercept | | .615 |
| | | (8.56) |
| Firm >1,000 workers | .64 | .092 |
| | | (6.26) |
| Plant >250 workers | .45 | .036 |
| | | (2.51) |
| Union | .20 | −.152 |
| | | (9.10) |
| Mean dependent variable | | .55 |
| Number of observations | | 5,143 |

Note: The dependent variable is a dummy variable equal to unity if the firm offers matching contributions, zero otherwise. The estimates are based on a logit model. The numbers are incremental effects: the difference in the probability that the dependent variable equals one when the independent variable is set alternatively to unity or zero (other variables set to their mean values). The intercept value is the probability of observing matching in a 401k plan when the worker is not covered by a union, plant size is less than 250 workers, and firm size is less than 1,000 workers. I also include dummy variables to denote observations for which either firm size or plant size is unknown (not reported). Numbers in parentheses are $t$-values. The sample includes workers who are covered by a 401k plan.
Source: Current Population Survey, May supplement, 1988.

of these differences in the data. I use data describing a sample of civilian army employees in October 1993.

### 10.3.1 Pay Increases

A central proposition in the sorting theory is that 401k contributors are higher-quality workers than noncontributors. A direct test of this proposition is to associate 401k contributions with higher wages. But given the two-way causality of the relation, this approach is problematic. One alternative is to evaluate pay increases over time: other things being equal, 401k contributors ought to be more likely to obtain pay increases than noncontributors. I test the hypothesis by looking at pay increases in the federal data over a three-month period.

The pay scale in the federal government is made up of fifteen grades, with ten steps within each grade. Pay increases take the form of either a change in grade (a promotion), worth as much as a 20 percent raise, or movements along the steps, each of which represents a 3 percent raise. Tenure explains most movements across steps,[14] but good workers can obtain extra step increases (merit-based increases). For my sample of workers employed in October 1993, I know their current wage and their wage in January 1994. Since their grade level also is reported, I can identify promotions in the data: 5.1 percent of the sample received a promotion over this period. Employees also received within-grade increases, though I cannot distinguish a merit-based increase from a normal tenure

Table 10.2  401k Contributions and Pay Increases

| Independent variable | % Change (1) | Promote (2) | % Change (3) |
|---|---|---|---|
| Sick leave balance ($\beta$) | .003 | .014 | .00 |
| | (2.73) | (2.45) | (1.06) |
| 401k contribution, $c$: | | | |
| $0 < c \leq 5\%$ | .0014 | .00 | .0011 |
| | (2.30) | (.25) | (2.69) |
| $5\% < c \leq 10\%$ | .000 | .008 | −.000 |
| | (.54) | (1.98) | (1.25) |
| Promotion | | | .092 |
| | | | (115.88) |
| Grade/step dummy variables[a] | X | X | X |
| Other variables[b] | X | X | X |
| Observations | 12,824 | 12,803 | 12,824 |
| Mean dependent variable | .016 | .051 | .016 |
| $R^2$ | .07 | | .53 |

Note: The dependent variable in columns 1 and 3 is the percentage change in the wage rate between 1 October 1993 and 1 January 1994; the estimates are made using ordinary least squares. The dependent variable in column 2 equals one if the worker received an increase in grade between the same two dates; estimates in column 2 are based on a logit model, where reported numbers are incremental effects: the change in the probability that the dependent variable equals one when the independent variable is set to one versus zero, all other independent variables set to their mean values. Numbers in parentheses are $t$-values on the underlying coefficients.

Source: Defense Manpower Center.

[a] I include fourteen grade dummy variables and nine step dummy variables denoting all the pay cells in the federal pay scale.

[b] Other variables included in the regressions (in addition to a constant term) are age, age-squared, tenure, tenure-squared, and dummy variables denoting gender (male omitted), race (black and Hispanic, white omitted), less than high-school graduate, some college, college graduate, and graduate degree (high-school graduate omitted), disability, Indian and Asian race dummy variables, and two SMSA locations different from the intercept location.

effect. However, I can ferret out these increases by controlling for tenure effects.

I estimate an ordinary least squares regression, where the dependent variable is the percentage change in pay over three months. I control for various demographic characteristics, tenure,[15] and dummy variables for each grade and step (minus one each) in the pay scale as of October 1993.[16] As indexes of discount rates, I include the sick leave balance and two 401k contribution dummy variables: one denotes contributions up to 5 percent of pay (which the government matches at a 50 percent rate); the other denotes contributions beyond 5 percent (which are not matched). The results are reported in table 10.2, column 1.

The results are generally consistent with expectations: the coefficients on two of the three discount rate dummy variables are positive and statistically different from zero at least at the 95 percent level of confidence. Since the data report promotions separately, I can divide the pay changes into those attributable to promotions and those attributable to quality step increases.

Column 2 reports the incremental effects from estimating a logit model (other variables set to their mean values), where the dependent variable equals unity if the worker receives a promotion over the three-month period, zero otherwise. In column 3, I reestimate the ordinary least squares equation from column 1, except I include a dummy variable equal to unity if the worker receives a promotion over the period, thereby disentangling the pay impact of merit increases from the effect of promotions.

The results show that workers making the highest 401k contributions are more likely to receive promotions (column 2), and those contributing less are more likely to receive the merit step increases (column 3). Overall, the results are consistent with the hypothesis that workers who have a higher propensity to save sick leave and to contribute to the 401k plan are more likely to receive pay increases.

### 10.3.2 Job Performance Ratings

Whereas pay increases over a short period affect only a small proportion of the workforce, all workers receive performance ratings. I therefore use these ratings as an alternative measure of worker quality across the entire sample. Workers are separated into three rating categories, with about half in the highest category and 14 percent in the lowest.[17] As discount rate index, I include the two 401k contribution variables and the worker's leave balance variable.

I estimate an ordered logit model where the dependent variable is set equal to the worker's most recent performance rating (zero for a low rating, one for a medium rating, and two for a high rating).[18] I control for various demographic effects (coefficients not reported).[19]

Table 10.3, column 1, reports the incremental effects. The coefficients on the discount rate proxies are positive and statistically significant at the 99 percent level of confidence. Workers who have all their accrued sick leave still available have a 31 percent higher probability of obtaining the two top ratings than those who use all their sick leave (all other variables set to their mean values).

The 401k contribution variables also are important. Workers who participate in the first tier of 401k savings (up to 5 percent of pay) have a 3 percent greater likelihood of obtaining the higher ratings than those who make no contributions. Second-tier contributors (contributions above 5 percent of pay) have a 6.1 percent higher probability of receiving the higher ratings than noncontributors. Both effects are statistically different from zero at the 99 percent level of confidence.

If I exclude the sick leave balance variable, the incremental effects of the 401k contribution variables increase markedly (column 2), confirm-

Table 10.3  401k Contributions and Performance Ratings

| Independent variable | (1) | (2) | (3) |
|---|---|---|---|
| Sick leave balance ($\beta$) | .31 | | |
| | (17.52) | | |
| 401k contribution, $c$: | | | |
| $0 < c \le 5\%$ | .030 | .047 | .031 |
| | (2.76) | (4.42) | (2.83) |
| $5\% < c \le 10\%$ | .061 | .084 | .062 |
| | (5.12) | (7.15) | (5.10) |
| Wage rate[a] | — | — | .084 |
| | | | (2.93) |
| Other variables[b] | X | X | X |
| Observations | 12,548 | 12,588 | 12,424 |
| Mean dependent variable[c] | 1.36 | 1.36 | 1.36 |

Note: The dependent variable equals zero, one, or two depending on whether the worker receives a low, medium, or high rating. Estimates are based on an ordered logit model. Reported numbers are incremental effects: the change in the probability of receiving the top two ratings when the independent variable is set to one versus zero, all other independent variables set to their mean values (the exception is the wage—see note a). Numbers in parentheses are $t$-values on the underlying coefficients. The incremental effects of receiving the top rating are .12, .013, and .026 for the variables in column 1.
Source: Defense Manpower Center.
[a] The wage and wage-squared are included as independent variables. The incremental effect on the wage measures the impact of the third versus first quartile wages, all other variables set to their mean values. The $t$-statistic on the square term is reported in the table: the coefficient on the wage variable itself was not statistically different from zero.
[b] Other variables included in the regressions (in addition to a constant term) are age, age-squared, tenure, tenure-squared, and dummy variables denoting gender (male omitted), race (black and Hispanic, white omitted), less than high-school graduate, some college, college graduate, and graduate degree (high-school graduate omitted), disability, Indian and Asian race dummy variables, and two SMSA locations different from the intercept location.
[c] Fourteen percent had a low rating (set to zero), 50 percent a high rating (set to two), and 36 percent had a medium rating (set to one).

ing the positive correlation between performance, sick leave balance, and 401k contributions.

Finally, to test whether the 401k contribution rates reflect an underlying wage effect, I reestimate the model including the worker's wage rate (and its square term). The results, reported in column 3, do not alter the qualitative conclusions: 401k contributors generally have higher ratings than noncontributors earning the same wages.

### 10.3.3  401k Contributors and Quits

Finally, I test whether quit probabilities are correlated with my measures of internal discount rates. Through matching in the 401k plan, employers pay low discounters more than high discounters. They also are more likely to choose 401k contributors for promotions to better jobs. In addition, in the federal 401k plan, each worker receives an unconditional contribution from the government equal to 1 percent of pay. The govern-

Table 10.4 Implied Discount Rates and Quit Rates

| Independent variable | (1) | (2) |
|---|---|---|
| 401k contribution, $c$:[a] | | |
|   $0 < c \leq 5\%$ | −.0087 | −.0036 |
| | (4.55) | (2.80) |
|   $5\% < c \leq 10\%$ | −.0069 | −.0016 |
| | (2.97) | (.94) |
| Wage rate[b] | — | −.005 |
| | | (4.37) |
| Other variables[c] | X | X |
| Observations | 13,114 | 12,874 |
| Mean dependent variable | .009 | .009 |

*Note:* The dependent variable equals one if a worker employed 1 October 1993 quit before 1 January 1994. Estimates are based on a logit model. Reported numbers are incremental effects: the change in the probability that the dependent variable equals one when the independent variable is set to one versus zero, all other independent variables set to their mean values (the exception is the wage—see note b). Numbers in parentheses are *t*-values on the underlying coefficients.

*Source:* Defense Manpower Center.

[a] The mean values for the two contribution dummy variables are .39 for the 0–5 percent category and .32 for the 5–10 percent category. The remaining 29 percent of eligible workers do not participate.

[b] The wage and wage-squared are included as independent variables. The incremental effect on the wage measures the impact of the third versus first quartile wages, all other variables set to their mean values. The *t*-statistic on the wage term is reported in the table: the coefficient on the wage-squared variable also is statistically significant.

[c] Other variables included in the regressions (in addition to a constant term) are age, age-squared, tenure, tenure-squared, and dummy variables denoting race (white omitted), gender (male omitted), less than high-school graduate, some college, college graduate, and graduate degree (high-school graduate omitted), and two SMSA locations different from the intercept location.

ment also holds back an additional 1 percent of pay, which also is retrievable as a lump sum upon quitting.[20] For all these reasons, the federal pay scheme encourages low discounters to stay and high discounters to quit.

Of the workers employed in October 1993 in my sample, I can identify those who quit the government over the ensuing three months. Although the quit rate in the government is low, there are ample quits to perform a strong test of the proposition that noncontributors quit more often than contributors (there were 102 quits in the sample).

I estimate a logit model, setting the dependent variable equal to one if the worker quits over the three-month period, zero otherwise. I construct two dummy variables: one is set equal to unity if contributions are positive, but not higher than 5 percent, zero otherwise; the other is set equal to unity if contributions are over 5 percent, zero otherwise. I control for various demographic characteristics, except that I exclude the sick leave balance.[21]

The incremental effects of setting each of the independent variables to one or zero are reported in table 10.4, column 1 (all other variables are set to their mean values). The incremental effects on both 401k contribution

Table 10.5  Distribution of 401k Contributions

| Category | 1988 (1) | 1993 (2) |
|---|---|---|
| Contributions | | |
| >0 | 52.8 | 59.2 |
| 0 | 47.2 | 41.8 |
| Percentage, if positive | | |
| <5 | 31.7 | 26.9 |
| 5 | 20.8 | 18.4 |
| 6–9 | 26.1 | 27.6 |
| 10 | 11.6 | 14.4 |
| 11–14 | 3.5 | 4.1 |
| ≥15 | 6.3 | 8.7 |
| Average | 6.4 | 7.0 |
| Overall average | 3.4 | 4.1 |

Note: Numbers in table are percentages.
Source: Current Population Survey, pension supplement, 1988 (col. 1), 1993 (col. 2).

variables are negative and statistically significant at the 99 percent level of confidence. The incremental effects are each about the same order of magnitude at the mean quit rate in the sample. Contributors to the 401k plan are less likely to quit the federal government than are noncontributors.

To control for underlying wage influences in the contribution variables, I repeat the estimates including the wage rate and its square term (column 2). Including the wage rate reduces the magnitude of the coefficients, but the coefficient on the first-tier contribution variable remains statistically significant at the 99 percent level of confidence.

## 10.4 MATCHING AND 401K CONTRIBUTIONS

It is interesting to use information about 401k contributions to infer something about the distribution of low and high discounters in the labor force covered by 401k pensions. Many workers participate in 401k plans without matching, some participate on the margin because of matching, and others do not participate even with matching. Within a model that revolves around internal discount rates, these choices seem to reflect three groups of workers: low discounters, high discounters, and middling discounters.

Table 10.5, column 1, lists the distribution of contribution rates (as a percentage of salary) from the 1988 Current Population Survey, pension supplement. About half of workers covered by 401k plans make zero contributions. Among those who contribute, the average contribution is 6.4 percent of pay, with approximately one in five contributing more than

Table 10.6  Impact of Matching on Contributions to 401k Plans

| Independent variable | Mean value | 1988 (1) | 1993 (2) |
|---|---|---|---|
| Employer match | .73 | .003 | .011 |
| | | (2.22) | (7.50) |
| Female | .43 | −.001 | −.002 |
| | | (.46) | (1.33) |
| Black | .07 | −.010 | −.009 |
| | | (3.69) | (3.05) |
| Hispanic | .03 | −.007 | −.010 |
| | | (1.88) | (2.88) |
| Less than high school | .05 | −.007 | .012 |
| | | (2.45) | (3.35) |
| College degree | .37 | .005 | .006 |
| | | (3.24) | (3.98) |
| Other independent variables[a] | | X | X |
| Number of observations | | 4,593 | 4,809 |

Note: Dependent variable is the percentage of pay a worker contributes to the 401k; estimates are made using a tobit model to accommodate left consoring at zero. Sample includes workers covered by a 410k plan. The underlying distribution of contributions is given in table 10.5, except that individuals who "don't know" whether the firm matches contributions are excluded. Mean values pertain to the 1988 data. Numbers in the table are incremental effects: the change in the dependent variable when the independent variable is set alternatively to one and zero, other independent variables set to their mean values.
Source: Current Population Survey, pension supplement, 1988 (col. 1), 1993 (col. 2).
[a] Other independent variables include dummy variables denoting marital status, children under 18 present in the home, and thirteen dummy variables denoting family income categories ($17,500–$19,999 income per annum omitted).

10 percent.[22] Column 2 lists the contribution percentages from the 1993 CPS pension supplement. Although the questions in 1993 are somewhat different, the reported contribution rates are somewhat higher than in 1988.

To estimate the impact of matching on the contribution rate, I exclude workers who report that they "don't know" whether the firm matches contributions. I set the dependent variable equal to the percentage of pay contributed to the 401k plan and use a tobit model to accommodate left censoring of observed contribution rates at zero. I include independent variables reflecting respondent's age, sex, race, and marital status, a zero-one dummy variable denoting the presence of matching in the plan, and thirteen dummy variables denoting family income categories.

Table 10.6, column 1, reports some of the results for the 1988 data.[23] The coefficient on the matching dummy variable is positive and statistically significant at the 99 percent level of confidence, but it is small. Matching elicits an increase in the average contribution rate of one-third of one percentage point.[24] Column 2 lists the results for the 1993 data: the incremental effect on the matching variable is somewhat higher at

1.1 percent, but still relatively small in relation to overall contribution rates (see table 10.5).

Otherwise, the coefficients on selected independent variables are similar in the 1993 and 1988 data. Contribution rates are about the same between men and women but are markedly lower for black and Hispanic workers. The effects of education and family income (coefficients not reported) are large and positive.

## 10.5 CONCLUDING REMARKS

If low discounters are higher-quality workers than high discounters, then firms will try to infer workers' (unobserved) discount rates. A candidate to perform this function is a 401k pension plan with matching. These plans coax workers to select wages commensurate with their internal discount rates without causing the firm to incur monitoring costs. Based on the results of my study, 401k contributors are less likely to quit than are noncontributors (see chapter 9), more likely to obtain pay raises, and more likely to obtain higher job performance ratings.

In the next chapter I pursue the idea that unobservable worker attributes are important sources of differences in worker qualities. I consider a measure introduced in chapter 9—a worker's reliability. The tendency to be unreliable can signify an employee's internal discount rate, a preference for leisure, or a propensity to be ill. Regardless of the reason, such workers are worth less in the workplace than those who show up for work consistently over long periods.

The key advantage of studying the reliability trait is that, contrary to internal discount rates, reliability can be measured. By implication, internal discount rates, though measured imperfectly, also have important implications for wage levels in the long run. In chapter 11 I introduce one additional concept: statistical discrimination.

That is, firms observe the correlation between low or high quality and attributes they can observe. Over time, they learn to infer underlying productivity attributes based on behavior they can see. Thus workers with some vector of attributes $V$ will be affiliated with expected underlying quality level $q$. Workers with this "brand name" initially will be assumed to have quality level $q$ until their own performance changes employers' notions of expected performance. The model has general application to any unobserved attribute that affects workers' value of marginal product.

## CHAPTER ELEVEN

# Reliability as a Hidden Worker Attribute

I have argued that hidden attributes importantly affect workers' value of marginal product. I have emphasized one particular attribute—internal discount rates—and have shown how pensions can be used to perform a sorting function based on this trait. Although I presented evidence consistent with the idea that high discounters are lower-quality workers, the inferences are indirect because discount rates cannot themselves be observed.

In this chapter I study a trait that also is hidden at the time of hire, but that has more potential for direct measurement over some period of performance: reliability—the propensity to show up for work. Since the repercussions of being unreliable might not be felt until far in the future, arguably a worker's reliability and internal discount rate are expected to be related—high discounters are more likely to be unreliable. But other factors like the individual's "taste" for leisure and his vulnerability to illness also affect reliability.

My purpose in this chapter is not to disentangle the separate contributions of these factors to the worker's level of reliability. Instead, I wish to treat reliability as a partially hidden worker trait and show that it plays an important role in wage determination. The results imply that other hidden attributes, like internal discount rates, have similar effects on wages.

I pursue the simple idea that reliability is an important determinant of a worker's value of marginal product; that the answer to a hypothetical query at the time of the job application (Is this applicant likely to show up for work reliably for a lengthy period?) importantly affects the firm's willingness to pay for the person's services. Workers who have a strong preference for leisure have more "performance failures." I show that the market discounts wages for workers who accumulate track records of unreliability.[1]

In addition, I argue that though firms cannot easily determine the reliability traits of workers at the time they are hired, they nevertheless find ways to form expectations of reliability based on observable traits. Thus, if previous hires from Smith University have been comparatively unreliable, the firm may infer that new hires from the same university will evince the same unreliability and make wage offers to its graduates based on this expectation. With time, individuals can distinguish themselves from their identifiable group, but their wage is partly determined by a de facto "brand name" effect.

## 11.1 NOT SHOWING UP FOR WORK

Perhaps the most fundamental determinant of being a "reliable worker" is the habit of showing up for work every day over an extended period. A firm must expend resources to accommodate workers who do not show up for work. If a secretary stays home, the supervisor who schedules output for the day must hire a temporary service and "retrain" the temporary on the location of forms, files, and the like or else must reschedule deadlines and such. If a sales representative does not show up, the firm must send an imperfect substitute to service the customer. When the firm's output is jointly determined, the absence of some workers reduces the productivity of the team.

Firms can work around unreliability by creating redundancy (for example, hiring four secretaries instead of three) to allow easier substitution on short notice, or by creating overlapping skills across team members. But redundancy is expensive. Workers who impose these costs on their employers are paid lower wages.

The problem is exacerbated as the time away from work increases. When workers take several days off, the firm loses the option of postponing key work until their return and increases its reliance on duplication. When workers are away for even longer periods—several weeks or months—or take all their remaining time off (quit) the firm incurs costs of hiring and retraining replacements.

The cost of unreliability presumably varies across jobs. Many clerical workers have similar skills. Among jobs that are either simple or similar, substitution of workers and jobs is less expensive. Other jobs are more complex and less alike. The director of sales in most firms is not similar in skill and experience to the production manager. And prominent workers make more day-to-day decisions in the firm that cannot be delegated to assistants.

Following the model in chapter 9, I suppose that the utility of taking a day off now is described by the function $\eta_i^\epsilon \log(1 + \mu)$, where $\mu$ is a unit of unscheduled time off, $\eta$ is a parameter that reflects the value of leisure, which may vary across individuals, and $\epsilon$ is a random variable that is positive when some reason arises to stay home (illness, home emergency, feeling a whim to take a day off).

There is some cost, say $\Delta$, to taking unannounced time off in the form of lower future wage increases. In a two-period model, assuming a zero interest rate, the net gain, $\pi$, to taking time off in period 1 can be written as

$$\pi = \eta^\epsilon \log(1 + \mu) - \Delta/(1 + r), \qquad (11.1)$$

where $r$ is the individual's internal discount rate. We can think of unreliable workers as having either higher $\eta$s, higher discount rates, or larger probabilities of drawing large values of $\epsilon$. From the firm's perspective, however, the cost of unreliability is the same regardless of its underlying cause.

If the market exploits all available information, it will not wait for each worker to evince his underlying reliability but instead will "assign" the individual to a group based on observable characteristics. Through experience, firms discern a relationship between observable characteristics and expected unreliability. In this way, compared with an agnostic approach, the firm sets wages sooner in tenure that more closely approximate values of marginal products across unobservable unreliability traits.

Early in the career, the wage is almost entirely dependent on the group's reputation. As experience accumulates, workers whose propensity for unreliability is not like that imputed to the group differentiate themselves through performance. Importantly, the market's discount for unreliability partly reflects observed performance and partly reflects the brand name effect.

## 11.2 A FIRST LOOK AT THE DATA

The data on the sample of federal workers are particularly well suited to a study of reliability. As discussed in chapter 9, a generous amount of paid sick leave is available in the federal government (thirteen days per year) and can be carried over indefinitely. The sick leave allowance is in addition to nineteen days of paid annual leave.[2] Thus, plenty of time off is made available to employees to accomplish personal errands, stay home with a sick child, and so forth without using sick leave. The data include information about accumulated use of sick leave, long periods of sick leave used, time off without pay, and quitting the government altogether, so I can measure more serious performance failures in the federal workforce.[3]

## 11.2.1 Reliability in the Federal Workforce

Personnel and pay information is available for about five thousand full-time employees of the federal government, as of December 1986. The data constitute a 10 percent sample of workers who were still employed in the government in December 1987 and a 100 percent sample of workers who had a significant personnel action during 1987.

The average federal worker in the sample used 73.6 percent of sick leave earned through current tenure.[4] Approximately one in four workers have less than 6.8 percent of their accumulated sick leave available; 10 percent have more than 61.2 percent of their earned sick leave available.

## 11.2.2 Wages and Sick Leave

I first estimate a wage equation that includes a conventional spot measure of unreliability, the number of sick days taken during 1986, as an independent variable.[5] The dependent variable is the log of the annual wage. I exclude workers over age 45.[6]

As shown in table 11.1, column 1, the coefficient on the sick leave variable is negative and statistically significant, but it is small. A worker who takes thirteen days of sick leave during 1986 has a wage only 1.3 percent lower than one who takes no sick leave. These results are not unusual; other studies find a weak relation between wages and absenteeism.[7] But observations of absenteeism over a short period are noisy measures of long-term unreliability, which biases the estimates toward zero.

I next consider a more informative measure of unreliability, the percentage of accumulated earned sick leave used, which I introduced in chapter 9.[8] The reestimated wage equation is shown in table 11.1, column 2. The results are markedly different from those based on a spot measure. The coefficient on the unused sick leave balance variable is large, negative, and statistically significant at the 99 percent level of confidence. Other things constant, workers who use all of their earned sick leave earn about 14 percent less than those who show up for work every day.

## 11.2.3 Selection of Supervisors

Another way to test for an occupation effect is to examine the characteristics of workers in jobs that require more responsibility. One index of job responsibility is supervision of other employees. Arguably, reliability in these jobs is more valued because supervisors are less likely to have close

Table 11.1  Wages and Worker Characteristics

| Independent variable | Mean value | (1) | (2) |
|---|---|---|---|
| Intercept | | 9.74 | 9.83 |
| | | (516.3) | (445.8) |
| Sick leave used—1986 only (days) | 9.3 | −.001 (2.46) | |
| Sick leave used—entire[a] tenure (%) | .76 | | −.137 (8.00) |
| White female | .28 | −.20 (24.47) | −.19 (23.40) |
| Black female | .09 | −.22 (17.25) | −.21 (16.43) |
| Black male | .12 | −.046 (4.20) | −.04 (3.76) |
| Other variables[b] | | X | X |
| Number of observations[c] | | 2,912 | 2,912 |
| $R^2$ | | .61 | .62 |
| Mean dependent variable | | 10.03 | 10.03 |

Note: The dependent variable is the log of annual wage; estimates are made using ordinary least squares; numbers in parentheses are absolute t-values. The data pertain to a sample of civilian workers under age 45 employed in the federal government as of December 1986.
[a] Cumulative sick leave used divided by cumulative sick leave earned through current tenure.
[b] Includes tenure, age, tenure-squared, age-squared, dummy variables equal to unity for supervisor job, less than high school, some college, highest degree college, highest degree master's or more (high-school graduate omitted), dummy variables denoting performance ratings ("outstanding," "exceeds fully satisfactory," "unsatisfactory," and no rating—"fully satisfactory" omitted), a dummy variable equal to one if worker is partially disabled, two dummy variables to denote SMSA location different from intercept location, and two interaction variables: tenure after college degree and tenure after graduate degree.

substitutes and are costly to replace if they either leave for long periods or quit. The selection argument suggests that unreliable workers are less likely to occupy positions of greater responsibility where the cost imposed by that trait is higher.

Table 11.2, column 1, shows the results of a logit model where the dependent variable is the probability of being in a supervisory job in the federal government. Reported numbers are estimated incremental effects: the change in the dependent variable resulting from setting the independent variable alternatively to one or zero (all other independent variables set to their mean sample values); numbers in parentheses are t-values. The reported intercept is the probability that the dependent variable equals one for the omitted sex and race category (white males), setting the values of the other independent variables equal to their mean sample values. The results show that a worker who does not use any sick leave is six times more likely to have a supervisory job than a worker who uses the average amount of sick leave (setting other variables to mean sample values).[9]

Table 11.2  Indexes of Quality and Worker Demographics

| Independent variable | Mean value | Supervisor job (1) | High rating (2) | Removed from job (3) | Sick leave used cumulative (%) (4) |
|---|---|---|---|---|---|
| Intercept | | .127 | .33[a] | .005[a] | .71 |
| | | (15.37) | (10.57) | (4.46) | (52.10) |
| Sick leave used cumula- | .76 | −.34 | −.35 | .008 | |
| tive (%) | | (9.97) | (9.68) | (3.78) | |
| White female | .29 | −.03 | .094 | −.004 | .081 |
| | | (2.07) | (5.03) | (3.81) | (10.63) |
| Black female | .08 | .005 | .00 | −.003 | .101 |
| | | (.21) | (.00) | (1.47) | (8.36) |
| Black male | .11 | .001 | −.06 | .005 | .035 |
| | | (.00) | (2.58) | (2.40) | (3.81) |
| Other variables[b] | | X | X | X | X |
| Number of observations | | 4,741 | 4,741 | 5,404[c] | 4,740 |
| −2 log $L/R^2$ | | 509.5 | 314.1 | 148.9 | .19 |
| Mean dependent variable | | .113 | .305 | .013[d] | .73 |

Note: Estimates in columns 1 and 2 are made using a logit model. Those in column 3 are based on a weighted logit model where the weights are the population-to-sample proportions in the choice-based sample. The reported numbers are incremental effects: the change in the dependent variable when the independent variable is set alternatively to one or zero, other related dummy variables are set to zero, and the remaining independent variables are set to their mean values. Estimates in column 4 are based on ordinary least squares. Numbers in parentheses are $t$-values.

The dependent variable equals unity if the worker occupies a job entailing supervisory duties (col. 1); receives either an "outstanding" or "exceeds fully satisfactory" rating in 1986 (col. 2); or is involuntarily removed from the federal government during 1987 (col. 3). The dependent variable in column 4 is the percentage of accumulated earned sick leave used as of December 1986. All data pertain to a sample of civilian workers employed in the federal government as of December 1986.

[a] Probability that the dependent variable equals unity if the sex and race dummy variables are set to zero, evaluated at the average values of the remaining independent variables. It is the probability that the dependent variable equals unity for a white male with mean sample characteristics.

[b] Includes age, tenure, age-squared, tenure-squared, dummy variables denoting less than high school, some college, highest degree college, highest degree master's or more (high-school graduate omitted), a dummy variable equal to one if worker is partially disabled, two dummy variables denoting SMSA location different from intercept location, and two interaction variables: tenure after college degree and tenure after graduate degree.

[c] Includes 663 removals from the oversample file.

[d] Weighted by the ratios of population-to-sample proportions in the choice-based sample and thus reflects the true mean in the population database.

## 11.2.4  Pay Differences across Groups

There is another striking result in table 11.1, one that provides a promising avenue for pursuing the reliability theory. Other things the same, females are paid about 20 percent less than males.[10] This result is not new. A substantial literature has arisen to explain why, after adjusting for differences in human capital and job experience, women earn lower wages than men.[11] The finding could be explained either by a "taste" for discrimination (for reasons unrelated to productivity, female workers are paid less for the same amount of work)[12] or by "statistical" discrimination (unobservable or imperfectly measured underlying economic traits are systematically different between the sexes).[13]

It is hard to make the first argument in the context of the federal data. First, if discrimination explains the wage discount to female workers, the same discrimination does not apply to black workers. Wages of black males are almost 95 percent of those of white males. Black females are paid about the same as white females (table 11.1).

Second, if sex discrimination exists, it does not affect performance ratings. Table 11.2, column 2, reports incremental effects from a logit model, where the dependent variable equals one if a worker received a high performance rating during 1986, zero otherwise. The ratings of 30 percent of the sample are in this category.[14] Evaluated at mean sample characteristics and compared with white males, black females are equally likely, and white females are about 30 percent more likely, to receive high ratings.[15]

Similar results are found when evaluating the likelihood of being fired or suspended (incremental effects are reported in column 3).[16] Compared with white males, black and white females are 60 and 80 percent less likely to be fired from the government, evaluated at mean sample characteristics. Thus, if sex discrimination is at work in the federal government, it is not reflected in either performance ratings or dismissals. The findings also are at odds with the idea that females exert less "effort" on the job.[17] There must be some attribute of females' employment that reduces the demand for their employ besides the quality of work they do while at their desks.

## 11.3 THE GROUP REPUTATION EFFECT

One explanation is that an index of unreliability—a reputation—is attached to brand names of workers in the labor market. If female employees as a group have a higher probability of not showing up for work, of taking off from work for long periods, and of quitting—employers will attach a higher predicted unreliability to females than to comparable male applicants. The demand for females will fall relative to the demand for males, creating a female wage discount. While the impact of differences in observed unreliability is reflected in the coefficient on indexes of unreliability in wage regressions, the fixed brand name effect is embedded in the gender dummy variable.

To explore this hypothesis, I estimate an ordinary least squares regression where the dependent variable is the percentage of earned sick leave used. The estimated coefficients are reported in table 11.2, column 4. The coefficients on the gender dummy variables provide the first evidence that

Table 11.3  Measures of Reliability across Worker Groups

| Category | | Twenty days[a] of sick leave (1) | Zero sick[b] leave balance (2) | LWOP[c] (3) | Quit[d] (4) |
|---|---|---|---|---|---|
| Male probability | M | .062 | .049 | .0043 | .0096 |
| Female probability | F | .086 | .096 | .0082 | .0149 |
| Difference | M − F | .024** | .047** | .0039** | .0053** |
| Ratio | F/M | 1.39 | 1.96 | 1.91 | 1.56 |

Note: Estimates reported in the first two columns are based on a logit model; those in columns 3 and 4 are based on a weighted logit model where the weights are the population-to-sample proportions in the choice-based sample. The numbers in the first (second) row are the probabilities that the dependent variable equals unity when the female dummy variable is set to zero (one) when other independent variables are set to their mean values. The underlying gender coefficients are statistically significant at the 95 percent level of confidence in all four estimates.

Other independent variables in the estimates are age, tenure, age-squared, tenure-squared, dummy variables denoting race, education (less than high school, some college, highest degree college, highest degree master's or more—high-school graduate omitted), a dummy variable equal to one if worker is partially disabled, two dummy variables to denote SMSA location different from the intercept location, and two interaction variables: tenure after college degree and tenure after graduate degree. All data pertain to a sample of civilian workers employed in the federal government as of December 1986.

[a]Dependent variable equals unity if the worker uses twenty days or more of sick leave during 1986, zero otherwise.

[b]Dependent variable equals unity if the worker has a zero sick leave balance on 1 January 1987, zero otherwise.

[c]Dependent variable equals unity if the worker takes leave without pay (LWOP) in 1987, zero otherwise.

[d]Dependent variable equals unity if the worker quits during 1987, zero otherwise.

**Statistically significant at the 95 percent level of confidence.

female workers are less reliable than their male counterparts. The coefficients are positive and statistically significant at the 99 percent confidence level.[18]

Although this result is significant, its magnitude is not sufficient to explain a 20 percent difference in wages across the genders. I thus consider more serious levels of performance failure—extended periods where a worker is out of service. I consider four indexes of serious reliability problems: the probability of a worker's taking more than twenty days of sick leave in one year, having a zero sick leave balance, taking leave without pay during 1987 (LWOP),[19] and the ultimate product failure, outright quitting during 1987.[20]

I estimate the likelihood of observing each of these events separately using a logit model and controlling for various demographic characteristics.[21] Table 11.3 reports gender effects for each estimate. The first row reports the predicted probability that the dependent variable equals unity for a male worker with mean sample characteristics. The second row reports the same probability for a female worker with mean sample characteristics. The third and fourth rows report the differences and ratios of these probabilities.

The results are consistent across indexes of unreliability. Depending on the measure, females are 39 to 96 percent more unreliable than their male counterparts. The differences are statistically significant at least at the 95 percent level of confidence.

## 11.4  SIGNALING RELIABILITY

Reliable female workers have an incentive to signal their superior work habits. This process gives rise to further tests of the theory. If efficient signals can be identified, we ought to observe smaller wage discounts for females who have acquired distinguishing signals. One obvious signal candidate is tenure. If a worker's expected reliability is correlated with the propensity to stay with the firm, then as females gain tenure their wage discount ought to fall.

### 11.4.1  Reliability and Tenure

Previous empirical work finds unusually high quit rates by female workers, but only in the first year or two of tenure.[22] These findings imply that simply by staying beyond three years in a firm, females ought to be able to eliminate the gender wage gap. Since the gap does not disappear in three years, the reliability theory seemingly is rejected.

I confirm these results in the federal database. In the first row of table 11.4, I report the quit probability for males with mean sample characteristics over four tenure categories. In the second row, I report the incremental quit probability for females with mean sample characteristics.[23] Females are more than twice as likely to quit in the first four years of tenure as males, and the result is statistically different from zero at the 95 percent level of confidence. But at higher levels of tenure, females' quit rates are not statistically different from those of males.

Quitting, however, is only one element of unreliability. In the third and forth rows of the table, I reproduce the estimates using a broader index of unreliability: the index equals unity if the worker either quit or took leave without pay during 1987, took twenty days of sick leave in 1986, or had a zero sick leave balance on 31 December 1986, zero otherwise. The results differ markedly. Unlike the quit results, the frequency of performance failure events for females remains relatively high—and statistically different from males—through twenty years of tenure.

The size of the differential, however, falls with tenure. Males are characterized by relatively stable unreliability between 9.4 and 12.8 percent per year over four tenure categories. Female workers' unreliability is twice as high as males' through ten years of tenure, and 150 percent as high during years ten through twenty. Among workers with twenty or

Table 11.4  Reliability and Tenure

| Category | Tenure level | | | |
|---|---|---|---|---|
| | ≤4 years | 5–10 | 11–19 | ≥20 |
| *Probability of quitting* | | | | |
| 1. Males | .027 | .020 | .016 | .0010 |
| 2. Female incremental effect | .031** | .010 | .003 | .0002 |
| *Probability of being unreliable* | | | | |
| 3. Males | .126 | .094 | .110 | .128 |
| 4. Female incremental effect | .127*** | .118*** | .059*** | .008 |
| 5. *Female wage discount* | −.27*** | −.21*** | −.17*** | −.13*** |

Note: Numbers in the first row are estimated quit probabilities for males with mean sample characteristics based on a weighted logit model where the weights are the population-to-sample proportions in the choice-based sample. Numbers in the second row reflect the incremental quit probability of females with mean sample characteristics. Numbers in rows 3 and 4 are the same except that the dependent variable is the probability of being unreliable (equal to unity if the worker took twenty days of sick leave during 1986, had a zero sick leave balance on 31 December 1986, or took leave without pay or quit during 1987). Numbers in the last row are coefficients on the female dummy variable when the dependent variable is the log of the annual wage. The latter estimates parallel those reported in table 11.1, column 2, using the same independent variables (except that the white and black female dummy variables are collapsed into a single female dummy variable—a race dummy variable separately included), but making the estimates separately within the tenure categories above.
**(***)Statistically different from zero at the 95 (99) percent level of confidence.

more years of tenure, there is no statistically significant difference between males' and females' reliability.

If the reliability theory is valid, the female wage discount ought to follow a similar pattern. The last row of table 11.4 presents the results of a reestimate of the wage equation from table 11.1, column 2, for the four tenure groups. The coefficients conform to the expected pattern. Among workers with fewer than four years of tenure, the female wage discount is 27 percent. Among workers with twenty or more years of tenure, the female wage discount is 13 percent.

### 11.4.2 Testing for Other Reliability Signals: Education and Superior Job Performance

An obvious question is whether there is a more effective way for females to signal reliability than by attaining long tenure. One appealing hypothesis is that females who are serious about performing reliably in the labor market engage in investments that connote an unusual commitment to a professional career.[24] For example, it is natural to think that females who either earn advanced degrees or achieve relatively high job performance ratings signal a higher than expected level of reliability.[25]

To test this hypothesis, I select workers with ten or fewer years of tenure and calculate the percentage of observations for which the unreli-

Table 11.5  Signals of Reliability

| Category | | Overall (1) | Average or below average rating and no college degree (2) | High rating and college degree (3) | Highest rating (4) | Master's degree or more (5) |
|---|---|---|---|---|---|---|
| Male | M | 10.8 | 14.9 | 4.5 | 4.9 | 3.8 |
| Female | F | 24.7 | 26.7 | 29.7 | 30.7 | 26.0 |
| Difference | M − F | 13.9** | 11.8** | 25.2** | 25.8*** | 22.2*** |
| Ratio | M/F | 2.3 | 1.8 | 6.6 | 6.3 | 6.8 |

Note: Percentage with unreliable index equal to unity. Sample includes 1,076 males and 876 females with fewer than ten years of tenure in the federal worker sample. Index equals unity if the worker takes twenty days of sick leave during 1986, takes LWOP or quits during 1987, or has a zero sick leave balance as of 31 December 1986.
**(***)Statistically different from zero at the 95 (99) percent level of confidence using the two-tailed test.

ability index is unity across categories of job performance ratings and attained education.[26] Table 11.5 reports the percentage of observations within each category for which the unreliability index equals unity. Column 1 shows that, overall, 24.7 percent of females are unreliable compared with 10.8 percent of males.

Column 2 shows the results for workers without a college degree and with performance ratings that are average or below average.[27] The distribution of failure rates for this group is similar to the overall results— 14.9 percent for males, 26.7 percent for females. Columns 3 through 5 show the results for workers with more human capital and higher job performance ratings.

The results in the first row show that, compared with workers with poor-quality signals—average or below-average ratings and no college education—the failure rate for males falls by at least two-thirds among those who have higher-quality signals (see columns 3–5). The results corroborate the intuitive notion that education and high job ratings are high-quality signals.

In contrast, female workers with high-quality signals evince no reduction in failure rates compared with females with low-quality signals. Females who earn graduate degrees and high job ratings have unreliability indexes that are statistically indistinguishable from those of females who have no college degree and no more than average job ratings. Thus, among workers with more education and higher ratings, the reliability of females compared with that of males is worse than among less-educated and lower-rated workers.

For example, females with graduate degrees are 6.8 times more unreliable than males with graduate degrees; females with the highest job performance ratings are 6.3 times more unreliable than males with the highest ratings. Females with the highest quality signals have failure rates (30.7 and 26.0 percent) that are almost twice as high as the failure rate for males in the lowest quality category (14.9 percent).

Within the context of the reliability theory, these results predict that females with high-quality signals suffer the same relative wage discount as those that have low-quality signals. The prediction is supported by the data.[28]

## 11.5 DATA FROM THE CURRENT POPULATION SURVEY

In this section I extend the analysis using data from the 1988 Current Population Survey, May supplement (CPS). The CPS has no information about accumulated use of sick leave, extended sick leave, or leave without pay or quitting. Instead, it includes a question asking whether individuals missed work during the week before the survey. Several personal reasons are included. To be consistent with the federal data, I base my estimates on absenteeism owing to "own illness."[29]

I study the data for approximately sixteen thousand full-time workers, aged 17 to 59, who are paid either an hourly wage or a salary.[30] Hourly workers report their hourly wage. For salaried workers, I convert their salary to an hourly wage by dividing usual weekly earnings by usual weekly hours.[31] I estimate a logit model where the dependent variable equals one if the respondent called in sick to his job during the week before the survey, zero otherwise. I also estimate a wage equation with predicted sick leave as an explanatory variable. The estimates are based on a two-stage process that is described in the appendix to this chapter.

The spot measure of absenteeism in the CPS serves as an index of workers' propensity for unreliability. The use of *predicted* unreliability in a wage equation measures the implicit brand name effect that is central to the reliability theory. The instrumental approach also is better suited to accommodate the problem posed by the potential influence of the two-way causality in the wage-reliability relation.

### 11.5.1 Empirical Estimates of the Sick Leave Equation

Table 11.6, column 4, reports the results from the second-stage logit model of sick leave use.[32] The estimates are incremental effects: the change in the dependent variable when the independent variables are each set to zero or unity (all other independent variables set to their mean values). The intercept term is the probability that a white male with mean sample characteristics calls in sick.

The incremental effects on the two gender dummy variables are posi-

# Table 11.6 Reliability and Wages

| Independent variable | Mean value | Log wage (1) | Log wage (2) | Log wage (3) | Sick leave (4) |
|---|---|---|---|---|---|
| Intercept | | 1.18 | 1.18 | 1.36 | .020[a] |
| | | (30.77) | (30.81) | (35.52) | (4.49) |
| Sick leave taken | .03 | — | −.065 | — | — |
| | | | (3.84) | | |
| Predicted sick | .03 | — | — | −6.45 | — |
| | | | | (25.53) | |
| Predicted log wage | 2.21 | — | — | — | .017 |
| | | | | | (1.05) |
| White female | .38 | −.21 | −.21 | −.11 | .011 |
| | | (34.14) | (33.96) | (15.42) | (3.10) |
| Black female | .05 | −.29 | −.29 | −.12 | .018 |
| | | (21.59) | (21.46) | (8.29) | (3.12) |
| Black male | .04 | −.12 | −.118 | −.10 | .004 |
| | | (8.32) | (8.29) | (7.11) | (.88) |
| Two-earner couple | .30 | — | — | — | −.012 |
| | | | | | (2.41) |
| Female interacted with children < 18 years at home | .18 | — | — | — | .013 (2.57) |
| Spouses earns higher wage | .13[b] | — | — | — | .016 (2.62) |
| If yes, percentage higher | .09 | — | — | — | .009 (2.09) |
| Other variables[c] | | | | | |
| Number of observations | | 15,976 | 15,976 | 15,594 | 16,835 |
| $R^2$/-2 log $L$ | | .39 | .39 | .41 | 2,216.6 |
| Mean dependent variable | | 2.18 | 2.18 | 2.18 | .030 |

Note: The dependent variable is the log of the hourly wage (cols. 1–3); a dummy variable equal to unity if the respondent called in sick during the week before the survey (col. 4). Estimates in columns 1 and 2 are based on ordinary least squares; those in columns 3 and 4 are estimated by a two-stage method (col. 3 least squares and col. 4 logit—see chapter appendix). Reported numbers are coefficients (cols. 1–3) and incremental effects (col. 4). The incremental effect is the change in the dependent variable when the independent variable is set alternatively to one or zero (other related dummy variables set to zero) and other independent variables are set to their mean values. The incremental effect on predicted log wage is calculated based on the mean log wage and 1 plus the mean log wage. Numbers in parentheses are $t$-values.

Source: Current Population Survey, May supplement, 1988.

[a]Probability that the dependent variable equals unity if sex and race dummy variables are set to zero, evaluated at the average values of the remaining independent variables. It is the probability that a white male with mean sample characteristics took sick leave during the week before the survey.

[b]These averages reflect zero entries for all not-two-earner participants; the averages within the two-earner category is found by dividing by the percentage of the sample that is a member of a two-earner household.

[c]Includes age and age-squared, a dummy variable for less than high school, college graduate, postcollege degree—high-school graduate omitted (all equations); pension dummy variable, health insurance dummy variable, union dummy variable, tenure, tenure-squared, three firm-size categories, a dummy variable indicating a plant size less than 250 workers (wage equations only); and dummy variables for marital status, homeownership, and three family income categories < $5,000, $5,000–$25,000 and > $50,000—$25,000–$50,000 omitted, and dummy variables denoting paid sick leave for respondent, its interaction with predicted wage level, and a dummy variable denoting paid sick leave for the respondent's spouse (sick leave equation only). See the chapter appendix.

tive and large, and the underlying estimated coefficients are statistically significant at the 99 percent level of confidence. White and black females without children at home are approximately 55 and 90 percent more likely to take a sick day than are males.[33] The results are larger for females with children at home.

The incremental effect on the dummy variable indicating the presence of children under 18 in the household is not itself statistically significant (not reported). Men with and without children at home are equally likely to call in sick. However, the coefficient on the interaction of this variable with a dummy variable equal to unity for female workers is positive and large, and the underlying coefficients are statistically significant at the 95 percent level of confidence. For example, white females with children in the home are twice as likely to call in sick as are their male colleagues, evaluated at mean sample characteristics.[34]

The results also show that the economics of staying home are in part influenced by spouse's wage. Workers who are part of a two-earner household take sick leave less often. More interesting, however, the coefficients on both the dummy variable denoting a higher-wage spouse and the continuous variable denoting the percentage higher spouse wage (if the spouse wage is higher) are both positive and large.

Within a two-earner couple, the partner with the lower wage is more likely to be the one who stays home; and the effect increases the larger the difference in the two earners' wage rates. Within a two-earner household, other things equal, a female worker with a spouse who earns 50 percent more than her own wage is twice as likely to take time off as is a female worker earning the same salary as her spouse.[35] In 72 percent of the two-earner couples in the sample, the male earns a higher wage than the female; and on average the male spouse earns 56 percent more than the female spouse.[36] Thus the wage difference most often favors the female spouse's taking time off from work.

### 11.5.2 Empirical Estimate of the Wage Equation

Table 11.6, column 1, shows the results of a traditional wage regression without a measure of reliability as an independent variable. Column 2 reports the same regression with a spot measure of sick leave reported in the CPS data—a dummy variable equal to unity if scheduled work is missed during the week before the survey owing to "own illness." The coefficient on the sick leave variable is somewhat higher than in some previous estimates—respondents who missed work because of "own illness" earn a wage about 6.5 percent lower than those who showed up for work all week—but consistent with previous studies, its inclusion has no effect on the measured wage discounts associated with female workers (compare the coefficients on the gender dummy variables in columns 1 and 2).[37]

Column 3 reports the results of the second stage estimate of the wage equation, where predicted sick leave is included as an independent variable. The coefficient on the predicted unreliability variable is negative and large, and the underlying coefficient is statistically significant at the 99 percent level of confidence.[38] Other things the same, a worker with a predicted probability of unreliability equal to 3 percent (the mean value in the sample) has a wage 17.5 percent lower than a worker with a predicted unreliability of zero.[39] The sizable wage effect suggests that predicted sick leave is correlated with other measures of more serious performance failure that are not observable in the data.

If expected reliability plays an important role in explaining gender differences in wages, then including it in the wage equation ought to diminish the importance of the gender dummy variables. It does. The coefficients on dummy variables representing white and black females are approximately 50 and 60 percent lower than the results reported in columns 1 and 2, which do not account for differences in predicted unreliability. These results are consistent with the hypothesis that expected reliability differences are important in explaining the female wage discount.

## 11.6 SORTING ISSUES

Given that there is a distribution of unreliability traits across the workforce, and that these attributes are at least partly unobservable to prospective employers, the question arises how the firm can arrange its compensation package to favor workers with high-quality characteristics.

One approach is to use a defined benefit pension plan. These plans impose substantial penalties on those who leave early. Applicants who have a higher expectation of quitting—or being dismissed—will be discouraged from entering these firms.[40] Another approach is to avoid offering paid sick leave. Workers with either the highest expected health problems or the highest value on unscheduled time off will be less likely to apply for a job at a firm that offers no paid sick leave.

As discussed in chapter 9, however, imperfect information ensures that some unreliable workers enter firms that are not designed for their employ. To the extent that unreliability is correlated with high discount rates, the use of defined contribution plans, with a lump sum available upon quitting, might be an effective way for the firm to rid itself of unreliable workers.

To the extent that internal discount rates and unreliability traits are not perfectly correlated, however, another alternative suggests itself: the firm can offer lots of paid sick leave. This approach attracts a larger number of unreliable workers into the firm, *but* it also has the advantage of encouraging workers to reveal their unreliability early in the contract.

That is, by eliminating the price effect in the decision to take time off, the firm encourages workers to make decisions based on the value they attach to leisure, as compared with the longer-term repercussions that result from taking time off. Workers who attach a high value to leisure relative to the delayed costs will take lots of paid sick leave. More reliable workers will forgo using it. In this way the firm learns about propensities for unreliability earlier in tenure. The firm can observe workers' use of sick leave to infer their reliability patterns and assign them to more suitable jobs. In this way job assignments depend less on brand name effects and more on individual performance earlier in the contract.


11.7 CONCLUDING REMARKS

Reliability is an important trait in the labor market. Firms attach a premium to workers who show up for work consistently over long periods. Workers who ignore the importance of reliability stand to lose substantial wage income over a lifetime.

Firms do not treat each observed labor input separately from those of other workers with similar attributes. Reliability indexes develop in the labor market much as brand name reputation does in product markets. This idea helps to explain why wages for females are lower than wages for males, despite their exhibiting human capital characteristics that look much like those of their male counterparts. The theory also explains why spot measures of reliability across particular workers do not explain gender differences in wages.

The model suggests that paid sick leave policies can be used to sort across workers' reliability. If no sick leave is offered, unreliable workers are discouraged from entering. If generous sick leave is offered, unreliable workers will be attracted, but the firm can observe their use of sick leave to determine their underlying reliability and then allocate them to suitable jobs with appropriate pay.

The same ideas potentially apply to the employment of older workers. Older workers are expected to be less reliable, both by not showing up for work and by taking long periods off or leaving the firm altogether.

In this sense defined benefit plans play a potentially important role in the firm. They erect a large cost to working at older ages, thereby reducing the costs of unreliability in its workforce. Moreover, because defined benefit plans can be arranged to encourage the exit of older workers at various ages, firms that suffer the worst productivity problems because of unreliability will most likely have pension rules to encourage the earliest retirement. It is hard to match this feature in a 401k plan without offering a supplemental lump sum to early retirees from the firm.

## APPENDIX: ESTIMATING EQUATIONS FOR SICK LEAVE AND WAGES

In this appendix I describe the two-stage model that underpins the results reported in table 11.6. I recognize that the choice to take sick leave and the wage rate are jointly determined. Thus I estimate the relations by two-stage methods. In particular, the two equations are

$$P(\mu = 1) = 1/[1 + \exp(DX + EZ + fw)] + \text{error}, \quad (11.2)$$

$$w = BX + CY + b\mu + \text{error}, \quad (11.3)$$

where $w$ is the log of the hourly wage, $\mu$ is a zero-one dummy variable equal to unity if the respondent missed some scheduled work in the week before the survey owing to "own illness," $X$ is a vector of attributes common to both equations,[41] and $Y$ and $Z$ are vectors specific to either the wage or sick leave equation ($f$ and $b$ are parameters, and $B$, $C$, $D$, and $E$ are vectors of parameters).

I estimate a first-stage logit model with $\mu$ as the independent variable and the vectors $X$, $Y$, and $Z$ as independent variables; I perform a similar first-stage estimate using ordinary least squares where the dependent variable is the log of wage. The predicted variables from the first stage are substituted into (11.2) and (11.3) for the second-stage logit and OLS estimates.

Although sick leave decisions might be related to age, presumably there is no rationale for including tenure as an independent variable in the $Z$ vector. But tenure surely affects wages, so tenure and tenure-squared are variables in the $Y$ vector. In addition, since the data include a zero-one dummy variable explicitly identifying the availability of paid sick time in the firm, I also include dummy variables in the $Y$ vector denoting firm characteristics that have been linked to wage levels—notably firm-size categories, pension and health coverage, and union status.[42]

To identify the effect of sick leave on wages, I use information in the CPS describing workers' personal living arrangements and wealth. Thus the vector $Z$ includes dummy variables indicating whether the worker has children under 18 at home, owns a home, has family income within various zero-one categories, has paid sick leave, is married, has a working spouse—and if so, whether the spouse has paid sick leave and whether the spouse has a higher wage.[43]

## CHAPTER TWELVE

# Tax Considerations and Plan Choice

To this point the book has focused on how pension plans can affect productivity in the firm, both by encouraging workers to work hard, attain long tenure, and retire before significant quality problems emerge in old age and by encouraging higher-quality workers to stay with the firm and lower-quality workers to leave. The optimum pension for a firm depends on what worker attributes the firm values most—and the price it is willing to pay for higher-quality workers. But the decision also depends on the cost of operating the pension plan and its tax consequences.

In this chapter I consider the features of the tax code that might influence this choice. I first consider the comparative tax treatment of defined contribution plans and defined benefit plans. In addition, I evaluate the rationale for using matching in 401k plans to satisfy discrimination rules. I conclude that regulatory and tax considerations favor defined contribution plans, particularly for smaller firms with younger workers. I also show that matching cannot be justified as a mechanism to ease the impact of discrimination rules in the tax code.

## 12.1 DIFFERENCES IN ADMINISTRATIVE COSTS

In chapter 7 I mentioned that one reason for the shift toward defined contribution plans is changes in administrative costs over the 1980s, primarily attributable to new federal legislation. These changes favor defined contribution plans, particularly for small firms.

The Hay-Huggins Company provides estimates of the administrative costs of defined benefit plans from 1980 through 1991.[1] For comparison, it calculates the administrative costs of operating a 401k plan with the employer matching contributions. Table 12.1 presents the results for four

Table 12.1  Administrative Costs

| Year | Number of participants | | | |
| | 15 | 75 | 500 | 10,000 |
| --- | --- | --- | --- | --- |
| | *Defined benefit plan* | | | |
| 1981 | $161 | $115 | $56 | $19 |
| 1991 | 455 | 259 | 133 | 53 |
| | *DB minus 401k cost* | | | |
| 1981 | 45 | 20 | 2 | −2 |
| 1981 | 49 | 22 | 2 | −2 |
| 1983 | 116 | 26 | 5 | −2 |
| 1984 | 64 | 17 | 3 | −4 |
| 1985 | 156 | 4 | 8 | −1 |
| 1986 | 103 | −36 | 36 | 7 |
| 1987 | 80 | −9 | 27 | 6 |
| 1988 | 289 | 86 | 39 | 16 |
| 1989 | 342 | 58 | 47 | 16 |
| 1990 | 220 | −24 | 61 | 16 |
| 1991[a] | 227 | 70 | 34 | 14 |

Note: Amounts are administrative costs per annum to operate a defined benefit plan, minus those required to operate a 401k plan with employer contributions, expressed in 1990 dollars.
Source: Hay-Huggins Company, *Pension Plan Cost Study for the PBGC*, at chapter 12, note 1.
[a]Includes ongoing costs assuming no new regulatory changes.

plan-size categories: ten thousand, five hundred, seventy-five, and fifteen participants. All cost figures are expressed per participant in 1990 dollars.

The various legislative requirements enacted over the period imposed both one-time costs and higher ongoing operating costs. The one-time costs came mostly from the need to rewrite the pension plan itself and reprogram computer algorithms to realign funding and benefit criteria mandated by the new provisions. These features explain why the cost figures are "lumpy" across years and why in 1991 the cost figures are lower than in some earlier years. The 1991 numbers include no one-time costs: they are estimates of ongoing operating costs for pension plans under the assumption that no new legislation is enacted after 1990.[2]

The results show that although the differential cost of operating a defined benefit plan increased across all size classes over the period, the increases are largest for smaller plans. For example, for the largest plan, the differential costs of operating a defined benefit plan increased by $16 per participant in real terms. The increase in differential costs for plans with five hundred participants is $32.[3] For small plans (fifteen participants) the cost increases are dramatic. In 1981 the differential cost of operating a defined benefit plan in this size class was $45 higher than for a 401k plan. By 1991 the difference had increased to $227. Moreover, owing to one-time adjustments to comply with new legislation, costs in some intervening years during the 1980s were even higher. For comparison, the average contribution per participant in plans like those used in the study is in the range of $1,400 in 1990 dollars.[4]

## 12.2 A DICHOTOMOUS PENSION TAX POLICY

Pension tax policy in the United States generally follows consumption tax treatment. That is to say, contributions to the pension are not taxable for either the worker or the firm. Earnings accumulate in a tax free trust fund. When pensions are withdrawn as retirement income, the proceeds are subject to normal individual income tax treatment. This tax treatment is favorable compared with tax assessments against earnings deposited in taxable savings vehicles, which are subject to comprehensive income tax treatment.[5]

In reality, tax policy depends on whether the firm uses a defined benefit or defined contribution plan. In the case of a defined contribution plan, the Internal Revenue Code extends full consumption tax treatment. Defined benefit plans are accorded partial consumption tax treatment and partial full income tax treatment. The difference in tax treatment imposes a penalty on defined benefit plans, with the size of the penalty depending on the demographic composition of the pension plan.

Consider a firm with a pension trust fund that invests in zero-risk securities yielding a zero real interest rate. The nominal interest rate and expected nominal wage growth are 10 percent. There is one worker in the firm. The chances of his quitting, being laid off, or dying before retirement are zero. The start age in the firm is zero, and retirement age is 25. The worker receives total compensation of $11 per year, $1 in the form of a pension benefit.

Suppose the firm uses a defined contribution plan. The firm contributes $1 annually in the pension fund in real terms. These amounts accumulate to a lump sum balance of $25 in real terms at age and service level 25. The accumulation of contributions is described by the linear schedule in figure 12.1.

Now suppose the firm uses a defined benefit pension that promises a lump sum at retirement equal to 10 percent per year of service times final salary. The present value of pension benefits in this plan is also $25.[6] Before 1988, the firm could deposit $1 in real terms in the trust fund every year, so that all contributions accumulated at the tax free rate, resulting in a $25 balance in real terms after twenty-five years.[7] Mechanically, the $1 annual real contributions occurred because the tax code permitted assets to equal *ongoing* liabilities.[8] If I normalize starting age to zero, the amount of ongoing liabilities in the example expressed in year-zero dol-

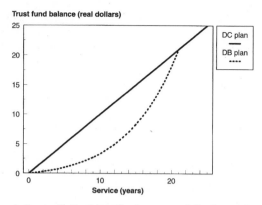

**Figure 12.1** Trust balances: Defined benefit plan versus defined contribution plan. Depicts the accumulation of assets in the pension trust fund in a defined contribution versus a defined benefit plan. Assumes that the plan has one person who works twenty-five years, then retires with a lump sum. See text for other assumptions.

lars is $L_O = \$1\, a$,[9] where $a$ is age and years of service. This limit is referred to as either the "old" full funding limit or, alternatively, the "ERISA" full funding limit.

Put simply, ongoing liabilities are pension accruals expressed in real terms, and thus liabilities are depicted by the linear schedule in figure 12.1. The same schedule depicts the accumulation of trust assets in a defined contribution plan when the firm contributes $1 per year in real terms.[10]

Since 1987, the firm faces an additional restriction on funding the defined benefit plan. It is labeled the "150 percent full funding limit," because contributions are not permitted unless pension assets are less than 150 percent of termination pension benefits.[11] For the one-person example, the new limit is $1.5L_T = 150\% \times \$1\, a\, e^{-i(R-a)}$, where $R$ is retirement age.[12]

If age of retirement is 25, and the interest rate is 10 percent, then after one year of service the new limit is approximately $0.13.[13] At age and service level 15, the old full funding limit is $15 in real terms: 150 percent of termination liabilities is $8.27.[14] As the individual approaches retirement age, 150 percent of termination liabilities exceeds 100 percent of ongoing liabilities and so the ERISA limit is constraining.[15]

The accumulation of assets under the 1987 Omnibus Budget Reconciliation Act (OBRA) limit is depicted by the nonlinear schedule in figure 12.1. The vertical difference between the two schedules is the amount of pension accumulations saved outside the pension fund. If the corporate tax rate is 33 percent and the nominal interest rate is 10 percent, then over

Table 12.2 Differential Tax on Defined Benefit Plans

| Interest rate | One worker each age, 0, 25 | |
| | No retirees (1) | 25% retirees (2) |
| --- | --- | --- |
| 5.0 | 0.0 | 0.0 |
| 7.5 | 3.7 | 0.0 |
| 10.0 | 9.9 | 3.8 |
| 12.5 | 17.2 | 9.4 |
| 15.0 | 25.2 | 15.9 |

Note: Numbers in table are percentages. Tax is expressed as a fraction of annual benefit payouts from the pension. See text for description of pension plans.

twenty-five years, the additional tax levied by OBRA is approximately 11 percent of the value of the pension.[16]

## 12.3 DISTORTION FAVORING DEFINED CONTRIBUTION PLANS

It is apparent from the figure that defined contribution plans have a substantial tax advantage over defined benefit plans. The distortion is highest for plans that are relatively immature. I can show this by expanding the model beyond a one-person pension.

A one-worker plan, averaged over lifetime tenure, is similar to, but not the same as, a plan that actually has workers at all age and service levels. For older workers and retirees collecting annuities, 150 percent of termination liabilities can exceed ongoing liabilities. Since the rules are applied in the aggregate, the "surplus" amounts for older workers and retirees can be applied to the "deficit" amounts for younger workers. The impact of the rules is therefore greater for firms with young to middle-aged workforces and relatively few retirees.

In addition, the tax depends on the nominal interest rate. At low interest rates, the income tax treatment is not dramatically different from consumption tax treatment. The higher the nominal interest rate, the larger the divergence between termination and ongoing liabilities (the more bowed the nonlinear schedule in figure 12.1), and so the greater the portion of pension savings accumulated outside the pension trust fund. (As the interest rate becomes very high, permissible trust funds approach zero at all ages.)

Table 12.2, column 1, shows the extra tax on a defined benefit plan that has a diffuse workforce, assuming all workers start at age zero and receive a lump sum pension after twenty-five years.[17] Column 2 reports the extra tax under the assumption that retirees receive annuities, not lump sums, and that there is one retiree for every three workers (roughly the average for all defined benefit plans).[18] I vary the nominal interest rate from 5 to 15 percent. The annual de facto excise tax is expressed as a percentage of annual benefit payouts from the pension plan, set at $25 in both cases.

At the 5 percent nominal interest rate, the OBRA excise tax on defined benefit plans is negligible. At this interest rate, 150 percent of termination liabilities is not substantially less than ongoing benefits at most ages. At a 7.5 percent interest rate, the tax rate increases to 3.7 percent for a pension plan with active workers of all ages but no retirees. The tax rate is still negligible for a plan with a three-to-ten retiree-worker ratio. At a 12.5 percent interest rate, however, the tax rate is significant for both plans. For pensions with no retirees, the effective excise tax is 17.2 percent of benefit payouts, and for the more mature plan, 9.4 percent

## 12.4 ILLUSTRATION OF TAX TREATMENT OF TWO DEFINED BENEFIT PLANS

I now illustrate the impact of the differential tax treatment on defined benefit plans that reflect typical demographics. I suppose that the OBRA rules were enacted in 1974 when ERISA was first passed, instead of in 1987.[19] I use two final salary plans from the group of "typical" pension plans as described by the American Academy of Actuaries. One depicts their "normal group." This plan is mature and stable and is projected to continue to grow. It has workers of all ages, but there are lots of long-service workers and retirees as well. The Academy describes it as typical of plans sponsored by many large companies.[20]

The second plan depicts their "new group." This one is sponsored by a relatively new firm initially formed by transfers from the parent company. Employment grows rapidly, and the plan is disproportionately populated by young and middle-aged workers. At the beginning of the simulation period, there are virtually no retirees.

I assume that the pension trust funds for both plans are invested entirely in one-year Treasury bills and that both exactly meet the pre-OBRA full funding limit at the start of the simulation period.[21] To perform the simulations, I use the funding model developed by Tepper Associates.[22]

Figure 12.2 demonstrates the results for the stable plan. The dotted line portrays the funding ratio under the old full funding limits. The solid line portrays the same funding ratios on the assumption that the OBRA full funding limit prevailed over the period. Figure 12.3 portrays the impact of the same full funding limits on the new, growing plan.

It is apparent from the figures that the OBRA full funding limit would

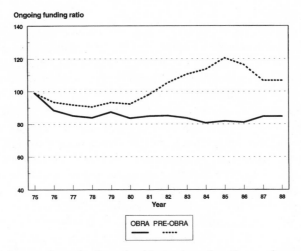

Figure 12.2 Impact of new funding rules: Mature, large firm. See text for assumptions.

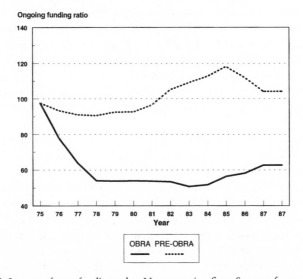

Figure 12.3 Impact of new funding rules: New, growing firm. See text for assumptions.

have had an important impact on funding levels in salary-related plans over the period 1975–87, particularly for new, growing firms. The mature plans would have been able to maintain assets in the trust fund equal to 80 percent of ongoing liabilities. The new, growing plans could have maintained assets equal to 60 percent of ongoing liabilities.

## 12.5 IMPLICATIONS FOR PLAN FORMATION

The combination of higher administrative costs and lesser tax advantages makes it hard to rationalize the choice of defined benefit plans over defined contribution plans. The tax problem is particularly acute for the firm that is a candidate to start a defined benefit plan—one that is relatively new, with lots of younger workers and few retirees. The after-tax cost of funding these benefits is substantially higher than for a comparable defined contribution plan. In this sense the extra tax imposed by the funding limits enacted in 1987 is particularly inefficient, because it creates the greatest distortions for the firms that are the prime entrants into defined benefit plans.

Although these distortions have implications for public policy (see chapter 13), from the firm's perspective there is a large incentive to find ways 401k plans (and perhaps other forms of defined contribution plans) can be arranged so as to replace some of the productivity advantages of defined benefit plans. The sorting ability of 401k plans, together with the large distortions in public policy that favor them, undoubtedly explains the impressive growth of these plans since 1981 (see chapter 7).

There is one aspect of 401k plans, however, that poses a special problem under the Internal Revenue Code. That is, because participation in these plans is voluntary, the Code requires that the ultimate savings rate of lesser-paid workers not be substantially different from that of higher-paid workers. These restrictions require the firm to monitor contributions to the 401k plan to ensure that the Code's discrimination rules are not violated.

This aspect of 401k plans suggests that the firm might wish to encourage participation, particularly among lesser-paid workers; and this idea often is suggested as an explanation for matching formulas. I will show, however, that if firms use matching to accomplish this objective, the economics are not favorable; that is, the firm likely would incur expenses that exceed the potential tax gains made available to the higher-paid workers. The calculus suggests that if matching is used profitably by the firm, it in fact is used to pay higher wages to better workers and to guide the firm in allocating high discounters to jobs that are suitable for them.

## 12.6 EFFICACY OF MATCHING TO SATISFY DISCRIMINATION RULES

In chapter 9 I show that matching in 401k plans effectively awards higher pay levels to low discounters, who I argue are higher-quality workers. I now consider the prevailing alternative theory—that matching is used not to remunerate higher-quality workers, but to satisfy Internal Revenue Service "discrimination rules," which require that pension savings vehicles not be "overused" by the so-called highly compensated employees. Given these constraints, it is natural to think that matching is designed to encourage more participation by lower-income groups so as to allow higher-paid workers to contribute higher amounts. In this section I show that the tax benefits from using matching for this purpose are trivially small.

### 12.6.1 Optimal Matching for Tax Gains

The rules define two groups of workers in the plan: "highly compensated" workers—those who earn more than approximately $66,000 per annum (in 1994 dollars) and are in the top 20 percent of the wage distribution among eligible participants[23]—and all other workers. The rules do not regulate participation rates, nor do they constrain contributions within each group. Instead, they restrict the (simple) average contribution rates between the two groups.

I denote 401k contributions, as a percentage of pay, as $c_i$. As a first-order approximation, the rules limit the contribution rate of the highly compensated group, $c_{HC}$, to within two percentage points of that of the lower compensation group, $c_{LC}$:[24]

$$c_{HC}^{\max} \sim c_{LC} + .02. \tag{12.1}$$

Suppose that this relation is constraining over the relevant range. And suppose the plan introduces some match rate $m$. The consequent change in the contribution rate for the highly compensated is proportional to the change in that for those not highly paid in the 401k plan:[25]

$$\Delta c_{HC} \sim \Delta c_{LC} = \Delta c. \tag{12.2}$$

Consider the tax benefit to the highly paid if the contribution rate of the group not highly paid can be increased by matching. These benefits, $B$, can be expressed as

$$B = \Delta c \, W_{HC} \, T, \tag{12.3}$$

where $W_{HC}$ is total wages of the highly paid and $T$ is the fraction of each dollar of contributions that represents tax savings (in comparison with tax-exposed savings vehicles). Now consider the direct cost of effecting the match scheme. Matching in the proportion $m$ raises the perceived return on savings in the 401k and encourages more contributions by those not highly paid. The cost of matching takes the form of inducing inefficient savings by those not highly paid.

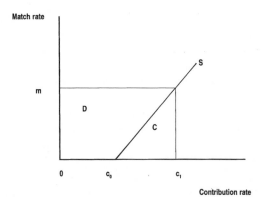

**Figure 12.4** Impact of matching on 401k contribution rate. Depicts 401k contribution rate of workers who are not highly paid as a function of the firm's match rate.

More specifically, assume that the 401k contribution rate (as a percentage of wage) of those not highly paid is related linearly to the match rate over the relevant range, that is,

$$c_1 = c_0 + b\,m, \qquad (12.4)$$

where $c_1$ is the contribution rate of those not highly paid with the match rate $m$ and $c_0$ is the contribution rate with a zero match. This solution is depicted in figure 12.4. Given the match rate, $m$, the total matching amount transferred to the not highly compensated workers is

$$M_{LC} = m\,c_1\,W_{LC}, \qquad (12.5)$$

where $W_{LC}$ denotes the wage base of those not highly paid. (This amount corresponds to the rectangular area in the figure times the wage base.)

The firm cannot reduce cash wages of this group by the entire amount, $M_{LC}$, because by inducing "too much" savings the firm induces lower-compensated workers to absorb a "triangle" loss, denoted by $C$, in the amount (corresponds to the triangular area labeled $C$ in the figure times the wage base)

$$C = \tfrac{1}{2}\,m\,\Delta c\,W_{LC}. \qquad (12.6)$$

Thus as a result of matching the compensating differential for the group not highly paid is the difference between expressions (12.6) and (12.5), the area labeled $D$ in the figure times the wage base:

$$\Delta W_{LC} = M_{LC} - C. \qquad (12.7)$$

The net gain from matching is the difference between the tax benefits (expression 12.3) and deadweight loss (expression 12.6), which I denote as $N$; substituting $\Delta c = b\, m$ from (12.4), we have:

$$N = B - C. \tag{12.8}$$

It is easily confirmed that the match rate, $m^*$, that maximizes the net gain, $N$, is[26]

$$m^* = \underline{T}\, W_{HC}/W_{LC}. \tag{12.9}$$

The optimal match is higher, the higher the tax advantage of additional permissible contributions to the highly paid and the higher the wage base of the highly paid compared with the wage base of those not highly paid. Using this result, I can write the net gain from the matching scheme as a percentage of wages paid to the highly compensated, $W_{HC}$:[27]

$$N^*/W_{HC} = \tfrac{1}{2}\, b\, \underline{T}^2\, [w_{HC}/w_{LC}]\, n_{HC}/n_{LC}, \tag{12.10}$$

where $w_j$ is the average wage of group $j$ and $n_j$ is the number of workers in group $j$.

### 12.6.2  Parameter Estimates

**The parameters $\underline{T}$ and $w_{HC}/w_{LC}$.** It is not difficult to develop an order of magnitude for this expression. Assuming that the horizon for savings in 401k accounts is twenty years, the income tax rate is 40 percent, and the nominal interest rate is 8 percent, the value of $\underline{T}$ in (12.10) is roughly .5. Its value varies between .3 and .6 within a reasonable bound of these parameters.[28]

Similarly, average wages of the highly compensated and those not highly paid, $w_{LC}/w_{HC}$, are estimable from the Current Population Survey, May supplement, and the Health and Retirement Survey. These data suggest that an estimate of this ratio on average is approximately 3.[29] Thus expression (12.10) can be rewritten as

$$N^*/W_{HC} \sim .375\, b\, n_{HC}/n_{LC}. \tag{12.11}$$

The gains from using matching to increase the tax advantages of the highly compensated therefore turn on the coefficient describing workers' reaction to matching, $b$, and relative numbers of highly compensated workers to those not highly paid, $n_{HC}/n_{LC}$.

**The parameter $b$.** The estimates for the parameter $b$ are given in table 10.6. Depending on whether data from the 1988 or 1993 pension supplements are used, the estimates range from .006 to .022.[30]

**The parameter $n_{HC}/n_{LC}$.** Finally, I consider the ratio of highly compensated workers to those not highly paid. Using CPS data, this ratio is 8 percent on average; thus we have[31]

$$n_{HC}/n_{LC} \sim .08. \tag{12.12}$$

Using form 5500 annual pension plan reports, this ratio is approximately the same.[32] Together with the higher-bound estimate of $b$ equal to .02, the net benefit for the typical firm is calculable from (12.11):

$$N^*/W_{HC} = .00066. \tag{12.13}$$

For an "average" 401k plan, then, the tax benefits of matching, $B$, less the subsidy given to those not highly paid, $C$, amount to about seven hundredths of one percent of wages paid to the highly compensated, or $0.66 for each $1,000 in salary. But there is a range of values in the data: the tenth and ninetieth percentile firms have ratios of $n_{HC}/n_{LC}$ from 2.1 to 27.9 percent, so the calculation in (12.11) ranges from $0.03 to $2.20 per $1,000 of the highly paid workers' compensation. Even at the upper limits, the order of magnitude of the tax benefits is minimal. Moreover, the tax gains do not net out the transactions costs of operating the matching scheme, nor do they account for the distortion it imposes on those not highly compensated.

The distortion arises from the compensating differential in (12.7). Assuming that the firm does not selectively reduce ex post the wages of workers who receive the matching amounts, the wages of all workers not highly paid must be reduced to offset the pure transfer aspect of the match, $W_{LC}$. But workers contribute different amounts to the 401k. And since in the discrimination theory values of marginal product are not related to contribution rates, the process creates a wedge between wages and values of marginal product across these workers.[33]

### 12.6.3 Tax Benefits and Plan Size

In chapter 10 I made the argument that the sorting theory of matching is consistent with the finding that the probability of finding matching in 401k plans is higher in large firms than in small firms. I now ask whether this finding is consistent with a tax theory of matching.

Consider the net gains from matching for tax purposes in expression (12.10). These benefits are related proportionally to the ratio of the numbers of highly compensated to lower-paid workers in the firm. If this ratio is higher in large firms, then the tax theory also is consistent with the matching data.

I use form 5500 data to address this issue. Three out of four 401k plans do not impose restrictions on participation (pension rules permit firms to exclude workers from participation within the first year of tenure, which some firms do) and thus are exempt from reporting information on highly compensated and not highly compensated workers on form 5500. The remaining plans are required to report the total number of highly compensated and not highly compensated workers in the firm.

Excluding duplicate firm data, there are 1,631 firms that report the portion of eligible workers who are highly compensated. I regress the relative share of highly compensated to not highly paid workers against five firm-size dummy variables. I find no evidence that the ratio is positively related to firm size.[34]

## 12.7 CONCLUDING REMARKS

Imposing income tax treatment on some portion of defined benefit pension trust funds encourages firms to abandon defined benefit plans in favor of defined contribution plans. The effect of the new law is akin to applying an annual excise tax on defined benefit plans, its size depending on the age distribution of the participants. For young, growing plans, the tax is large. Workers can still obtain full consumption tax treatment of their implicit pension savings by using defined contribution plans. Tax considerations therefore clearly favor defined contribution plans. The relative increase in regulatory costs for smaller defined benefit plans reenforces this decision for new, smaller firms.

These results do not mean that older, established firms with lots of older workers and retirees are better off terminating their defined benefit plans. For these firms, the defined benefit excise tax may be relatively small compared with the benefits yielded by the plan. But for plans making prospective decisions, particularly those with younger workforces, the tax effects clearly favor defined contribution plans. And the discussion in previous chapters clearly suggests that the appropriate combination of defined contribution and 401k plans can be constructed to mimic many of the attributes of defined benefit plans, except for the powerful effects of defined benefit formulas on retirement age.

Matching provisions almost certainly are not valuable to the firm as ways to reduce high earners' income tax liability. They are more suited to sorting workers based on their inclination to save. The information embedded in observed contribution rates is revealing: despite matching, four in ten workers do not contribute to 401k plans. Yet an equal number of workers make 401k contributors even without matching.[35] The implicit distribution of discount rates implied by these observations reveals the potential value of sorting workers according to their inclination to value the future.

The potential importance of workers' internal discount rates to firm productivity means that firms can benefit from paying attention to this attribute of the workforce. Sorting minimizes the problem of high discount rates for individual firms and pays low discounters more than high discounters, which makes sense in a market context. But from a broader societal viewpoint, the issue of high discounters remains and is central to the "retirement income problem" faced at a more global level.

That is to say, even though managers are successful in sorting out high discounters from the firm, or aligning pay so as to pay them lower wages, low discounters as a group may end up transferring tax dollars to support high discounters in old age. I next consider these issues from a broader policy context.

*Part Three*

INTERNAL DISCOUNT
RATES AND
PUBLIC POLICY

## CHAPTER THIRTEEN

# A Pension Tax Policy for Low Discounters

In part 3 I switch the focus of the book to public policy. I continue the theme of separating the workforce into broad groups based on their natural attributes, especially their internal discount rates. I consider the social problem posed by high discounters' disinclination to save for retirement and assess viable economic solutions. In this chapter I consider pension policy. In the ensuing chapters, I consider how these issues are intertwined with the social security system. My policy suggestions encompass both private pensions and the public system from a broad perspective.

Through tax policy, the federal government can encourage low discounters to pursue their natural tendency to save, or it can encourage low discounters to act like high discounters. Pension tax rules affect the relative price of postponed versus current consumption, so they can importantly affect retirement and savings decisions. Comprehensive income tax rules penalize savings: they artificially increase the price of future versus present consumption, thereby encouraging immediate consumption. Put differently, imposing comprehensive income tax rules can aggravate the high discounter problem by penalizing the savings behavior of low discounters.

In addition, pension policy influences the number of high discounters in pension plans. It does this through various regulations (notably nondiscrimination rules) that work to extend pension coverage across workers in the firm, regardless of their internal discount rates. Presumably there is some positive externality to these provisions. As long as society supports the consumption of the poor elderly, then overall tax rates must reflect this burden. If low discounters (as taxpayers) are faced with the responsibility for financing part of the old age consumption of those who do not save, they have a stake in the savings decisions of high discounters. If some high discounters voluntarily participate in pensions that pay annuities, they impose less burden on the public in future years, thereby reducing low discounters' future tax burden.

The impact of nondiscrimination rules may be significant when firms offer defined benefit plans. As long as some high discounters take jobs in these firms, they will receive annuities in old age that they would not otherwise choose outside the job. The private pension system, however, is undergoing dramatic change. Although defined benefit plans have provided an annuity for two out of three private-sector workers,[1] there has been a growing trend in favor of defined contribution plans, especially 401k plans (chapter 7).[2]

For low discounters the trend may have few consequences. They will arrange their resources to ensure adequate retirement consumption. But high discounters will have lower pension coverage. Plain defined contribution plans and their more complex counterparts, 401k plans, tend to sort high discounters out of pension coverage (chapter 9). And even if high discounters participate and accumulate savings, these plans almost always pay benefits in lump sums and thus are less likely to support consumption in old age than are annuities.[3] This trend implies a higher future burden on the social security system or on other public welfare programs like Supplemental Security Income.

## 13.1 HOW PENSION TAX POLICY MATTERS

Two aspects of the tax code dominate the treatment of savings for retirement. First, ordinary income tax rules are modified to award "consumption tax treatment" of savings in pension plans. For the most part this treatment is available to individuals only through firm-sponsored pensions.[4] Second, to qualify for this treatment, plan sponsors must write pension rules to conform to rules set out in the Internal Revenue Code and in the ERISA statute. These rules regulate fiduciary behavior, reporting and disclosure, funding, mandatory insurance, vesting, and discrimination rules. Costs are imposed by all of these requirements, but my emphasis on worker attributes implies a particularly important role for discrimination rules.

### 13.1.1 The Price of Future Consumption

Contributions to a pension trust fund are tax deductible to the firm, and investment earnings are exempt from tax. Pension benefits are taxed as ordinary income during retirement. This policy is often referred to as consumption tax treatment, because wages saved for later consumption are taxed once when they are spent.[5] This policy contrasts sharply with ordinary income tax treatment. Under income tax rules, wages saved for later consumption are taxed once when earned and again in the form of taxes on nominal earnings during the accumulation process. The so-called double tax biases individuals toward current consumption and away from postponed consumption.

The compelling case for consumption tax treatment of savings is that the effective tax rate on wages does not depend on the period in which the earnings are used to support consumption. Income tax treatment encourages workers to ignore their future consumption requirements, a problem of special magnitude during older ages, when their productive capabilities typically wane.

One way to characterize income tax treatment of savings is as an extra income tax on wages at the time they are earned. In effect, there is a two-tier tax rate. If earnings are used to support *current* consumption, they are assessed a tax rate equal to the statutory rate prescribed in the Internal Revenue Code. If earnings are used to support *future* consumption, they are assessed at the statutory rate *plus* some increment.

Consider a worker twenty-five years from retirement. The real interest rate is zero, and the marginal income tax rate is 40 percent. The nominal interest rate is 10 percent. If the worker uses $1 of income to support immediate consumption, he pays a 40 percent income tax, leaving $0.60 to spend. If the worker saves $1 in a tax-free pension trust, his after-tax income available for consumption at retirement is $12.18; after applying the 40 percent tax on pension income, his after-tax amount is $7.30. In present value terms, this amount is equivalent to $0.60.[6] The consumption tax treatment does not impart a bias to spend now or later.

The price of future consumption changes if savings are subject to ordinary income tax treatment. Under an income tax rule, income in my example is taxed at 40 percent, and the after-tax amount, $0.60, is accumulated at an *after-tax* return of 6 percent, not the 10 percent applied to pensions. This treatment of earnings in the savings vehicle penalizes savings. After twenty-five years, the $.60 is worth $2.68, not $7.30 as in the pension. The present value of $2.68 is $0.22. Thus, if the worker spends $1 of his income immediately, he has $0.60 to spend. His effective tax rate is the statutory rate, 40 percent. If he saves the $0.60 for retirement twenty-five years later, he has $0.22 to spend in real terms.[7] His effective tax rate is 78 percent.

Consider two identical workers earning the same wage, both twenty-five years from retirement. The high discounter saves nothing and so relies on public support of his consumption during old age. The federal government assesses a tax rate against his wage income of 40 percent. The low discounter saves a portion of his wages to support his own consumption during old age. If he saves in a pension, he pays the same 40 percent tax on income deferred for future consumption. If he saves in a vehicle that is subject to income tax rules, he faces two tax rates. On the portion of

Table 13.1 Effective Tax Rate on Savings, Income Tax Rules

|  | Interest rate | |
| --- | --- | --- |
| Years to save | 5% | 10% |
| Statutory tax rate 40% | | |
| 25 | 64% | 78% |
| 10 | 51% | 60% |
| Statutory tax rate 20% | | |
| 25 | 38% | 48% |
| 10 | 28% | 35% |

*Note:* The numbers in the table depict the de facto income tax rate on income used to support consumption either ten or twenty-five years in the future on the assumption that workers use tax-exposed savings vehicles. If the tax rate on income is $t$, the nominal interest rate $i$, and years of savings $y$, then the present value of $1 saved in a tax-exposed vehicle is $PV = (1 - t) e^{(1-t)iy} e^{-iy}$. The efffective tax rate is $1 minus $PV$.

his income immediately consumed, he pays a 40 percent tax. On the portion he saves for consumption at retirement age, he pays a 78 percent tax.

The higher tax is paid *if and only if* income is used to support future consumption. The second-tier tax is higher the higher the nominal interest rate, the higher the statutory marginal income tax rate, and the longer the period of accumulation (see table 13.1).

It is apparent that eliminating consumption tax treatment of pensions would discourage saving for retirement. Yet this change effectively has been made in part by restricting the full funding limit to 150 percent of accrued liabilities (see chapter 12).[8]

### 13.1.2  Nondiscrimination Rules

A second feature of the Internal Revenue Code pension tax policy is the concept of nondiscrimination. The discrimination rules are complex,[9] but essentially firms that offer pensions are encouraged to make them available in substantially the same form to all their employees. In defined benefit and defined contribution plans, the rules usually mean that essentially the same formula applies to all employees;[10] in the 401k context, plans usually offer the same provisions to all workers, and high-wage voluntary contributions are constrained by contributions of the lower-paid workers (see chapter 12).

From an efficiency perspective, discrimination rules are undesirable because they inhibit firms from arranging pensions to maximize labor productivity. For example, firms might gain substantial value from using a defined benefit plan to reduce quitting of high-wage workers, but the firm may be less concerned with quitting by lesser-skilled workers. Yet the firm may find it very difficult to cover some workers with a defined benefit plan and others with a defined contribution plan.[11] Similarly, in some jobs the firm may be indifferent to hiring high or low discounters and thus be unwilling to pay the indenture premium that accompanies defined benefit plans (chapter 9). In other jobs the firm may attach high value to long tenure of low discounters and be willing to pay the premium. Yet the discrimination rules do not permit the firm to exclude workers from a defined benefit plan based on their internal discount rate.

From a public perspective, discrimination rules confer a positive externality on taxpayers as a whole. Although pension firms naturally attract low discounters, imperfections in the labor market mean that some high discounters take jobs in pension firms (chapter 9). Once in a pension firm, discrimination rules ensure pension coverage. Some private pension annuities accrue to high discounters, thereby reducing the overall burden high discounters place on public retirement systems.

Discrimination rules, however, are unlikely candidates to substantially increase high discounters' savings rates. High discounters are not expected to take jobs in pension firms: they have a natural aversion to deferred compensation schemes. To the extent that high discounters enter pension firms, the externality effect of discrimination rules is waning as the pension market shifts toward defined contribution plans and lump sum payments (chapter 7). High discounters are more likely to depart the firm before they attain long tenure to gain access to the lump sums and are less likely to participate in 401k matching formulas (chapter 10). Even if they stay until retirement, high discounters likely will dissipate their lump sums long before they grow old.

In addition, it is important to recognize that we already have a mechanism to require savings by high discounters. And the system is universal. The social security system requires that 15.4 percent of workers' value of marginal product be set aside in exchange for the right to a retirement annuity, access to medical coverage, and access to disability and other insurance programs. Moreover, the formula is tilted to benefit lower-wage workers. It is not efficient to regulate all private pension savings in exchange for additional retirement support for some portion of high discounters. A more effective means is to use the social security system to deal with the "high discounter problem." I address these issues in the next chapter.

Eliminating the regulatory burden on private pension plans confers economic efficiencies. First, firms will face lower direct administrative costs of enforcing discrimination rules.[12] Second, low discounters will not face artificial restrictions on their savings rates (as in 401k plans) if others in the firm do not wish to save. Third, pension firms will be allowed to craft their pension plans to attain the highest value added across their workforces.

## 13.2 SOME POLICY PROPOSALS FOR PENSIONS

Public policy toward pensions, at a minimum, should not distort the price of future versus current consumption: it should not discourage low discounters from following their natural inclination to save for retirement. It also should not bias decisions against pensions that pay annuities as their normal form of benefit. These plans tend to ensure the delivery of a retirement income stream to high discounters who otherwise would use their savings long before old age. Public policy has drifted in the opposite direction, increasing the regulatory burden on defined benefit plans and reducing the tax advantages for these plans relative to defined contribution pension plans (chapter 12).

If future retirement security is to be ensured without imposing a further burden on a public retirement system, a few pension policy changes suggest themselves.

*Eliminate the 150 percent full funding limit.* The new full funding limit imposed in 1987 creates a large tax disadvantage on defined benefit plans in firms dominated by young and middle-aged workers (chapter 12). In addition, since the effect of the limit varies with the nominal interest rate, a large amount of uncertainty about allowable contributions is introduced into these plans. Eliminating the limit ensures that consumption tax treatment extends to pension savings and recreates a "level playing field" between defined benefit and defined contribution plans. This change leaves the "old" full funding limit in place, restricting contributions when plan assets exceed *projected* pension benefits, which is equivalent to extending tax policy for defined contribution plans to defined benefit plans.

*Eliminate auxiliary restraints on funding.* The Internal Revenue Code also artificially restricts funding of defined benefit plans in other ways, specifically by placing restrictions on projected nominal salaries or nominal pension benefits for funding purposes.[13] The rules are complex and subject to periodic changes, making them costly to administer. They constrain firms' pension funding below the economic value of pension accruals.

If the government wishes to constrain the amount of pension savings by higher-wage workers, then the goal can be satisfied more cheaply by relying on an existing rule in the Code that restricts the amount of income a retiree can take from all tax-qualified funds and IRAs (currently $150,000 per year).[14] Excess distributions are taxed at 15 percent. Put simply, contribution limits are costly to enforce and are redundant with the excessive distribution rule currently in place. These changes allow low discounters to follow their natural inclination to save and permit firms to maximize the productive value of pensions.

*Eliminate the nondiscrimination rules.* All discrimination rules in the Internal Revenue Code should be eliminated. The problem posed by high discounters' disinclination to save should be handled by the social security system. In the same vein, regulatory restrictions on the pension formula (preventing different percentage accruals by age, service, wage level, or occupation) could be eliminated, as well as restrictions on vesting.

*Eliminate restrictions on IRAs.* These changes have an obvious corollary: the preferential tax treatment afforded firm-offered pensions ought to be extended to Individual Retirement Accounts (IRAs). The purpose of restricting pension tax treatment to firm-offered pensions[15] is to expand coverage to workers who otherwise might not contribute to pensions, given a free choice. But if the discrimination rules, broadly defined, are eliminated, the raison d'être for excluding IRAs from full consumption tax treatment is no longer relevant.

The expansion of tax preferences creates an efficient market for pensions. In arranging their pensions, firms will weigh the advantages of pension restrictions against the wage premiums that workers might require to accept the risk or indenture implicit in these contracts. Firms will choose pension rules to maximize the value of pensions in the firm.

Since workers will have the option of saving in IRAs, the market will be characterized by pension coverage that is economical. All low discounters will save for their retirement at optimal levels; most high discounters will not participate either in pensions or in IRAs.[16]

## 13.3 CONCLUDING REMARKS

Government policy toward retirement income is intertwined with the natural conflict between high and low discounters. The role of government in setting tax policy and public retirement benefits is to avoid policies that encourage low discounters to act like high discounters. Mostly this means that pension savings should be subject to consumption tax treatment, but pension tax policy also has been used to encourage some savings by high discounters.

The latter goal has been met by imposing nondiscrimination rules that require comparable treatment of workers in the firm. As long as some high discounters take jobs in pension firms, then pensions that include all workers and pay annuities confer some benefit on taxpayers in the long run. But developments in the pension market have sharply diminished the efficacy of these rules. The development of defined contribution and 401k plans, and the proliferation of lump sum payments, make it unlikely that large numbers of high discounters will have higher retirement income from pensions.

Discrimination rules, broadly defined, should be eliminated. Pension policy should focus solely on two goals: facilitating savings decisions among those inclined to save for retirement, and giving firms maximum flexibility in using these plans to augment productivity. As a corollary, I would permit unlimited IRAs, so that pension tax rules are not intertwined with firm-sponsored pensions. The consequence of pursing these goals is to extract the highest value attainable from the pension system, in terms of higher productivity, more retirement savings, and a larger capital stock.

Pension policy, however, cannot be considered in a vacuum. Other policies effected through the social security system and other public programs must work in concert with private pension policy. For example, a pension policy that encourages low discounters to save may be offset by social security policy that penalizes retirees with pensions. In the next chapter I show that many factors in the social security system penalize individuals who can be labeled "savers" and "workers." Instead, they reward "leisure preferrers" and "spenders." A sound policy that encourages savings and deals with the high discounter problem requires a coordinated effort in both pension and social security policy.

## CHAPTER FOURTEEN

# Incentives, High Discounters, and Social Security

I have argued that a worker's wage is determined in part by his internal discount rate. Low discounters earn more than high discounters. Low discounters also have a higher propensity to save. Thus low discounters are expected to have more wealth in old age than high discounters. This disparity has implications for federal retirement policy.

If high discounters save nothing, then when they are old, unproductive, and impoverished, they turn to society for support. If society responds by awarding them generous public retirement benefits, it eliminates the mechanism that disciplines high discounter behavior, thus encouraging them to free ride off low discounters.[1] Perhaps more important, the promise of substantial benefits for "free" when old encourages low discounters to take the same free ride—to act more like high discounters.

As high discounters take advantage of public money, the tax rates on savings and work that finance these benefits must increase, thereby making it less attractive to work and save and more tempting to take the free ride. In the end no one saves, thereby reducing the overall standard of living in the economy. One way to prevent a degenerate solution is to erect a forced savings vehicle: it could involve a national mandatory savings scheme. In the United States it takes the form of a pay as you go social security system.

An important economic function of social security is to prevent a degenerate solution brought about by free riders.[2] It is one way to correct the distortion caused by high discounters' inclination to ignore their future consumption requirements. Although participating in social security does not engender capital accumulation,[3] it is a pseudosavings scheme in the sense that all workers forgo current consumption when young in exchange for a claim on consumption when old. Once in place, the system frees low discounters to save extra amounts to finance higher levels of their own future consumption. If the system operated on this principle, the distortions caused by the system would be limited to its effects on the capital market.[4]

In this sense social security can be viewed as a mechanism to fix a free rider problem, one that is aggravated by the wide dispersion of internal discount rates in the economy. If workers' contributions (plus interest) are commensurate with expected benefits in the system, then the threat of a degenerate solution is ameliorated without introducing distortions in the labor market. If a wedge is created between contributions and expected benefits, however, distortions arise that can discourage work and savings.

In reality, the social security system[5] has been transformed from a vehicle that eliminates the free ride to one that transfers funds to those who neither work nor save, creating deteriorating prospects for those who finance most of the retirement benefits in the system. In this chapter I consider reform in the Old Age and Survivors Insurance program (OASI). In chapter 15 I consider the disability and health insurance programs in social security.

In developing proposals to reform the system, I focus on preserving the primary function of social security: to maintain a required retirement program for all workers in the economy. Second, I propose changes that improve economic efficiency. In this sense I try to apply principles learned from the private pension market. That is to say, since participants in the private sector must make choices that reflect the marginal costs and benefits of various provisions in private pension plans, I can use observed outcomes in this market as a guide to what others might be willing to pay in similar circumstances if they had to make a choice of benefits and costs on the margin.

## 14.1 TRANSFORMING THE SOCIAL SECURITY ASSESSMENT TO A PURE TAX

The potential for social security to affect the incentive to work and save is driven by the assessment against wages that funds the program. In particular, the OASI assessment that covers retirement benefits is 10.7 percent of wages (separate assessments are made to cover disability and health benefits).[6] If the money collected is transferred to those currently retired, then in principle the assessment is just like other income taxes used to support other transfer programs administered by the federal government and therefore can be viewed as a pure tax.

The nature of the tax is altered by a promise made by the federal government: In exchange for sacrificing wages for OASI support to those currently old, workers acquire a quasi property right that entitles them

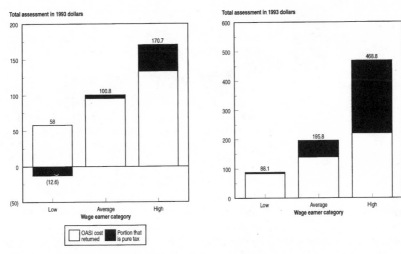

Figure 14.1 Pure tax portion of OASI assessment, single male. Assumes an OASI assessment of 10.5 percent. In reality, a balanced budget requires an assessment of 12.4 percent (see table 15.2), and thus the tax portion of the assessment is understated at all wage levels. From Steuerle and Bakija, *Retooling Social Security for the 21st Century,* at chapter 14, note 9.

to retirement benefits when they become old, financed by similar assessments on future generations. If for each dollar of OASI assessment workers expect at least one dollar of benefits (in present value terms), then the assessment is viewed as "savings" rather than a tax.[7]

In reality, the inter- and intragenerational transfers in the system make part of the assessment a pure tax. The intergenerational transfers are attributable to the changing profile of workers and retirees over time.[8] The intragenerational transfers are attributable to the ways the system favorably treats particular groups of covered workers.

Eugene Steuerle and Jon Bakija construct estimates of present value benefits and contributions for different categories of workers and different generations.[9] They assume a real interest rate of 2 percent and use the so-called intermediate assumptions of the Social Security Trustees' Report.[10] Some of their results are reproduced in figure 14.1.

The bar chart depicts lifetime OASI assessments for single males with low, medium, and high wages.[11] The black areas denote the portion of assessments *not* offset by future benefits (in a present value sense)—this portion is a pure tax. The white areas represent the "savings" portion of the assessment. The numbers are portrayed for two generations, those

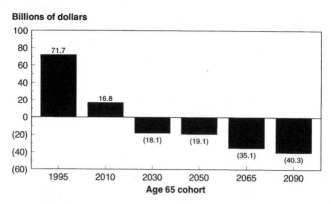

**Billions of dollars**

Figure 14.2 OASI transfers across cohorts. From Leamer, "Cohort-Specific Measures of Lifetime Net Social Security Transfers," at chapter 14, note 13.

retiring at age 65 in 1995 and in 2030. The results are different for females, one-earner and two-earner couples, and so on, but the results for single males shown in the chart illustrate the essential point: the portion of assessments that constitute taxes is higher for higher wage earners and younger cohorts.

Among workers attaining age 65 in 1995, lower-wage workers receive some net subsidy from the system. About 30 percent of high-wage workers' assessments represent a tax. For workers attaining age 65 in 2030, high-wage earners expect to pay about $469,000 in OASI assessments in exchange for $266,000 in benefits (1993 dollars): 43 percent of their assessments effectively are a pure tax.

The 10.5 percent OASI tax rate reflected in these estimates is insufficient to finance projected benefits in the social security system. Some changes must be made to recreate a balance in the trust fund. The Social Security Advisory Board estimates that under intermediate assumptions, the assessment must be increased to 12.4 percent immediately to attain a long-run balance in the trust fund.[12] Steuerle and Bakija do not account for these increases, so their estimated tax portion of the assessments is importantly understated for the future retiree cohort.

Dean Leamer has estimated net transfers across generations in the OASI system, on the assumption that assessments increase gradually over a long period to create a long-run balance in the trust fund.[13] His estimates, expressed in constant 1989 dollars, are shown in figure 14.2. The cohort that reached age 65 in 1995 received a subsidy of $71.7 billion. The cohort aged 65 in the year 2030 pays a net tax of $18.1 billion. Clearly, the portion of the social security assessment that is a pure tax increases for each succeeding cohort.

I next outline a series of reforms to the OASI system. My policy proposals are guided by a simple principle: The system should primarily address the free rider problem, which is aggravated by the presence of high discounters in the economy. This objective should be attained with minimum distortions imposed on the labor market.

Toward this end, I try to minimize the portion of assessments that are pure taxes. I suggest changing that portion of the system that awards extra benefits for reasons unrelated to work (for example, the spouse benefit). I also reconsider aspects of the system that award benefits far beyond what participants would be willing to pay for in a free market (for example, some portion of survivor benefits).

I retain the tilt in the benefit structure toward lower-wage workers. We can think of the tilt as a sort of negative income tax on low-wage earners. It provides a stronger incentive for low-wage individuals to participate in the workforce and decreases the likelihood that lower-wage earners will have insufficient retirement income when old. As a complement to this policy, I oppose Supplemental Security Income benefits. This program penalizes low-wage workers who participate in the social security system over a lifetime and engage in private savings.

As a guide to realigning social security benefits, I use observations on private pensions, which better reflect workers' willingness to pay for various kinds of retirement benefits. In general, private pensions closely align benefits to contributions made during the work life.

## 14.2 APPLYING PRIVATE PENSION PRINCIPLES TO SOCIAL SECURITY

### 14.2.1 The Spouse and Survivor Benefits after Retirement

In private pensions, firms pay benefits to their retirees based on their work and earnings in the firm. Married workers are not treated appreciably differently from single workers. In defined contribution plans, this outcome is evident. In defined benefit plans, annuities are set so as to generate similar present values for different types of benefit forms. Typically, married workers take a joint and survivor (J&S) benefit. This form awards some survivor benefit to a surviving spouse upon the retiree's death, but the annuity is reduced to accommodate the spouse benefit.[14]

The principle of equivalence does not characterize the social security system. Two workers with the same wage history and identical contributions are treated differently depending on their marital status and spouse's wage. Consider two workers, each of whom earns a social security retirement benefit of $600 per month.[15] Worker A has a spouse who contributed the same amount over her work life and also earns a $600 benefit. Worker B has a spouse who contributed nothing to the system.

Worker B receives a free spouse benefit equal to 50 percent of his benefit, or $300 per month.[16] In addition, if the insured retiree dies first, the spouse receives the insured's $600 benefit in place of $300.[17] The benefit discourages work by the spouse.

For example, if worker A's spouse could earn a benefit of less than $300 after a lifetime of paying social security benefits, then the entirety of her social security assessments results in no additional benefits. Effectively, the entire assessment is a pure tax on labor.[18]

Steuerle and Bakija compare unmarried and married males with the same average wage history. The married worker's spouse does not participate in the workforce. Both males retire in the year 2030 at age 65. Each pays a lifetime OASI assessment of $195,000 (in 1989 dollars), but the single male expects to collect $139,600 in present value benefits; the married male and spouse together expect to collect $312,800 in benefits. The difference of $173,200 represents the cost of a spouse and survivor benefit.[19] Clearly, the spouse benefit increases the pure tax burden of social security on single workers and discourages second earners in a family from entering the workforce.

### 14.2.2 Survivor Benefits before Retirement

Most medium and large firms in the private sector provide life insurance to employees before retirement.[20] The amounts usually are in the range of one to two times annual earnings.[21] Higher amounts are available at a cost to workers. In addition, defined benefit plans convey some benefits to surviving spouses. Upon the death of a worker, his benefit is calculated on a J&S basis as though he had retired at the earliest age he was entitled to based on service at the time of death. The survivor benefit is usually 50 percent of the J&S annuity. Often the present value of this benefit is given to the survivor immediately as a lump sum.

As an example, consider a worker earning the average social security wage in 1994 ($24,444) who dies at age 40 after twenty years of service. Suppose the firm has a life insurance policy of 1.5 times salary and that the pension pays an annuity at normal retirement age (55) equal to 1 percent times service times final salary. In this case the firm awards the survivor $36,666 in life insurance proceeds, plus a lump sum of $9,355 representing the present value of the survivor benefit.[22] Thus total survivor benefits amount to $46,021, or about 1.8 times salary.

Moreover, all life insurance benefits are payable to any designated survivor, so unmarried workers are treated like married workers. The pension lump sum is not available to the heirs of a single person, but married workers as a whole pay for the benefit in the form of a lower J&S benefit payable at normal retirement.[23] In defined contribution plans, even this distinction is erased, because the value of the worker's pension account passes to his heirs.

Social security survivor benefits operate differently, because they are not proportional to contributions. First, survivor benefits do not depend on contributions, but rather are based on the worker's marriage and parental status. Unmarried workers receive virtually no survivor benefits. Married workers, particularly those with children, have large survivor benefits. Second, survivor benefits are not related to the amount of contribution: in fact, because of child benefits, workers who contribute for the fewest years are more likely to receive the most generous survivor benefits.

Consider how the same 40-year-old worker is treated in social security. Using rules in place in 1995, if this worker lived and retired at age 65, his monthly benefit would be approximately $880.[24] Upon death at age 40, his spouse is entitled to this same benefit without reduction for fewer years of service. Using a 2 percent real interest rate and social security mortality tables (assuming the survivor is female), the present value of this annuity at age 65 is $168,146. Discounting back to age 40 at 2 percent and ignoring mortality before age 65, the present value of this benefit is $101,985.[25] Thus, compared with an unmarried worker with the same history of contributions, married workers in effect have about a $100,000 life insurance benefit, or four times annual salary. If the benefit were proportional to contributions only through age 40, the present value would be $45,326.[26]

These benefits understate survivor benefits if the deceased worker has children. For the sake of illustration, suppose the worker has two children both 2 years old at the time of his death. In addition to the deferred spouse annuity, which remains unchanged, the spouse also is entitled to an immediate annuity of 75 percent of the full annuity, or $660 per month (indexed to inflation). If she remains unmarried, the annuity continues for the next fourteen years (until both children are 16).

In addition, each child is also entitled to an annuity of 75 percent of the worker's full annuity until age 18—but subject to an overall cap of $1,608 in 1995.[27] In this case the cap is binding, so the family's survivor benefit is $1,608 monthly (indexed) for fourteen years, followed by two years (when the children are 16 and 17) during which the children receive an annuity of $1,320 (two times each child's entitlement of $660). The present value of these benefits is $259,047.[28] If these benefits are added to the survivor benefit ($101,985), total survivor and life insurance benefits are $361,032, or almost fifteen times current salary (see table 14.1).

Compared with benefits derived in the private sector, the social security system has a large implicit life insurance policy on some covered workers. But the implicit cost of these policies is not assessed in propor-

Table 14.1  Life Insurance and Pensions versus Social Security

| Category | Unmarried | Married, no children | Married, two children |
|---|---|---|---|
| Private | | | |
| Life insurance[a] | $36,666 | $36,666 | $36,666 |
| J&S benefits[b] | | 9,355 | 9,355 |
| Total | $36,666 | $46,021 | $46,021 |
| Social security | | | |
| J&S benefits[c] | 0 | $101,945 | $101,945 |
| Parent and children benefits[d] | 0 | | $259,047 |
| Total | 0 | $101,945 | $361,032 |
| Alternative calculation | | | |
| J&S benefits based on service until death | | $45,326 | $45,326 |

Note: Worker earns the average social security wage in 1994 of $24,444 per year.
Sources: U.S. Department of Labor, Employee Benefits, at chapter 2, note 3, and U.S. Social Security Administration, Social Security Bulletin, Annual Statistical Supplement, 1996, 70, at chapter 14, note 6.
[a] Assumes that the firm awards an average life insurance benefit of 1.5 times annual salary.
[b] Assumes that the pension pays 1 percent of salary times service; service is twenty years at the time of death; the interest rate is 7 percent; and the spouse is female and lives to the expected death age using social security life expectancy tables. Normal retirement is 55. Upon death, the age 55 benefit is calculated based on service to death, multiplied by 90 percent for the J&S benefit, and multiplied by 50 percent for the survivor benefit. The present value at age 55 is discounted to age 40.
[c] Assumes an indexed monthly benefit of $880 (the primary insurance amount—PIA) from age 65 to death for a female spouse, discounted to age 40 using a 2 percent real interest rate assumption.
[d] Assumes spouse is 40 years old, and two children each 2 years old. Assumes that the family maximum benefit is binding ($1,608 monthly). Mortality for the spouse and children is ignored, and the discount rate is 2 percent. See text for more detail.

tion to their value. Those who have no implicit insurance pay as much as those who have extraordinary life insurance coverage.

If social security policies were changed to align benefits and costs across workers earning similar wages, the distortions and inequities in the system would be significantly reduced. In addition, the imbalance in the OASI trust fund also would be alleviated, thereby reducing the implicit future tax increases embedded in the current equilibrium. Two changes that work toward this reform mimic rules in the private pension system.

*Establish economically equivalent J&S benefits.* Upon attaining retirement age, workers with similar wage histories should receive similar present value benefits. This means eliminating the 50 percent spouse benefit and reducing the postretirement survivor benefits so they are comparable with common practice in private pension plans. Typically, this means that married workers take a lower annuity in exchange for joint and survivor protection and that the surviving spouse receives a benefit after the recipient's death equal to 50 percent of this benefit. In this way workers who pay similar amounts into the system over a lifetime are treated the same during retirement.

*Reduce the level of mandatory life insurance.* The amount of implicit life insurance coverage in the system can be reduced to levels commonly found in the private sector. However, recognizing the role social security plays in securing retirement income, a convincing argument can be made that the insurance should be geared toward old age protection. One way this outcome can be accomplished is to retain the surviving spouse's old age benefit—award the spouse entitlement to the worker's annuity at age 65—but scale back the annuity to reflect fewer years of contributions by the deceased worker.

In the example used above, a monthly annuity of $400 (indexed) would accrue to the surviving spouse at age 65.[29] The value of this annuity is approximately $45,000 at age 40,[30] compared with approximately $360,000 currently.

There is a well-developed market for life insurance. For most workers with young children, the price of insurance is low. In addition, the demand for life insurance may not be high, owing to the high likelihood that young survivors will marry another productive earner.

### 14.2.3 The Means Test and Tax Policy

The social security system ostensibly is not means tested. In fact, the income tax treatment of some benefits accomplishes the same effect. The means test is based not on the level of wages, but instead on taxable income during retirement. Social security benefits are partly offset against other sources of retirement income, in the form of wages for part-time work, pension income, or other income from savings for retirement.

Consider various couples who have earned a joint $12,000 social security annuity. Couples with taxable income less than $32,000 receive the benefits tax free. Others with the same social security benefits, but who also have invested in a pension annuity or have accumulated other income-producing assets for retirement (or both) that push their taxable income beyond $32,000 have 50 percent of their benefits taxed at normal income tax rates.[31] Couples with more than $44,000 in taxable income pay a tax on 85 percent of benefits. If their marginal income tax rate is 30 percent, they in effect rebate $3,060 of their annuity to the social security system (85 percent times $12,000 times 30 percent tax rate).

The tax revenue is sent directly to the OASI trust fund, making the implicit means test explicit. Two workers in the same job with the same lifetime contributions and with the same family circumstances are treated differently based solely on taxable income during retirement.

The means test creates a disincentive to save for retirement. Low discounters are penalized for having a higher savings rate than high discounters who save at low rates.

*Tax social security benefits like pensions.* Social security benefits should be taxed on consumption tax principles, like pensions. Consumption taxes can be applied either when contributions are made or when benefits are taken. Since 50 percent of contributions are taxed as ordinary income, 50 percent of benefits should be taxed during retirement. In this way, half of all social security benefits are taxable income to all recipients.[32] Normal exemptions, deductions, and progressivity in the United States Internal Revenue Code award older Americans with lower incomes the same tax treatment as their younger counterparts with the same taxable income.

## 14.3 INCENTIVE EFFECTS OF SUPPLEMENTAL SECURITY INCOME

The Supplemental Security Income program (SSI), though financed from general revenues, has a strong potential interaction with the social security system because it effectively imposes a tax on work for lower-wage earners. SSI is a federal welfare program that entitles older (or disabled) individuals to a minimum level of income, regardless of their social security participation. This entitlement has a curious corollary: workers at low wage levels who pay into social security for a lifetime essentially receive the same retirement, disability, and health benefits as those who make no contributions.

There is little incentive for lower-wage individuals to work and contribute to the social security system. In 1995 supplemental social security guaranteed $687 per month, or $8,244 per annum (plus medical coverage) to an elderly couple with no other source of income. (States supplement this amount, so that the guarantees are generally higher than federal payments.) By comparison, a person working at the minimum wage in 1995 earned an annual salary of approximately $8,500 for two thousand hours of work. The average social security retirement benefit in 1995 was $697 per month, or $8,364 per year.[33]

In short, for lower-wage workers, SSI effectively transforms the entire social security assessment to a pure tax on their labor. Moreover, SSI often "tops up" benefits collected from the Disability Income program, creating an even stronger incentive to quit the workforce early to gain entry into the disability program (chapter 15). In effect, the SSI program entirely offsets the negative income tax aspect of social security for lower-wage workers. The following change in policy can reestablish the incentive to work and contribute to the social security system.

*Eliminate the SSI program.* Individuals who contribute little to the social security system over their work life should not be provided income support in old age commensurate with that of workers who contribute over a lifetime. If individuals are impoverished in old age because they have not contributed to the social security system, they should be treated like other adults in poverty; that is, they should be included in state welfare systems.

Moving responsibility for welfare to the states increases the likelihood that older individuals will not easily qualify for benefits (that is, they will be required to work later in their lives). In addition, states more likely will be responsive to local conditions so as not to pay welfare benefits that are "too high" in relation to those of workers who contributed to the social security system over a lifetime.

States themselves have an incentive to encourage their citizens to work, contribute to social security, and accumulate social security credits so as to reduce the burden on the states' tax base when they become old.

## 14.4  POLICY CHANGES TO REDUCE OLD AGE POVERTY FOR HIGH DISCOUNTERS

The discussion above implicitly assumes that calculations about social security are made by low discounters. High discounters naturally attach less value to social security benefits, especially when young, but they are fully aware of the payroll deduction from current wages. Thus high discounters are expected to perceive a higher portion of the social security assessment as a pure tax. The distortion against work for high discounters is implicitly accepted in return for overcoming their tendency to free ride on low discounters when they become old and have no source of income.[34]

There are other features of the social security system, however, that can be changed to reduce the high discounter problem in old age. The first is to reconsider the earnings test in the system. The second is to revisit the early retirement option at age 62.

*The earnings test.* For social security recipients older than 65 (but less than 70), benefits are reduced by $1 for every $3 of outside earnings above some predetermined level ($11,280 in 1995). Beginning in the year 2005, actuarial adjustments will be made to fully compensate workers who forgo their benefits until age 70. In effect, low discounters will not be discouraged from working when older because they will perceive that the loss of current benefits is fully offset by actuarially fair adjustments in the form of higher benefits levels at age 70.[35] High discounters, however, will not perceive the advantage of postponing their benefits and still will be encouraged to quit work early. In this sense the full actuarial adjustments in the new formulas are not neutral in all older workers' decisions.[36]

*The early retirement option.* Other things being equal, high discounters are expected to retire earlier because they do not account for the higher replacement rates available if they postpone retirement. If leisure preferrers and high discounters did not have a call provision against low discounters' income, the clear optimal solution would be to permit everyone to retire when he wishes. In reality, the call provision exists, and low discounters have an incentive to minimize its value. In effect, by retiring at earlier ages, workers who have no other savings partly undo a principal goal of social security: to ensure that the some portion of the workforce does not free ride on others for retirement security.

At age 67, for example, projected formulas in the system deliver a 41 percent replacement rate to an average worker. The replacement rate is only 28 percent if retirement occurs at age 62. Retiring early increases the chances that more transfers to these individuals will be required later on owing to their "inadequate income." These factors suggest the following changes:

*Eliminate the earnings test.* Given the challenge posed by high discounters on a system that depends on capital accumulation, the last goal public retirement policy should strive for is to encourage high discounters to exit the workforce. The disincentive is eliminated by abolishing the earnings test.

*Restrict the early retirement option.* To reduce the cost of the free ride, and to preserve the goal of adequate retirement income, retirement eligibility should be changed to age 67. Individuals are free to retire earlier if they can provide their own support.

## 14.5 CONCLUDING REMARKS

The rules governing the social security retirement system stray far from the principle of aligning rewards and work: the system is characterized by important disincentives to work and save. It can be improved by implementing some of the principles of the private pension system.

These ideas include the application of economically equivalent benefit formulas for joint and survivor benefits; taxing social security on a consumption tax basis; reducing welfare insurance benefits levels that compete with those earned by participating in the OASI system over a lifetime; eliminating (or establishing a price for) life insurance benefits payable before retirement age; and so on. Not only do these reforms reduce distortions and inequities in the system, they reduce the portion of social security assessments that are viewed as a pure tax.

At the same time, some special features of social security—notably its function of mandating savings of sorts—can be emphasized to reduce the high discounter problem. These changes include eliminating the earnings test and restricting early retirement benefits to later ages.

Even these changes, however, may be insufficient to create a balance in the OASI trust fund. Moreover, many other features of the public retirement system are not addressed, and these also play an important role in discouraging work and savings. In particular, the disability and Medicare-Medicaid features are central to an overall retirement policy designed to encourage work and savings and to ensure a viable social security system in the future. I turn to reforms in these programs in the next chapter.

## CHAPTER FIFTEEN

# Reforms for the Disability and Medicare Programs

In chapter 14 I considered social security issues as they applied to the Old Age and Survivors Insurance program that funds retiree benefits. This program accounts for only a portion of money expended by the social security system. The Disability Insurance (DI) and Hospital Insurance (HI) programs also are large parts of the system (see table 15.1).[1]

Only about half of the public resources spent on the aged and disabled come from OASI. Of the combined 15.3 percent social security assessment against wages, almost 30 percent is attributable to the disability (1.7 percent) and medical (2.9 percent) programs. Moreover, the DI and HI fund projections portend their growth relative to basic retirement benefits. The 1996 Social Security Trustees' Report[2] shows that DI and HI assessments of 2.2 and 7.4 percent need to be implemented immediately to attain a long-term balance in the funds (table 15.2).

The free rider component of OASI also is present in the disability and medical programs in social security. If individuals encounter poor health during their lifetimes, they may be tempted to rely on the generosity of their fellow citizens rather than purchasing health and disability insurance. As in the retirement program, however, the operation of the auxiliary programs in the social security system can impose distortions on decisions to save and work. I first address the disability program, then turn to reforms of the hospital program.

In evaluating these programs, I emphasize their incentives for work and savings. Again, I keep in mind the disparate savings propensities of covered individuals (high and low discounters). I also use the selection idea introduced in chapter 11: that some individuals are naturally inclined to work, while others have a strong preference for leisure ("workers" and "leisure preferrers"). Thus policies that make it affordable to retire at early ages will encourage leisure preferrers to exit the workforce earlier

**Table 15.1 Social Security and Other Federal Payments to the Aged and Disabled (billions of dollars, 1995)**

| Category | | Amount |
|---|---|---|
| Retirees and beneficiaries (OASI fund) | | $291.6 |
| Disabled | | |
|   Cash payments (DI fund) | $ 40.9 | |
|   Medicaid payments[a] | 48.5 | |
|   Supplemental Security Income (SSI)[a] | 20.2 | |
|   Subtotal | 109.6 | |
| Medical benefits (to retirees and disabled) | | |
|   Hospital (HI trust fund) | $116.3 | |
|   Supplemental medical[b] | 64.9 | |
|   Medicaid for over age 65[a] | 36.5 | |
|   SSI to over age 65[a] | 3.4 | |
|   Subtotal | 221.1 | |
| Total disabled and medical | | 330.7 |
| Grand total | | $622.3 |

Source: U.S. Social Security Administration, *Social Security Bulletin, Annual Statistical Supplement, 1996,* 181, 304, 343, at chapter 14, note 6.
[a] Payments made from general federal revenues.
[b] Federal subsidy to part B of Medicare, financed from general revenues.

than otherwise, thereby increasing the tax burden on those who stay. This effect decreases the rewards from work, encouraging "workers" to act more like "leisure preferrers."

## 15.1 DISTORTIONS FROM THE DISABILITY PROGRAM

### 15.1.1 Description of the Program

The social security disability program is intended to provide benefits to covered workers who have physical or mental impairments that prevent them from holding "substantial gainful employment." Compared with regular social security retirement benefits, disability awards typically are made at relatively young ages. For example, almost half of new disability awards are made to men and women under age 50.[3]

Disability awards are based on the OASI formula except that benefits are not reduced for fewer years of contributions, and benefits are unreduced from their age 65 equivalent. The awards are increased for the presence of spouse and children. Thus the average disability annuity ($662 in 1995) is comparable to the average OASI benefit ($697).[4] In addition, those on the disability rolls are entitled to Medicare coverage after two years in the program.

Workers need not be truly disabled to win a benefit. The aggregation

Table 15.2 Social Security Wage Assessments

| Trust fund | 1997 actual | Balanced budget |
|---|---|---|
| Old Age and Survivors Insurance (OASI) | 10.7 | 12.4 |
| Disability (DI) | 1.7 | 2.2 |
| Medicare (HI) | 2.9 | 7.4 |
| Total | 15.3 | 22.0 |

Note: Numbers are percentages. OASI and DI assessments are collected against wages and salaries up to $65,400 in 1997; there is no limit to the HI assessment. Numbers in the second column assume "intermediate assumptions."

Sources: Board of Trustees, Federal OASIDI Trust Funds, 1996 Annual Report of the Board of Trustees of the Federal OASI and DI Trust Funds, 7, 113, at chapter 14, note 10; Board of Trustees of the Federal HI Trust Fund, 1996 Annual Report of the Board of Trustees of the Federal HI Trust Fund, 44, at chapter 15, note 2; and U.S. Social Security Administration, Annual Statistical Supplement to the Social Security Bulletin, 1996, 35, at chapter 14, note 6.

of numerous smaller impairments can lead to qualification, depending on the worker's age and occupation. And so-called age and vocational factors justify one-third of disability awards.[5] Once a recipient is on the rolls, it is difficult to terminate benefits—even if a review finds he is capable of "substantial gainful employment"—unless it can be shown that his medical condition has improved since the time of the award.[6] Although social security finances DI payments, the states determine eligibility, and an extensive appeals system is in place that often overturns denials by state employees.

### 15.1.2 Potential for Distortions in the Labor Market

Although the program is intended to award generous benefits to the severely disabled, the high level of benefits at early ages provides an incentive for workers to try to win an award, whether or not they are truly incapable of work.[7] Not counting the value of Medicare coverage, replacement rates can be as high as 80 percent for disability recipients with other family members and 55 percent for single recipients.[8] The data support the hypothesis that workers react to the incentive.

Studies find that the DI program encourages those who can (and do) work to leave the workforce in exchange for a generous early retirement program. If entrants in the program were truly unable to work, its introduction in 1957 should not have caused a reduction in labor supply. Yet the data show a convincing relation between the availability of disability benefits and lower rates of labor force participation.[9]

In addition, studies find a positive correlation between downturns in the economy and the number of disability awards, suggesting that states use the program as a quasi unemployment program, financed by social security.[10] The probability of getting awards also varies across states. Acceptance rates vary from 22 percent in some states to 48 percent in others.[11]

Either the disabled are concentrated in particular areas of the nation, or some states use more lenient criteria to admit candidates to the program.

Other evidence supports these findings. For example, in 1983 a review by the Social Security Administration of one million cases, previously approved by the states, resulted in disqualification of 45 percent of the beneficiaries.[12] (Legislation soon followed making removal from the rolls more difficult, so that in 1989 such reviews resulted in a termination rate of only 10 percent.)[13]

In addition, even those found to be capable of work by state boards often find their way onto the rolls. In 1989, for example, 37 percent of applicants were found to satisfy the standards for disability; the rest were determined to be fit for work. Yet after a series of appeals, the acceptance rate increased to 45 percent.[14]

The large number of entrants itself raises questions about the legitimacy of the program. For every 1,000 people who work during ages 60–64, the Social Security Administration (SSA) classifies 285 people in the same age group as incapable of work. For every 1,000 workers aged 45–59, SSA classifies 83 as incapable of work.[15] Thus in 1994, for every 2.5 workers who retired on regular OASI benefits, one worker retired on disability benefits.[16]

The social security system makes about 5.1 disability awards per 1,000 insured workers each year; the distribution of awards is fairly uniform across young and old ages.[17] At these rates, for each cohort entering the covered workforce at age 18, about one in five will be declared disabled before age 62.[18]

If these statistics reflect the expected health status of the workforce, then perhaps the insurance feature in the DI program is fully valued by all workers. That is, if the each covered worker perceives an equal chance of becoming disabled and all awards represents true disabilities, then the entire DI assessment might be viewed as a fair insurance premium.

If, however, a large portion of awards are perceived not to be given to those truly incapable of work, but to be made to leisure preferrers who exaggerate their disability, then workers who are not inclined to feign an inability to work view most of the DI assessment as a pure tax. The DI tax rate is 1.7 percent, compared with 1.2 percent in 1993, and the Trustees estimate an equilibrium assessment of 2.2 percent under intermediate assumptions.[19]

## 15.2 A PROPOSAL FOR REFORM IN THE DISABILITY PROGRAM

Like the OASI retirement program discussed in chapter 14, the disability program is operated in ways that seem to reward those who are disinclined to work for exaggerating their physical or mental shortcomings so they can leave the workforce early. Other workers contribute for a lifetime with little expected benefit from the program. I propose numerous changes to the program to bring contributions and expected benefits into closer alignment.

### 15.2.1 Introduce Economically Equivalent Benefits and Limit Replacement Rates

As in the OASI program, disability benefits are not closely tied to contributions; they vary depending on the perceived "need" of those entering the program. Family supplements create a mismatch between contributions and benefits: two covered workers with the same rate of contributions to DI receive markedly different benefits depending on whether they are married or have children. In addition, given the moral hazard that besets the program, high awards (and thus high replacement rates) are unlikely to characterize a rational disability program. If workers can receive benefits that closely approximate the wages they can earn for full-time work, the temptation is great to try to get into the program.

Two changes can be made to reduce the incentive to quit work imparted by the current system. First, disability benefits should be based on contributions; they should not be enhanced for the presence of other family members without a commensurately higher disability insurance assessment to those who want the extra coverage. Second, replacement rates should be lower than those available to workers who retire from the system at normal retirement ages.

The hypothetical benefit at age 65 can still be calculated as under current law (counting service as though retirement occurred at age 65), but these benefits should be scaled back so as to be economically equivalent to the age 65 benefit. In this way those who enter the DI program at the earliest ages would not receive a higher present value than those who enter at older ages.[20]

Supplemental Security Income also must be altered to accommodate these changes; otherwise disability benefits would be offset by higher amounts received from SSI. Thus the reform outlined in chapter 14—to eliminate SSI—is a prerequisite to successful reform of the disability program.

### 15.2.2 Create a Budget for the Disability Insurance System

As long as the disability program is an entitlement, states face no discipline for placing able-bodied workers on the rolls. This problem is largely eliminated if the DI program is put on a fixed budget. The baseline budget could be determined by having a panel of medical experts review of a broad sample of new awards. They would determine the portion of awards that are eligible in a strict interpretation of the law.

Suppose the national panel found, as they did in 1983, that half of new recipients are disabled in the sense that they are truly incapable of working at any job. This puts the number of new awards under a modified system at roughly 300,000 per year. The study also would estimate the number of legitimate recipients expected to improve sufficiently over time to return to work.

Next, the combined tax rate of 1.7 percent should be reduced to a rate consistent with the legitimate numbers determined by the study. The new tax rate might be in the range of 1 percent.[21] This rate—and the number of awards and terminations consistent with this rate—provides a budget for the system.[22]

### 15.2.3 Introduce a Scoring System

The question naturally arises how the budget will be allocated to those truly disabled. Several approaches are possible. I propose instituting a scoring system. Panels of medical personnel could be affiliated with each Social Security Administration office. Each applicant would be sent to three panels, which would assign him a score.

Those obviously qualified as truly disabled would be scored highest; obvious frauds would be scored lowest, with most applicants scored across the continuum. Those with the highest combined scores would be admitted to the program, subject to the budget constraint—in my example, 300,000 awards per year nationally.[23] To discourage frivolous applications, an application fee could be set equal to the cost of the panel evaluations, with a rebate to those accepted into the program.

In the next year, recipients of these awards would be required to reenter the pool and be reevaluated by three panels, and they would be included in the larger pool now comprising two cohorts of applicants.[24] The budget would be expanded to accommodate two cohorts, recognizing that some previous recipients from the first cohort are expected to regain their ability to work. Again, those with the highest scores would be chosen.

To facilitate the transition, all current DI recipients over some chosen age (say age 60) could be grandfathered under existing rules. Others would be included in the scoring process (with appropriate expansion of slots to accommodate some portion of the stock of existing recipients younger than the grandfathered age). Congress could require periodic audits of the system. If it decided that the recipient pool was insufficient, it could enact a tax increase to pay for expansion of the rolls. If it decided too many were being admitted, it could reduce the allowable number of new awards and reduce the tax assessment.

Reforming the disability program would make it possible to reduce and stabilize the current and projected DI tax rates into the indefinite future. The DI system would be viewed more as an insurance program and less as a mechanism to transfer resources from those inclined to work to those inclined to take full-time leisure. As such, the DI assessment would more closely approximate an insurance premium rather than a tax on individuals who are inclined to work.[25] Those truly disabled would be included in the program without fear that their benefits would ultimately be reduced to accommodate ever-increasing numbers of those unwilling to work at their market wage.

## 15.3 MEDICARE AND MEDICAID

I next consider medical benefits conferred upon retirees in the social security system. Upon qualifying for Medicare or Medicaid, an individual is granted an asset of substantial magnitude. Moreover, unlike the old age benefit program, which still preserves some relation between contributions and benefits, there is no effort to align medical benefits in the social security system according to lifetime contributions. Those who contribute little or nothing to the hospital trust fund receive the same treatment under Medicare as those who pay large amounts over a lifetime of work.

In 1995, of all old age, disability, and medical payments (including hospital payments, supplemental coverage subsidies, and federal Medicaid payments to the elderly), 43 percent was paid in the form of Medicare and Medicaid reimbursements to recipients who were over age 65 or disabled (see table 15.1).[26] This amount is unrelated to payments made to the social security system during the work life. Since medical benefits are unrelated to contributions, workers properly perceive the entire HI assessment as a pure tax on labor.

In addition, Medicaid for the elderly is means tested: those who save through pensions or other vehicles for retirement are penalized by Medicaid policy. Elderly individuals who have zero assets qualify for nursing home care if they need it. Those who retire at older ages, save more, or both must dissipate their savings and turn over their private pension annuities in order to qualify for the same nursing home care that is automatically given to those who have no savings. The means test in Medicaid discourages workers from accumulating private savings and earning pension annuities.

The Medicare system is far removed from the discipline that the market exerts on an industry beset with moral hazard. The most problematic elements of the system are that it fits one plan to all recipients, regardless of their underlying willingness to pay for medical care; makes no attempt to align the magnitude of the benefits to workers' lifetime contributions to the HI system; applies a standard for reimbursements for new medical innovations that accounts for the benefits of technology but not its cost; and awards property rights to almost unlimited use of medical resources at little or no marginal cost.

Given these characteristics, it is not surprising that older Americans overuse medical resources to the exclusion of other goods and services that might be more valuable to them. As one index of the problem, while covered individuals in their last year of life represent approximately 5 percent of the Medicare population over age 65, they account for approximately 30 percent of total expenditures. Fully one in every eight dollars of Medicare expenditures on those over age 65 is spent during the last thirty days of life.[27] The United States expends far more of its national resources on medical care than other countries, a statistic that commands some attention given the zeal with which they spend resources on national programs.[28]

The average retiree on social security collects a regular retirement annuity of about $8,400 per year.[29] The federal government spends another $6,200 a year per retiree in Medicare and old age Medicaid funds.[30] (Other amounts are financed by states' contributions to Medicaid and cross-subsidies from private insurers.) The obvious question is whether, if given a choice how to spend $14,600 a year, retirees would opt to devote over 40 percent to a medical insurance policy. A potentially large efficiency could be obtained by permitting retirees flexibility in allocating their own resources to medical and nonmedical consumption during old age.

I make several proposals to enhance the efficiency of old age medical programs. Two principles serve as guides: Some minimal health insurance is mandated to deal with the free rider problem; in this context, the problem occurs when older individuals eschew insurance, figuring that society will accommodate their health care needs regardless of their ability to pay. And otherwise, individuals' have freedom to allocate their scarce retirement resources according to their values and preferences.

## 15.4 A VOUCHER SOLUTION FOR MEDICARE AND MEDICAID

### 15.4.1 Value of the Voucher

The essence of my proposal is to retain the existing HI assessment against wages but replace the Medicare program with a voucher system,[31] thus establishing a budget for medical care. I would set the voucher amount so that it is related to contributions made to the HI system over a lifetime of work. One useful approach might be to set the voucher at some percentage of the regular OASI retirement benefit. This approach awards a subsidy for low-wage workers and thus extends the negative income tax feature in the system to retiree health benefits.

The formula setting the voucher's value is chosen to meet an overall budget. One approach is to set the average voucher equal to the average per capita expenditure of Medicare and Medicaid on the elderly ($6,200).[32] In this case the overall budget increases over time owing to the growth of the elderly population. Alternatively, the budget can be fixed so as to rationalize a constant tax rate, in which case the real value of the voucher can be set to some lower number, and so on. Once the budget is determined, the structure of the system can be established.

*First tier.* The voucher in my proposal has two tiers: the first tier, a fixed dollar amount, is not redeemable for cash. It can be used to purchase a basic policy from a private insurance company. Those who do not make a choice are assigned a carrier through a competitive bidding process administered by the Social Security Administration or its agent.

The basic policy includes coverage for hospice care for the terminally ill or for nursing home care for the old and disabled. It includes a high deductible, imposes strict limits on the damages obtainable from malpractice suits, and amortizes payments in a way that discourages large end of life expenditures (see below).

First-tier policies must be term renewable; and insurance carriers must accept all applicants at a price strictly determined by age as long as they are younger than the social security normal retirement age (preexisting conditions restrictions can apply at older ages for those who wish to change coverage).[33] A term renewable policy—common in life insurance coverage—eliminates the problem in term insurance of companies' dropping retirees who become seriously ill.[34]

*Second tier.* The second-tier voucher has a face value equal to the total voucher amount, less the first-tier value.[35] The second-tier voucher is redeemable for cash. Individuals who choose to have more medical coverage during old age, including those who want access to expensive technology and efforts to extend life for short periods, can opt to spend their entire second-tier voucher on additional private insurance coverage, plus any amount of other insurance they can support with other sources of income and wealth. A wide range of options will develop covering different combinations of medical services available in the market, each carrying a different price. Retirees could opt for any of these coverages or none.

*Efficiencies.* The proposal is a close approximation to a free market solution. First, the ability to pay concept is reintroduced into the demand for second-tier coverage. Second, through the price-service combinations chosen in the competitive process, retirees convey how much they are willing to pay for either unlimited technology, or elective procedures, or costly procedures with small marginal effects, or improved diagnostics, or unlimited use of resources at the end of life. The exercise of free choice, subject to income and price constraints, likely will generate a pattern of expenditures that favors other competing uses of funds during old age. A wide distribution of choices is predictable.

Third, workers currently have little incentive to accumulate private assets. If they save, they have an incentive to dissipate their wealth early in retirement to qualify for means-tested federal Medicaid benefits. The voucher system reestablishes the incentive to participate in the social security system, to save for retirement, to subscribe to annuity pensions, to spend money rationally during their entire retirement period, and to leave bequests.

In addition, because a link is established between the voucher amount and the HI assessment, two-earner families receive benefits more in proportion to their additional social security contributions, thereby reducing the distortion that discourages second earners' participation in the labor market.[36] Owing to the same proportionality principle, the HI tax assessment would be limited by the social security maximum wage. There is no reason to force higher-wage earners to purchase more medical benefits though social security: it is merely an additional tax on wage income.[37]

Finally, since the voucher amounts are proportional to retirement benefits, the market is forced to devise ways to accommodate older individuals' demand for medical care *within a budget*. By construct, total medical expenditures will increase in proportion to social security benefits[38] *unless* the elderly decide they wish to devote a greater portion of their retirement resources to the purchase of new medical technology they find worthwhile. In this way the current HI tax rate is sufficient to fund the system into the indefinite future.

### 15.4.2 Tax Treatment of the Voucher

The voucher is taxed in the same manner as regular social security benefits (chapter 14) and private pensions (chapter 13), thereby eliminating the bias in favor of medical consumption now in the tax code.[39]

### 15.4.3 The Property Right to Unlimited Medical Care

Since all first-tier policies (and presumably most second-tier policies) will be written to explicitly limit expenditures in situations where the costs clearly outweigh the benefits—that is, the contracts recognize both the benefits and costs of incremental treatment and technology—federal law must be amended to insulate hospitals and doctors from liability for terminating treatment not covered by patients' insurance policies. Otherwise the elderly will be inhibited from making decisions about the level of care they are willing to pay for. This change in property rights explicitly introduces the economics of medical care into law.

### 15.4.4 A Reimbursement Policy for Expenditures toward the End of Life

Finally, I consider how to limit uneconomical expenditures in the last part of life. The approach I outline is part of the first-tier benefit, but a variant might also characterize some voluntary contracts offered under second-tier coverage. Currently, patients and their families have a de facto property right to medical resources to extend life. There is no incentive on the margin to refrain from wasteful spending when remaining life expectancy does not justify the expenditures.

Given this system, each person individually is rational in spending without limit. As a group, however, they prefer a more economical expenditure of retirement resources. If retirees and medical care suppliers are free to write contracts that reflect costs, reimbursement systems will arise that value life-increasing expenditures consistently with consumers' willingness to pay for increasing life expectancy.

The trade-off between spending to reduce deaths and competing uses of resources is constantly made by individuals and their governments. For example, a decision is made about the value of lifesaving when government pays or mandates others to install safety features affecting highways, factories, and airlines. Individuals decide to spend money for fire alarms, sprinkler systems, and the like in their homes; and they may sacrifice some valued consumption of cigarettes and fat to extend their life expectancy. Similarly, if they are free to purchase their preferred insurance package, each cohort of retirees could and would make a choice about how much insurance to buy to extend their expected lives in the face of life-threatening illnesses.

Studies of individual and government lifesaving expenditures in other contexts are widespread. There is a wide range of estimates. But on average the studies find that consumers are willing to spend about $1 million to save the life of a 40-year-old person (in an expected sense).[40] If normal life expectancy for such a person is forty more years, this estimate amounts to a price of about $25,000 per year of life saved.[41]

An insurance policy that incorporates a rational level of major medical care has two characteristics: it pays off the medical expenditure according to an amortization schedule that reflects the value set on each year of lifesaving; and it stops reimbursements at the death of the patient.

Suppose for illustration that the first-tier insurance policy pays off medical bills at the rate of $25,000 plus interest for each year a patient lives beyond a major medical intervention. And suppose the policy uses the most liberal assumption about the efficacy of medical procedures: that expected life is zero at the time of the procedure (that is, that every day of life following the date of a major medical procedure is attributable solely to the procedure). With this policy in place, a procedure costing $100,000 is performed only if the individual is expected to live four years beyond it, and so on.[42]

This particular policy will have some insurance premium attached to it. Other policies with more or less liberal payoff procedures will have different prices. The first-tier rule will be set according to the budget determined by the HI assessment. Second-tier rules will depend on retirees' willingness to pay for more generous contract conditions. The elderly could choose the combination of medical intervention policy and price that maximizes their expected utility during retirement.

## 15.5 CONCLUDING REMARKS

Government policy toward retirement income is intertwined with the natural conflict between high and low discounters and between leisure preferrers and workers. Public policy ought to ensure that some individuals' exercise of free choice does not unreasonably impinge on the freedom of others—that high discounters cannot free ride off the savings habits of low discounters and that leisure preferrers cannot take advantage of those more inclined to work. Otherwise the temptation is great for individuals to reduce their level of work and savings.

If the free riding is not restricted, a degenerate solution can set in that makes everyone worse off. These factors provide the rationale for some mandatory participation in programs designed to support old age. However, with the way the social security program has developed, it is not clear that its basic purpose is satisfied at a reasonable cost to those supporting the system.

Although the overt problem of social security is reflected in trust fund imbalances, its problems are more deeply rooted. The system is characterized by a vague relation between contributions and benefits. The most obvious "mismatch" derives from the pay as you go nature of the system, which separates those benefiting and those providing the financing. But the problem also is endemic within cohorts. The way disability, Medicaid, Medicare, SSI, and ancillary benefits are awarded has created a large wedge between the benefits received and contributions paid to the system. Workers and savers are treated much less generously than leisure preferrers and spenders.

The long-run effect of these policies is hard to measure. The propensities of individuals and their children to save and work are formed over long periods, and these inclinations are not quickly altered as public systems gradually tilt in favor of those who are disinclined to produce and save. The danger is that over the long run, as the retirement system effectively becomes more of a means-tested transfer program, the incentive to be a contributor to the system will gradually fade into an inclination to take the free ride.

The proposals in the last two chapters are designed to reestablish a basic equity principle in the social security system: individuals who work and contribute to the program over a lifetime should receive benefits commensurate with the sacrifices they make throughout their lives to support the system and their own retirement. Applying this idea reduces the distortions in the system. The reforms reestablish the basic function of social security—to reduce the free rider problem—without introducing large disincentives to work and save, and they allow individuals to choose a more rational allocation of retirement resources between medical and nonmedical consumption.

These reforms complement the tax and pension reform proposals outlined in chapter 13. By making social security a more efficient mechanism to address the high discounter problem, pension policy can be set so that corporations can use pensions to maximize productivity. Individuals can either choose higher compensation levels in pension firms or save outside firms in competitive Individual Retirement Accounts. In either case, savings through pensions are not penalized by public policies that implicitly tax savers and reward those disinclined to save and work. Together these reforms markedly improve the long-term outlook for corporate efficiency, wages, and retirement income for future generations.

CHAPTER ONE

1. See Samuel Williamson, "The First Industrial Pensions," unpublished paper, Center for Pension and Retirement Research, Miami University, Oxford, Ohio, 1992, and M. Latimer, *Industrial Pension Systems* (New York: Industrial Relations Counselors, 1932).

2. The dominance of the theory is made apparent in recent reviews of the pension literature. For example, see Stuart Dorsey, "Pension Portability and Labor Market Efficiency: A Survey of the Literature," *Industrial and Labor Relations Review* 48 (January 1995): 276–92; Alan Gustman, Olivia Mitchell, and Thomas Steinmeier, "The Role of Pensions in the Labor Market: A Survey of the Literature," *Industrial Labor Relations Review* 47 (April 1994): 417–38; and Joseph Quinn, Richard Burkhauser, and Daniel Myers, *Passing the Torch: The Influence of Economic Incentives on Work and Retirement* (Kalamazoo, Mich.: Upjohn Institute, 1990).

3. The tax advantages of pensions are well known, and thus I do not review tax issues here. For a full treatment of pension tax issues, see Richard A. Ippolito, *An Economic Analysis of Pension Tax Policy in the United States* (Homewood, Ill.; Richard D. Irwin, 1990).

4. The plans were made feasible after the Internal Revenue Service issued regulations in 1981 defining the permissible boundaries within which the plans would be tax qualified. Before the legislation, thrift plans could exist, but employees' contributions could be made only on an after-tax basis. When benefits were paid, individuals received a tax exclusion of only the nominal amount of their original contributions. Thus the tax advantages on employees' contributions were clearly inferior to those characterizing 401k plans.

5. The Internal Revenue Code generally precludes pensions from paying proportionally higher pensions to higher-wage workers, though some exceptions are allowed. For a detailed discussion of the discrimination rules, see Everett T. Allen, Joseph Melone, Jerry Rosenbloom, and Jack VanDerhei, *Pension Planning,* 7th ed. (Homewood, Ill.: Richard D. Irwin, 1992).

CHAPTER TWO

1. See Dorsey, "Pension Portability," Gustman, Mitchell, and Steinmeier, "Role of Pensions," and Quinn, Burkhauser, and Myers, *Passing the Torch,* all at chapter 1, note 2.

2. Economic pension liabilities is a term used to distinguish the real pension liability of the firm, as distinguished from various accounting or actuarial concepts of pension liability. For a discussion of economic liabilities, see Richard Ippolito, "The Implicit Pension Contract and True Economic Pension Liabilities," *American Economic Review* 75 (December 1985): 1031; for a discussion of various pension liability concepts, see Dan McGill, K. Brown, J. Haley, and Sylvester Schieber, *Fundamentals of Private Pensions,* 7th ed. (Philadelphia: University of Pennsylvania Press for Pension Research Council, 1996).

3. While 61 percent of workers explicitly have benefits indexed to final wages, 22 percent earn credits in flat amounts per year of service (the rest have benefit formulas based on career earnings and other things). Flat benefit formulas, which are typically found in union plans, are periodically increased to reflect wage growth; hence, as a practical matter, flat benefit formulas can be treated analytically like final pay plans. Distributions of types of formulas are found in the U.S. Department of Labor, *Employee Benefits in Medium and Large Firms 1993,* BLS Bulletin 2456 (Washington, D.C.: GPO, 1994), table 137.

4. This estimate is as of 1996, based on unpublished information from the U.S. Department of Labor.

5. A description of the growth of the pension system and a discussion of its causes and consequences are given in Richard A. Ippolito, *Pensions, Economics, and Public Policy* (Homewood, Ill.: Dow Jones–Irwin for the Pension Research Council, 1986). A discussion of the tax treatment of pensions can be found in Congressional Budget Office, *Tax Policy for Pensions and Other Retirement Savings* (Washington, D.C.: GPO, 1987).

6. One important exception is Latimer, *Industrial Pension Systems,* at chapter 1, note 1.

7. For example, see Phillip Cagan, *The Effect of Pension Plans on Aggregate Savings: Evidence from a Sample Survey,* National Bureau of Economic Research Occasional Paper 95 (New York: Columbia University Press, 1965), and Alicia Munnell, "Private Pension Savings: New Evidence," *Journal of Political Economy* 84 (October 1976): 1013.

8. For example, see William Sharpe, "Corporate Pension Fund Policy," *Journal of Financial Economics* 3 (June 1976): 183–93, and Irwin Tepper and A. Affleck, "Pension Plan Liabilities and Corporate Financial Strategies," *Journal of Finance* 29 (December 1974): 1549–64.

9. Richard V. Burkhauser, "The Pension Acceptance Decision of Older Workers," *Journal of Human Resources* 14 (winter 1979): 63–75.

10. For example, see Joseph Quinn, "Microeconomic Determinants of Early Retirement: A Cross-Sectional View of Married Men," *Journal of Human Resources* 12 (summer 1977): 329–46.

11. See, for example, Richard Burkhauser and Joseph Quinn, "Is Mandatory Retirement Overrated? Evidence from the 1970s," *Journal of Human Resources*

18 (summer 1983): 337–58: Gary S. Fields and Olivia S. Mitchell, *Retirement, Pensions, and Social Security* (Cambridge: MIT Press, 1984); and Alan Gustman and Thomas Steinmeier, "A Structural Model of Retirement," *Econometrica* 54 (1986): 555–84.

12. Normal retirement age in a pension plan is the age at which a worker is entitled to take a full pension annuity. Workers often are allowed to retire "early," but they must accept a reduction to accommodate more years of collecting the pension. A common age for normal retirement is 65; early retirement age might be 55. See discussion in chapter 5.

13. Before 1987, approximately 50 percent of pension-covered workers were in plans that froze benefits at normal retirement (see U.S. Department of Labor, *Employee Benefits in Medium and Large Firms*, at chapter 2, note 3). The Omnibus Reconciliation Act (OBRA) of 1986 outlawed the freezing of credits solely as a function of age. However, the firm can freeze benefits after a certain level of service is attained.

14. If the worker retires at age $N + 1$ in this plan, he loses his pension annuity $bRW_R$ during the extra year he works; that is, $P_{R+1} - P_R = bRW_R$, and thus the effective wage rate during his last year of work is $W_{R+1} = W_R(1 - bR)$.

15. In terms of the previous note, $b = .01$ and $R = 30$. Recent work suggests that in some circumstances the firm may selectively increase wages for some workers to offset the pension penalty, thereby inducing them to stay with the firm past normal retirement age. See Robert Clark and Ann McDermed, "Earnings and Pension Compensation: The Effect of Eligibility," *Quarterly Journal of Economics* 100 (1986): 341–61.

16. Fewer than 10 percent of pension plans offer full actuarial adjustments to workers after normal retirement age (U.S. Department of Labor, *Employee Benefits in Medium and Large Firms*, BLS Bulletin 2363 [Washington, D.C.: GPO, 1989], table 90). Also see Bankers Trust Company, *Corporate Pension Plan Study* (New York: Bankers Trust, 1980). Some empirical estimates of late retirement penalties are found in Fields and Mitchell, *Retirement, Pensions*, at chapter 2, note 11; and Burkhauser, "Pension Acceptance," at chapter 2, note 9.

17. There is some evidence that adjustments during the age interval $[E,R]$ are not always economically equivalent, that is, that early retirement may be favored in some formulas and discouraged in others. See discussion in chapter 5.

18. See, for example, U.S. Department of Labor, *Labor Mobility and Private Pension Plans*, BLS Bulletin 1407 (Washington, D.C.: GPO, 1964).

19. Jeremy Bulow, "What Are Corporate Pension Liabilities?" *Quarterly Journal of Economics* 96 (August 1982): 435.

20. This is not the first paper that modeled the defined benefit pension contract in a labor market context. See, for example, B. Barnow and R. Ehrenberg, "The Costs of Defined Benefit Plans and Adjustments," *Quarterly Journal of Economics* 93 (November 1979): 523–40. The Bulow paper, however, was the first to reconcile the model with workers' effective pension savings rates over their tenure cycle.

21. Accountants label their calculations "accrued pension liabilities." They appear in a footnote to the firm's balance sheet.

22. The model presented in this section is based on one developed more fully

in Ippolito, "Implicit Pension Contract," at chapter 2, note 2; and *Pensions Economics,* at chapter 2, note 5. The idea of the implicit pension is not new. The notion that pensions affect worker tenure in the firm was suggested in Gary S. Becker, *Human Capital: A Theoretical and Empirical Analysis* (New York: Columbia University Press, 1964). Also see Gary Becker and George Stigler, "Law Enforcement Malfeasance, and Compensation for Enforcers," *Journal of Legal Studies* 3 (January 1974): 1–18. The idea that pensions are implicit contracts was also beginning to emerge in the finance literature. See Jack L. Treynor, "The Principles of Corporate Finance," *Journal of Finance* 32 (May 1977): 627–38; and Patrick Regan, W. Priest, and Jack L. Treynor, *The Financial Reality of Pension Funding under ERISA* (Homewood, Ill.: Dow Jones–Irwin, 1976).

23. Several of the early papers in the "new" pension economics were directed at testing for compensating wage differentials in firms where pensions were offered. Although these studies generally confirmed a wage-pension trade-off, they suffered in part from lack of a theory of how workers saved for pensions over the tenure cycle. See Ronald Ehrenberg, "Retirement System Characteristics and Compensating Wage Differentials in the Public Sector," *Industrial and Labor Relations Review* 33 (1980): 470–83; Bradley Schiller and Randall Weiss, "Pensions and Wages: A Test for Equalizing Differences," *Review of Economics and Statistics* 62 (1980): 529–38; and Robert Smith, "Compensating Differentials for Pensions and Under-funding in the Public Sector," *Review of Economics and Statistics* 63 (1981): 463–68.

24. More precisely, if a worker does not quit now, he may quit before retirement age sometime in the future. The potential for a future quit works to reduce the capital loss from quitting now because the probability of collecting a "stay pension" by not quitting now is less than unity. See Edward Lazear and Robert Moore, "Pensions and Mobility," in *Pensions in the U.S. Economy,* ed. Zvi Bodie, John B. Shoven, and David A. Wise (Chicago: University of Chicago Press, 1988).

25. That is, if expression (2.5) is differentiated with respect to $a$, it is apparent that the change is increasing in $a$.

26. See Clark and McDermed, "Earnings and Pension Compensation," at chapter 2, note 15; Ippolito, "Labor Contract," at chapter 2, note 2; Christopher Cornwell, Stuart Dorsey, and Nasser Mehrzad, "Opportunistic Behavior by Firms in Implicit Pension Contracts," *Journal of Human Resources* 26 (fall 1991): 704–25; and Olivia Mitchell and S. Pozzenbon, "Wages, Pensions and the Wage-Pension Tradeoff," paper presented at the American Economic Association Meetings, New Orleans, 1986.

27. See, for example, Lazear and Moore, "Pensions and Mobility," at chapter 2, note 24; Olivia Mitchell, "Fringe Benefits and Labor Mobility," *Journal of Human Resources* 17 (spring 1982): 286; and B. Schiller and R. Weiss, "The Impact of Private Pension Plans on Firm Attachment," *Review of Economics and Statistics* 61 (August 1979): 369.

28. See Steven Allen, Robert Clark, and Daniel Sumner, "Post-retirement Adjustments of Pension Benefits," *Journal of Human Resources* 21 (winter 1986): 118–27, and "Post-retirement Benefit Increases in the 1980s," in *Trends in Pensions 1992,* ed. John Turner and Daniel Beller (Washington, D.C.: GPO, 1992).

Also see Alan Gustman and Thomas Steinmeier, "Cost of Living Adjustments in Pensions," in *As the Workforce Ages: Costs, Benefits, and Policy Challenges,* ed. Olivia Mitchell (Ithaca: ILR Press, Cornell University, 1993), 147.

29.   See Robert Clark, "Employer Health Care Plans for Retirees," unpublished paper, North Carolina State University, 1987.

30.   The relation between compensation structure and self-selection is described in Steven Salop and Joanne Salop, "Self Selection and Turnover in the Labor Market," *Quarterly Journal of Economics* 90 (November 1976): 620–27.

31.   The wage profile idea is found in Becker, *Human Capital,* at chapter 2, note 22. Although Becker recognizes pensions as a possible substitute for twisting wage profiles, this idea was not developed in subsequent literature. A more recent wage twist theory of worker tenure is found in Edward Lazear, "Why Is There Mandatory Retirement?" *Journal of Political Economy* 87 (December 1979): 1261–84. In this paper, mandatory retirement is invoked to force "overpaid" older workers to retire.

CHAPTER THREE

1.   See Becker, *Human Capital,* at chapter 2, note 22.

2.   Presumably, workers who have a high propensity to quit are not attracted to jobs that award full compensation only on condition that the worker stay with the firm over the long run. See Salop and Salop, "Self Selection," at chapter 2, note 30.

3.   Workers who evade the responsibilities of their jobs increase the likelihood of getting fired. In a wage tilt scheme, getting fired is costly because it denies dismissed workers the opportunity to earn high wages in later tenure years. As a result, workers presumably work harder to increase their chances of staying with the firm over the long run. See Lazear, "Why Is There Mandatory Retirement?" at chapter 2, note 31.

4.   In chapter 8 I advance the idea that wage tilt creates an indenture of sorts, and thus the firm is required to pay workers a premium.

5.   In year one the worker's wage is $7,350; in year two it is approximately $7,524; in year three, $7,700; and so on. The accumulated difference between these wages and the $10,000 alternative wage (in real terms) is $20,000.

6.   See, for example, Katherine Abraham and Henry Farber, "Job Duration, Seniority and Earnings," *American Economic Review* 77 (June 1987): 278–97, and Joseph Altonji and Robert Shakotko, "Do Wages Rise with Seniority?" *Review of Economic Studies* 54 (July 1987): 437–60.

7.   Compared with saving in a tax-exposed vehicle (including accumulation of deferred wages in the firm), the worker's lifetime tax burden can easily be 40 percent lower using the pension vehicle. See Ippolito, *Economic Analysis,* at chapter 1, note 3.

8.   When mandatory retirement was legal, an explicit mandatory retirement age was seen as a way to close out the contract. See Lazear, "Why Is There Mandatory Retirement?" at chapter 2, note 31. For a discussion of mandatory retirement and the implications of the Age Discrimination Act, see Burkhauser and Quinn, "Is Mandatory Retirement Overrated?" at chapter 2, note 11.

9.   Alternatively, the firm can rely on penalties in the social security system to encourage retirement no later than age 65. See Burkhauser and Quinn, "Is Mandatory Retirement Overrated?" at chapter 2, note 11.

10.   See discussion in chapters 2, 4, and 5.

11.   The wage tilt theory can be modified so that a defined benefit pension plan is also offered in the firm to provide the means (through economically unfair pension annuities) to terminate the contract. In this case the question arises why wage tilt is needed if a defined benefit plan already effects a deferred wage scheme on a tax-favored basis. In chapter 8 I suggest some situations in which *both* pensions and wage tilt are required to effect long tenure in the firm.

12.   See Becker, *Human Capital,* and Becker and Stigler, "Law Enforcement Malfeasance," at chapter 2, note 22.

13.   The theory is related to Jovanovic in the sense that no real distinction is required between quits and layoffs. See Boyan Jovanovic, "Job Matching and the Theory of Turnover," *Journal of Political Economy* 87 (October 1979): 972–90. Empirical work supports this notion: pensions appear to be negatively related to quits and layoffs. See Steven Allen, Robert Clark, and Ann A. McDermed, "Pensions, Bonding and Lifetime Jobs," *Journal of Human Resources* 28 (summer 1993): 463–81; Ann Bartel and George Borjas, "Middle-Age Job Mobility: Its Determinants and Consequences," in *Men in Their Pre-retirement Years,* ed. S. M. Wolfbein (Philadelphia: Temple University School of Business Administration, 1977); Mitchell, "Fringe Benefits and Labor Mobility," at chapter 2, note 27, and Cornwell et al., "Opportunistic Behavior," at chapter 2, note 26.

14.   Even though the notion of pension capital losses is relatively new in the literature, many studies have demonstrated empirically that pensions and mobility are negatively related. For example, see Gustman, Mitchell, and Steinmeier, "Role of Pensions," at chapter 1, note 2. In contrast, wage tilt seldom, if ever, appears in quit studies. One exception is George Borjas, "Job Mobility and Earnings over the Life Cycle," unpublished paper, University of California at Santa Barbara, 1980. Ann Bartel and George Borjas study the relation between mobility and *future* wage growth; see their chapter "Wage Growth and Job Turnover: An Empirical Analysis," in *Studies in Labor Markets,* ed. Sherwin Rosen (Chicago: University of Chicago Press, 1981).

15.   See David McCarthy, *Findings from Survey of Private Pension Benefit Amounts* (Washington, D.C.: GPO, 1985).

16.   Consider a two-period model: individuals work for two periods, then retire. For simplicity, suppose the firm maintains an equal age density of workers in both periods, and workers turn over with probability $q$ during each period (the result survives relaxation of both assumptions, albeit with somewhat more complicated expressions). The firm replaces quitters at the beginning of each new period with workers of the same age as those who quit. Those retiring consist of two groups, one that survived both periods in the firm (these number $(1 - q)(1 - q)$), and one that joined the firm to replace those that quit after one period and did not quit during the second period (these number $q(1 - q)$). To be consistent with the database used below, quits are assumed unvested in the pension (the data do not include vested quits); hence there are $1 - q$ retirees each

period. Average tenure is related to the quit rate in the following way: $S_R = [q(1 - q) + 2(1 - q)(1 - q)]/(1 - q) = 1 + (1 - q)$.

17.   See Robert Hutchens, "Delayed Payment Contracts and a Firm's Propensity to Hire Older Workers," *Journal of Labor Economics* 4 (October 1986): 439–57.

18.   To make this test, I use the 1979 Current Population Survey (CPS), May supplement. For each three-digit SIC industry that has at least twenty observations, I calculate a simple wage-tenure equation: ln wage = $a_1$ + $a_2$ ln tenure + $a_3$ age + $a_4$ union + $a_5$ education + $a_6$ female + $a_7$ black. Because of the lack of data, I used a double-log wage-tenure estimating equation rather than single-log with tenure and tenure-squared as independent variables.

I then calculate the age of each worker with less than two years of tenure in each SIC industry, excluding individuals aged 55 or older (see below): This is my estimate of average age of hire (Age Hire). Industries that have fewer than ten hires are excluded. The following regression is estimated for the eighty-three SIC industries left in the data: Age Hire = 27.1 − 3.16 $a_2$ − .11 PENS + other variables. The $t$-statistics on these three coefficients are 9.22, .85, and .06, respectively. (Other variables in the regression include the mean percentage of two firm-size dummy variables, the mean industry wage rate, and the percentage of the industry's workforce unionized, female, and nonwhite). $R^2 = .066$.

The variable $a_2$ is the estimated coefficient on the tenure variable in the within-industry wage estimates, and PENS is the percentage of workers in the industry covered by a pension. The $t$-values on the coefficients of these variables are close to zero, suggesting no statistically significant relation between age of hire in the industry and wage tilt and pension coverage.

19.   I control for firm size, union coverage, sex, race, and one-digit industry code. I do not have measures of workers' skill levels, such as education, and thus I include a measure of the worker's wage. To estimate average wage, I start with the wage for each worker for the last year of full-time work before retirement, then reduce it for prior tenure years back to the average midcareer tenure using the estimated wage growth parameter in the firm. The median of these wages for workers in each firm is used to measure the average firm wage.

20.   The May supplement includes workers in the third and fourth rotations; these are matched against the seventh and eight rotations in March.

21.   I control for age, tenure, their square terms, years of education, firm-size dummy variables, gender, race, dummy variables denoting city and SMSA location, and one-digit industry and occupation codes.

22.   The point estimate on wage tilt is $b_j(1 - p)p$, where $p$ is the portion of positive values for the independent variable and $b_j$ is the estimated coefficient on wage tilt. The incremental effect on the pension term is found by calculating the quit probability setting the pension variable to one or zero, all other variables set to their mean values.

23.   The coefficients on the other independent variables, reported in the notes to table 3.4, are similar to those found in other quit studies. For example, see Mitchell, "Fringe Benefits," at chapter 2, note 27.

24.   I calculate the probability of quitting when the pension dummy variable is set alternatively to one and zero, setting other variables to their mean values.

25. The results are not specific to particular firm sizes or unionization. To test these ideas, I include interaction terms between the pension and wage tilt variables with various firm-size dummy variables and unionization. The coefficients on the wage tilt–firm size interaction terms exhibit $t$-statistics less that .67 in all cases. The pension effect is negative and statistically significant across all firm-size categories. The interaction terms between wage tilt and unionization and between pension coverage and unionization are insignificantly different from zero.

Additionally, the results are not specific to the 1979 CPS. I reestimated the same equation using the May 1988 CPS pension supplement. In these estimates, the $t$-value on the tilt variable is .54; the incremental effect on the pension variable is $-.188$ with a $t$-value on the underlying estimated coefficient equal to 4.46. The mean of the dependent variable in the 1988 data is .26.

26. Similar findings are reported elsewhere. For summaries of this literature, see Alan L. Gustman and Thomas L. Steinmeier, *Pension Incentives and Job Mobility* (Kalamazoo, Mich.: Upjohn Institute, 1994), and Gustman, Mitchell, and Steinmeier, "Role of Pensions," at chapter 1, note 2.

27. I discount using a 3 percent interest rate, which is reasonable given the prevalence of inflation adjustments during retirement. See Allen et al., "Postretirement," at chapter 2, note 28. The inclusion of year dummy variables in the regression mitigates the importance of the particular interest rate used.

28. Usually, benefits with J&S provisions are reduced to account for longevity of both spouses. Accounting for this discount prevents the dummy variable from being biased downward for firms that have disproportionate numbers of annuitants covered by J&S provisions.

29. Usually survivor benefits are 50 percent of those collected while the retiree is living. Including the beneficiary dummy variable prevents pension amounts from being biased downward in some plans owing to a disproportionate number of surviving beneficiaries' collecting pensions after the death of the retiree.

30. That is, pension benefits are those paid in 1978, not the year of first receipt; wages are expressed in 1978 dollars. Thus, if some inflation erosion occurs during retirement, benefits for workers retiring before 1978 are underestimated as a percentage of lifetime wages. The year dummies correct for this problem.

31. Wages in the social security wage history are limited by the maximum social security wage base. When this constraint is binding, I use an algorithm provided by Fox to impute wages. His algorithm is based on knowledge of the quarter of coverage within each year when the maximum is reached. My own tests of this algorithm, using data for which actual wages are known, show that his estimates are not biased. Moreover, to ensure that these imputations are not driving the results, I reestimate the equations using only wage profiles not affected by the algorithm. The qualitative results are the same as those reported in table 3.3. See Alan Fox, "Earnings, Replacement Rates and Total Income," *Social Security Bulletin* 45 (October 1982): 3–23, and Ippolito, "Labor Contract," at chapter 2, note 2.

The median average annualized rate of within-firm wage growth for the 109 plan sample is .74 percent per year. This result is consistent with those reported in Abraham and Farber and Altonji and Shakotko (at chapter 3, note 6), who find that wages grow with tenure at an average rate of less than 1 percent per year. Of the firms in the sample, 25 percent evince average wage growth (net of inflation and economywide real wage increases) less than −.40 percent per year and 25 percent evince growth of more than 2.81 percent.

32.  The midcareer wage is calculated using expression 3.2.

33.  Since the careers of retirees in my sample preceded ERISA vesting rules enacted in 1974, I cannot be sure when vesting occurred. I therefore assume that vesting requirements are satisfied in all plans at the midcareer tenure level. This is not an important assumption because, as shown in the discussion above, unless vesting provisions are very conservative, most of the pension capital loss is attributable not to vesting, but to the loss of benefit indexing to final wages. If vesting occurs beyond the midpoint of careers in some firms, the estimates of pension capital losses are understated.

34.  Interest rates during the late 1950s and 1960s were in the range of 5 percent. Allowing for some inflation adjustments after retirement, a 3 percent discount rate is reasonable. The ten-year Treasury bond rate was less than 4.33 percent during the 1950s and ranged from 3.88 to 5.07 from 1960 to 1967.

CHAPTER FOUR

1.  In this chapter I describe the federal retirement system for federal workers who started their federal employment before 1984. Those hired in 1984 and after are covered by a pension more closely aligned with private sector standards.

2.  See McCarthy, *Findings from Survey,* at chapter 3, note 15.

3.  See Allen et al., "Post-retirement," at chapter 2, note 28.

4.  See McCarthy, *Findings from Survey,* at chapter 3, note 15; U.S. Department of Labor, *Employee Benefits,* at chapter 2, note 3; and Bankers Trust, *Corporate Pension Plan Study,* at chapter 2, note 16.

5.  The composite is drawn from data describing the characteristics and generosity of private sector pension plans (see sources cited in previous note). The private sector firm is assumed to have normal retirement at age 62 and early retirement at age 55 (subject to a 4 percent reduction for each year of retirement before age 62). The annual benefit is set equal to 1 percent times service at retirement times final wage.

6.  The latter assumption understates the relative quit costs in the federal sector because the federal pension explicitly indexes for inflation after retirement, whereas in the private sector adjustments are ad hoc and incomplete. However, since research has shown that in the private sector ad hoc inflation adjustments during retirement have accommodated as much as 75 percent of inflation, this bias is not important. See Allen et al., "Post-retirement," at chapter 2, note 28.

7.  The numbers in figure 4.1 are invariant to taxes as long as income taxes are proportional. In this case, after-tax losses are $(1 - t)CL$, where $t$ is the tax rate and $CL$ is the pension capital loss. Compared with the after-tax wage $(1 - t)W$, the ratio remains $CL/W$. The proportionality assumption is made for these calculations for simplicity, but if tax rates are typically lower during retire-

ment than during work years, the numbers demonstrated in table 4.1 and used in the empirical work below understate the importance of capital losses compared with after-tax wages.

8.    Moreover, as demonstrated in chapter 11, firms that impose penalties on quitters must pay a wage premium, which is more attractive to workers who are natural "stayers."

9.    This model is based on one described in Salop and Salop, "Self Selection," at chapter 2, note 30, or Jovanovic, "Matching," at chapter 3, note 13.

10.    An alternative method is to include actual pension capital losses in a quit equation. This method is appropriate if workers affiliate randomly with firms that have different pension capital losses. My choice of the self-selection model is based on empirical work that demonstrates its superiority over competing models. See, for example, Allen, Clark, and McDermed, "Job Mobility," at chapter 3, note 13.

11.    The CPS data yield ten-month turnover rates (which include permanent layoffs) equal to 25 and 11 percent for private and federal workers. The actual twelve-month turnover rate (including permanent layoffs) for manufacturing industries was 24 percent (U.S. Department of Labor, Bureau of Labor Statistics, *Employment and Earnings, United States,* [Washington, D.C.: GPO, 1979]). The twelve-month quit rate for federal workers was 10.7 percent in 1979 (U.S. Office of Personnel Management, *Report of Federal Civilian Employment* [Washington, D.C.: GPO, 1979]); there are virtually no permanent layoffs in the federal government. Thus the pseudo turnover rates are higher than true turnover rates, but the ratio of private to federal turnover rates is close to its natural relation using actual turnover data.

12.    These variables include age, tenure, their square terms, education, union coverage, race, gender, firm size, nine major occupational variables, and seven major industry dummy variables. The results were not sensitive to the inclusion of the wage rate.

13.    Approximately once each five years, the CPS includes a pension supplement, usually in May. I compared these data with the reinterviews the following March for both the 1988 and 1993 data.

14.    I calculate the quit cost for both the private and federal workers as a percentage of the wage, using the same assumptions underlying figure 4.1. If this calculation is denoted by $x$, then the resulting equation is $\ln(x) = -6.3 + .17$ Age $- .0023$ Age$^2 + .28$ Tenure $- .008$ Tenure$^2 + 1.35$ FEDERAL, $R^2 = .72$, Observations $= 4,465$, where all the coefficients are significant at the 99 percent level of confidence (the $t$-statistic on the coefficient 1.35 is 33.4). The value of $\exp(1.35)$ is 3.85.

15.    See James Long, "Are Government Workers Overpaid? Alternative Evidence," *Journal of Human Resources* 17 (winter 1982): 123–31.

16.    See U.S. Office of Personnel Management, *Reforming Federal Pay: An Examination of More Realistic Pay Alternatives* (Washington, D.C.: GPO, 1985).

17.    Ibid.

18.    If the plan so provides, the worker is often given the balance in the account on departure. The balance can be rolled over to an Individual Retirement Account to continue accumulating tax free until retirement age (age 59.5 or later).

19.   This is a slight simplification. In reality, the first ten years of service are rewarded at rates between 1.5 and 1.75 percent. And the wage used in the formula is the average of the high three salary years.

20.   For convenience, I ignore other fringe benefits like health coverage and vacation time.

21.   These workers can retire with full benefits after thirty years, or at age 60 after twenty-five years of service, or at age 62 if they have at least five years of service. In all cases, there is no "early" retirement option: workers must wait until they attain the age at which full benefits are available. This somewhat peculiar characteristic of the federal pension means there is a unique age for each employee at which the penalties for leaving the government are zero.

22.   Retirements exclude special situation retirements owing to reductions in force and the like; they also exclude disability retirements.

23.   The oversample works to improve the efficiency of the estimates. The weights eliminate the bias in the coefficients imparted by the choice-based sample.

24.   The 2 percent estimate is derived by solving the logit model setting the independent variables to their mean values and setting the eligibility variable to zero.

25.   This number is derived in the same way as in the preceding note, except the eligibility variable is set to unity.

26.   That is, $(1 - .235)^5 = .26$, where .235 is the retirement rate of those who attain eligibility for full pension benefits.

27.   The layouts of the tapes change somewhat over the samples, and the industry designation for federal workers also changes somewhat, requiring some care in setting up the data. For the most part, however, the data are comparable.

CHAPTER FIVE

1.   That is, $e^{.08 \, 10 \, \text{years}} = 2.225$, and thus the projected wage is $2.225 \times \$30,000$, which is \$66,766.

2.   That is, $1\% \times 20 \text{ years} \times \$66,766 = \$13,353$.

3.   That is, using continuous discounting at 8 percent, and assuming death at age 80, the present-value factor of an annual annuity at age 65 is 8.73. Discounting to age 55, I multiply by .449 ($= e^{-.08 \, 10 \, \text{years}}$), which gives the amount: $8.73 \times .449 \times \$13,353 \approx \$52,400$. Additional service accruals from ages 55 to 65 lead to higher benefits, but presumably these will be offset by implicit pension contributions in the form of lower cash wages over these years. Thus net pension wealth at age 55 is not expected to be affected by the option to accumulate additional service accruals. I have illustrated this point in chapter 4 for the case of federal pensions.

4.   That is, $1\% \times 20 \text{ years} \times \$30,000 = \$6,000$.

5.   The calculation uses the same discounting factors as note 3, except that the age 65 annuity is set to \$6,000 instead of \$13,353.

6.   That is, using continuous discounting at 8 percent, and assuming death at age 80, the present value of a \$1 annuity starting at age 55 is \$10.80. Thus $\$52,400/10.8 \approx \$4,850$.

7.   Using the same discount factor as in note 6, we have $\$23,500/10.8 \approx \$2,180$.

8. That is, $e^{-.021 \; 10 \; \text{years}} \approx .811$, which is approximately equal to the ratio of the age 55 annuities to the age 65 annuities ($4,850/$6,000).

9. That is, $e^{-.10 \; 10 \; \text{years}} \approx .36$, which is approximately equal to the ratio of the annuities $2,180/$6,000.

10. If I recognized the possibility of death between ages 55 and 65, the reduction factors would increase slightly, but the results would closely approximate those depicted above. For example, if I used a 6 percent interest rate in the calculation, the actuarial reduction factor would be 6 percent per year. McGill et al. calculate the reduction to be 6.3 percent per year using the same interest rate and the UP-84 mortality table. See McGill et al., *Fundamentals,* at chapter 2, note 2.

11. The divergence between actuarial and economic equivalencies in pension plans does not extend in the same way to the social security system between ages 62 and 65. The actuarial formula in social security equilibrates the present value of the benefit streams over this age range in real dollars, recognizing full indexing of the primary insurance amount during the period when the benefit is postponed.

12. If the pension follows the practice of increasing benefits during retirement to offset 50 percent of inflation, the latter reduction would be 2.6 percent. Cost of living adjustments after retirement typically amounted to half the inflation rate during the late 1960s and 1970s. See Allen et al., "Post-retirement Adjustments," at chapter 2, note 28.

13. Usually the early benefit is available if the worker has ten years of service. See U.S. Department of Labor, *Employee Benefits,* at chapter 2, note 3.

14. For example, consider a worker who leaves the firm at age 50. Suppose the firm permits him to collect his subsidized benefit starting at age 55. His benefit is calculated based on his age 50 salary and service level and the annuity collected from age 55 until 80 (the assumed death age), discounted at 8 percent to age 50. Label this number $E$. The alternative is for the worker to stay until age 65, in which case I calculate his annuity based on his age 65 wage (which by assumption is equal to his age 50 wage plus accumulated wage growth, where the growth rate is assumed equal to the interest rate) but retain his age 50 service level. This annuity is discounted back to age 50. Label this number $N$. If the age 50 wage is denoted by $W_{50}$, then the pension loss depicted in figure 5.2 is $(N - E)/W_{50}$.

15. See U.S. Department of Labor, *Employee Benefits,* at chapter 2, note 3. The survey excludes firms with fewer than one hundred workers.

16. That is, 48 percent award full benefits at age 65, and 21 percent at age 62.

17. For example, if the rule of 85 prevails, a worker aged 55 with thirty years of service can retire with full benefits.

18. See Council of Economic Advisers, *The Economic Report of the President* (Washington, D.C.: GPO, February 1995), table B-72.

19. For example, a plan might award a 3 percent per year reduction for the first three years of early retirement, and 5 percent per year for earlier retirement ages.

20. This number corresponds to the lighter-line schedule (solid boxes) in figure 5.4, because the firm acts like a low discounter—it discounts at the market interest rate. Even though the choice of early retirement is perceived as advantageous by the high discounter, in fact his decision confers a gain to the firm.

21.  That is, I set the interest rate and wage growth to 8 percent per annum; the benefit is 1 percent times final wage times tenure at retirement; benefits are not indexed to inflation after retirement.

22.  Recall that death is assumed to occur at age 80, that normal retirement age is 65, and that early retirement age is 55.

23.  See U.S. Department of Labor, *Employee Benefits*, at chapter 2, note 3.

24.  For example, see Lynn Karoly and Jeanette Rogowski, "The Effects of Health Insurance on the Decision to Retire," *Industrial and Labor Relations Review* 48 (1994): 103–23. Some work suggests the effect is modest; see Alan Gustman and Thomas Steinmeier, "Employer Provided Health Insurance and Retirement Behavior," *Industrial and Labor Relations Review* 48 (1994): 124–40.

25.  See U.S. Department of Labor, *Employee Benefits*, at chapter 2, note 3.

26.  See chapter 4 for the case of the federal government. Also see Fields and Mitchell, *Retirement*, at chapter 2, note 11; Burkhauser, "Pension Acceptance," at chapter 2, note 9; Laurence J. Kotlikoff and David A. Wise, "Labor Compensation and the Structure of Private Pension Plans: Evidence for Contractual Versus Spot Labor Markets," in *Pensions, Labor, and Individual Choice,* ed. David A. Wise (Chicago: University of Chicago Press, 1985); and James Stock and David Wise, "Pensions, the Option Value of Work, and Retirement," *Econometrica* 58 (September 1990): 1151–80.

27.  The survey is described in detail in McCarthy, *Findings from Survey,* at chapter 3, note 15.

28.  The provisions of ERISA and their likely impact on labor markets can be found in Richard Ippolito, "A Study of the Regulatory Effects of ERISA," *Journal of Law and Economics* 31 (April 1988): 85–125.

29.  Tenure is measured by service credited in the pension plan. Since virtually all defined benefit plans award past service credit when they begin (particularly plans established in the 1950s, as most of these were), this is likely an accurate measure of starting ages in the firm.

30.  This point is made forcefully by Hutchens, "Delayed Payment Contracts," at chapter 3, note 17.

31.  The point estimate is equal to $p(1 - p)b,$ where $p$ is percentage of the mean of the dependent variable and $b$ is the estimated coefficient on the service variable. Thus, we have $.053 \times .4 \times .6 \times 10$ years $\approx .13.$

## CHAPTER SIX

1.  Also see Olivia Mitchell and R. Luzadis, "Changes in Pension Incentives through Time," *Industrial Labor Relations Review* 42 (October 1988): 100–108.

2.  For a good summary, see Quinn, Burkhauser, and Myers, *Passing the Torch,* at chapter 1, note 2.

3.  One exception is Donald O. Parsons, "The Decline in Labor Force Participation," *Journal of Political Economy* 88 (February 1980): 117–34.

4.  The definition of retirement is taken from the Current Population Survey. Here retirement is defined as withdrawal from the labor force. Individuals who are retired from their main jobs but still employed part time are considered to be still working.

5.  A summary of much of this literature is found in Lawrence Thompson,

"The Social Security Reform Debate," *Journal of Economic Literature* 21 (December 1983): 1425–67.

6.   See Robert Moffitt, "Trends in Social Security Wealth by Cohort," in *Economic Transfers in the United States,* ed. Marilyn Moon (Chicago: University of Chicago Press, 1977).

7.   See U.S. Social Security Administration, *Social Security Bulletin, Annual Statistical Supplement, 1993* (Washington, D.C.: GPO, 1994).

8.   The problem occurred because of the nonlinear social security benefit formula. Higher replacement rates were given for the first portion of average monthly wages than for subsequent amounts. By not fully indexing average wages but indexing the formula (including the so-called kink points), the system assigned a relatively high replacement rate to an ever larger portion of average wages for each succeeding retiree cohort. See Alicia H. Munnell, *The Future of Social Security* (Washington, D.C.: Brookings Institution, 1977).

9.   See Phillip Rones, "Using the CPS to Track Retirement Trends among Older Men," *Monthly Labor Review* 108 (February 1985): 46–49.

10.   The disincentive does not exist between ages 62 and 65 because appropriate adjustments are made to postponed benefit receipts.

11.   See Alan Blinder, Roger Gordon, and Donald Wise, "Reconsidering the Work Disincentives of Social Security," *National Tax Journal* 33 (December 1980): 431–42, and Richard Burkhauser and John Turner, "Can 25 Million Americans Be Wrong?" *National Tax Journal* 34 (December 1981): 467–72.

12.   See Parsons, "Decline," at chapter 6, note 3.

13.   U.S. Social Security Administration, *Social Security Bulletin, Annual Statistical Supplement, 1993* at chapter 6, note 7.

14.   See Gary Burtless, "Social Security, Unanticipated Benefit Increases and the Timing of Retirement," *Review of Economic Studies* 53 (October 1986): 781–805.

15.   See Fields and Mitchell, *Retirement, Pensions,* at chapter 2, note 11; and Gary Burtless and Robert Moffitt, "The Choice of Retirement Age and Post-retirement Hours of Work," *Journal of Labor Economics* 3 (April 1985): 209–36.

16.   The difference that remains after accounting for the 1977 wage indexing is attributable to the inclusion of two zero-wage years in the calculation for the age 55 retiree, and growth in real wages.

17.   See Alan Gustman and Thomas Steinmeier, "Changing the Social Security Rules for Workers over 65," *Industrial and Labor Relations Review* 44 (1991): 733–45.

18.   I am indebted to the authors for reestimating their model at my request to specifically address this question. Their model was set up to analyze the social security effects with the 1983 Amendments in place. They changed their model to include nominal wage histories in the benefits formula instead of indexed wages, holding the PIA constant at age 62. The results represent the average effects for cohorts reaching age 55 in 1976 through 1997, though their model does not generate significant changes among cohorts. During this projection period, they did not put in place the scheduled changes in the social security retirement ages, the

delayed income credit, and the reduction in the earnings test as specified under the 1983 Amendments.

19.   See Harold Iams, "Characteristics of the Longest Job for Newly Retired Workers: Findings from the New Beneficiary Survey," *Social Security Bulletin* 48 (March 1985): 5–21.

20.   See Alan Gustman and Thomas Steinmeier, "Partial Retirement and the Analysis of Retirement Behavior," *Industrial Labor Relations Review* 37 (April 1984): 403–16.

21.   Bankers Trust Company, *Corporate Pension Plan Study,* at chapter 2, note 16. These data have been augmented by another sample comprising one hundred collectively bargained pension plans compiled by Olivia Mitchell using Bureau of Labor Statistics data over the period 1960 to 1980. See Mitchell and Luzadis, "Changes in Pension Incentives," at chapter 6, note 1.

22.   Bankers' publications employ somewhat confusing terminology. "Early" retirement in the Bankers' data is retirement before age 65; normal retirement generally refers to age 65. Usually, normal retirement age is the age of eligibility for full benefits, and early retirement refers to retirement with reduced benefits. I changed Bankers' terminology in the text to conform to the norm by substituting "age 65" for "normal retirement age" in the Bankers' data.

23.   The remaining plans had formulas in between: they offered either actuarially subsidized benefits at the earliest ages of eligibility but not full benefits until age 65, or else actuarially fair benefits at early ages but full benefits before age 65.

24.   U.S. Department of Labor, *Labor Mobility,* at chapter 2, note18; and U.S. Department of Labor, *Employee Benefits,* at chapter 2, note 3.

25.   For calculating these numbers, I include in the age 55 category plans that have a service requirement only (no age requirement); a requirement involving the total of age plus service (with no specific age restrictions); or an age of eligibility less than 55. In the 1964 report, ages of eligibility for full benefits before age 65 are found in early retirement tables under the heading "no reduction." All numbers are derived from U.S Department of Labor, *Labor Mobility,* at chapter 2, note 18; and U.S. Department of Labor, *Employee Benefits,* at chapter 2, note 3.

26.   Several effects can stem from the availability of earlier retirement. First, the actuarial subsidy—even if not economically fair—reduces the cost of leaving the firm compared with a full actuarial reduction. Second, high discounters may have found the early out option attractive, using their higher subjective discount rates. And third, some reaction could have occurred owing to a liquidity effect. That is, in the face of dramatic unanticipated wealth effects in the social security system after 1970, workers may have wanted to retire earlier than planned, perhaps earlier than age 62. If they had not set aside savings for such a contingency, the availability of economically equivalent pension annuities at earlier ages over the period may have eased some of this adjustment. Recall from figure 6.1 that the liquidity effect may have been constraining for many workers over the period, as evinced by the sudden shift from age 65 to age 62 during the 1970s as the most popular age of retirement.

27.   See Iams, "Characteristics of the Longest Job," at chapter 6, note 19.

28.   These data are based on the 1969 and 1983 Newly Entitled Beneficiaries

Surveys conducted by the Social Security Administration. Actual pension coverage ratios were 52 and 68 percent over the two surveys, but I multiplied these numbers by 80 percent to account for some defined contribution plan coverage (Ippolito, *Pensions, Economics,* at chapter 2, note 5).

29.  I analyzed plans in the U.S. Department of Labor's Benefit Amounts Survey (see chapter 5). Of those that permitted retirement with full benefits before 65 (as evinced by some retirees' actually taking retirement with full benefits before 65 during the period 1976 to 1978), only about one-third retired on full benefits before age 65. In addition, an unknown portion of those retiring on reduced benefits may have satisfied the requirements for full benefits before age 65 had they chosen to postpone retirement. And Bazzoli's estimates suggest that some of those eligible for early full benefits nevertheless postponed retirement until at least 65. These data suggest that the assumption of eligibility of 50 percent in these plans is reasonable. See Gloria Bazzoli, "The Early Retirement Decision: New Empirical Evidence," *Journal of Human Resources* 20 (spring 1985): 214–34.

30.  The proportion of the labor force affected increases because more pension plans permitted early retirement with full benefits (table 6.4) and more male workers of retirement age were covered by a pension. See Iams, "Characteristics of the Longest Job," at chapter 6, note 19.

31.  See Bazzoli, "Early Retirement Decision," at chapter 6, note 29.

32.  See Rones, "Using the CPS," at chapter 6, note 9.

33.  Recall that the social security wealth effect on retirement age was estimated to be .4 years, and the change in the recalculation effect .2 years. Together with a pension effect in the range of .5 years, the total reduction in retirement age owing to this factor is approximately 1.1 years. This can be compared with the actual decrease of 2.1 years in average retirement age from 1970 to 1985 (see table 6.1).

34.  All employees hired after 1983 have been covered by a new plan, but this had no effect on the data reported in the text.

35.  These data, although calculated continuously, have been published in different sources over time. These include U.S. Civil Service Commission, *Retirement Report* (1955–76); U.S. Office of Personnel Management (OPM), *Federal Fringe Benefit Facts* (1977–80); and OPM, *Compensation Report* (1981–85).

36.  That is, I estimated the equation, $FA = a + b$ time for the years 1955 through 1969, where $FA$ is average federal retirement age. The data in figure 6.2 reflect the variable $FA^* = FA - b$ time, where $b$ is a negative number.

37.  See, for example, Finis Welch, "Effects of Cohort Size on Earnings: The Baby Boom Babies," *Journal of Political Economy* 87 (October 1979): 65–98, and Philip Levine and Olivia Mitchell, "The Baby Boom's Legacy: Relative Wages in the 21st Century," *American Economic Review* 78 (May 1988): 66–69.

38.  See, for example, Burkhauser and Quinn, "Is Mandatory Retirement Overrated?" at chapter 2, note 11.

39.  See Donald Parsons, "The Industrial Demand for Older Workers," unpublished paper, Ohio State University, 1983; Randall K. Filer and Peter A. Petri, "A Job-Characteristics Theory of Retirement," *Review of Economics and Statistics* 70 (1988): 123–29; and Joseph Quinn, "Job Characteristics and Early Retirement," *Industrial Relations* 17 (1978): 315–23.

## CHAPTER SEVEN

1. See U.S. Department of Labor, *Pension Plan Bulletin,* no. 5 (1996), table E5, and its unpublished data and projections based on trends in the form 5500 data and the labor force.

2. Kruse studies form 5500 data over time to show that the share of defined contribution plans is primarily attributable to new plan choice. See Douglas Kruse, "Pension Substitution in the 1980s: Why the Shift towards Defined Contribution Plans?" *Industrial Relations* 34 (April 1995): 218–41. Also, U.S. Department of Labor data show that the number of workers covered by defined benefit plans has fallen from a peak almost 30 million in 1980 to about 25 million in 1993. See U.S. Department of Labor, *Pension Plan Bulletin,* at chapter 7, note 1, table E5, and unpublished data for 1993.

3. See Angela Chang, "Pension Plan Choice: A Review," Congressional Research Service, 1991; Robert Clark and Ann McDermed, *The Choice of Pension Plans in a Changing Environment* (Washington, D.C.: American Enterprise Institute, 1990); and Employee Benefit Research Institute, *What Is the Future of Defined Benefit Plans?* (Washington, D.C.: Employee Benefit Research Institute, 1989).

4. This statistic is drawn from the form 5500 reports that pension plans submit to the Internal Revenue Service each year.

5. In defined benefit plans, 96 percent (weighted by participants) use cliff vesting. Most cliff vesting occurs at the statutory maximum (usually five years for cliff vesting or seven years graduated vesting). In defined contribution plans, only 23 percent of covered workers have vesting at the statutory maximum, and 34 percent have immediate vesting. See U.S. Department of Labor, *Employee Benefits,* at chapter 2, note 3.

6. See Dorsey, "Pension Portability"; Gustman, Mitchell, and Steinmeier, "Role of Pensions"; and Quinn, Burkhauser, and Myers, *Passing the Torch,* all at chapter 1, note 2.

7. See chapter 7, note 18.

8. Results based on different ending years, such as 1988 or 1993, produce qualitatively similar results.

9. In terms of calculations in the chapter appendix, column 4 reports the value of $U$ in expression (7.3) by category.

10. See Clark and McDermed, *Choice of Pension Plans,* at chapter 7, note 3.

11. The difference between actual defined benefit plan market share in 1991 and the share predicted from 1979 coefficients across plans sizes is as follows:

| Plan Size | Reduction in the Predicted Probability of DB Participant Market Share |
|---|---|
| <200 | −30.6 |
| 200–500 | −28.3 |
| 500–1,000 | −21.3 |
| 1,000–2,000 | −15.5 |
| 2,000–5,000 | −13.8 |
| >5,000 | −05.4 |

Note that since these results are calculated on the 1979 database, then by defini-tion they exclude employment shift effects.

12.   American Academy of Actuaries, *Preliminary Report: Results from the American Academy of Actuaries Survey of Defined Benefit Plan Terminations* (Washington, D.C.: American Academy of Actuaries, 1992).

13.   The plans were made feasible after the Internal Revenue Service issued regulations in 1981 defining the permissible boundaries within which the plans would be tax qualified. Before the legislation, thrift plans could exist, but employ-ees' contributions were permitted only on an after-tax basis. When benefits were paid, individuals received a tax exclusion of only the nominal amount of their original contributions. Thus the tax advantages on employees' contributions were clearly inferior to those characterizing 401k plans.

14.   For a detailed discussion of the discrimination rules; see Allen et al., *Pen-sion Planning*, at chapter 1, note 5.

15.   Some portion of the defined contribution plan share in 1979 is attribut-able to old thrift plans that existed before 401k legislation, but their tax advan-tages were inferior to those of regular defined contribution plans and thus they are not expected to constitute an important part of the defined contribution market in that year. Also, see chapter 7, note 13.

16.   Figure 7.2 depicts the prominence of 401k plans in 1991 and the corre-sponding fall in defined benefit market share from 1979 to 1991.

17.   Also see Clark and McDermed, *Choice of Pension Plans*, at chapter 7, note 3, and Alan Gustman and Thomas Steinmeier, "The Stampede towards De-fined Contribution Plans," *Industrial Relations* 31 (spring 1992): 361–69. These studies analyze pension market developments through the mid-1980s using a sim-ilar method to disentangle employment and preference shifts.

18.   Primary coverage refers to the worker's main source of retirement in-come on the job. In many cases workers have two plans. The second plan is often a 401k or profit sharing plan that is somewhat less valuable than the main pen-sion. The U.S. Department of Labor uses an algorithm to assign primary or sec-ondary status to each form 5500 on their tapes.

In brief, the algorithm assigns primary defined benefit status if participants within a taxpayer EIN (employer identification number) either are all covered by a defined benefit plan only or are covered in approximately the same numbers by a defined benefit plan and a defined contribution plan. (In the latter case, it is assumed that the defined contribution plan is providing secondary coverage.) Participants are assumed to be covered primarily by a defined contribution plan if either no defined benefit plans exists in the EIN or the defined benefit plan covers a substantially different number of participants than are covered by a de-fined contribution plan. (In the latter case, both the defined benefit and defined contribution plans are considered primary coverage for some employees in the EIN observation.)

19.   Plans with fewer than one hundred participants are subject to more le-nient filing requirements. The sample also excludes plans that had missing data.

20.   This presence of other union participants in the firm is determined by examining the form 5500 reports for other plans where the plan sponsor has the same EIN.

21.  In effect, it is the incremental effect relative to the firm and industry represented by the intercept term.

22.  That is, the bracketed term on the intercept is the value of the logistics equation, when all the independent variables (all of which are zero-one dummy variables) are set to zero.

23.  The estimates for firm size for the omitted industry are found by adding the incremental effect for the size category to the bracketed term on the intercept.

24.  The employment shift effect also incorporates the interaction between employment shifts and preference changes.

25.  These shares do not match the population shares presented at the beginning of the chapter because the sample omits plans with fewer than one hundred participants. Also see note 24 above.

26.  Workers cannot simply choose among plans within the same firm. The Internal Revenue Code requires that workers in the firm are covered by plans that do not discriminate based on wage level. Exceptions are made for collectively bargained plans and plans across plant locations.

CHAPTER EIGHT

1.  The arguments that surround defined benefit plans in this chapter also apply to any other deferred wage scheme.

2.  See Armen Alchian and Harold Demsetz, "Production, Information Costs and Economic Organization," *American Economic Review* 62 (1972): 777–95.

3.  The model does not depend on the assumption that higher utility arises from higher wage offers. The main results hold, for example, if workers get bored doing the same things and thus attach value to occasionally changing jobs over the life cycle.

4.  First, since the marginal product of each team member is by definition identical in the long-tenure firm, the firm presumably does not want to have a two-tier wage scheme based on criteria that develop outside the firm: the two-tier wage schedule works to erode the team concept on which firm productivity depends. Second, ex ante, workers themselves would prefer to insure against the possibility of getting an unlucky draw in period 2. (If I introduce diminishing marginal utility, the insurance clearly is optimal.) Third, if those with the lucky draws are not immediately apparent, so that the firm must incur transactions costs to ferret out those with higher outside offers and those who pretend to have higher offers, it might be more economical to set the wage schedule in advance.

5.  This assumption is the equivalent of setting vesting at retirement age, which is not legally permitted. But since vesting does not prevent large capital losses from quitting (chapter 2), the economic content of the assumption is consistent with reality.

6.  If the job offer is sufficiently high, it may not be feasible to deter quitting by erecting pension capital losses. I pursue the conditions for efficacious deferred wages in the appendix.

7.  See, for example, Costas Aziadis, "Implicit Contracts and Underemployment Equilibria," *Journal of Political Economy* 83 (1975): 1183–1202.

8.  These findings originally came from studies searching for the expected compensating differential for pensions in cash wages. Most studies find either no

compensating differential or one that is less than one-to-one. See, for example, Stuart Dorsey, "A Test for a Wage-Pension Tradeoff with Endogenous Pension Coverage," unpublished paper, Baker University, 1990; Ehrenberg, "Retirement System Characteristics," at chapter 2, note 23; William Even and David MacPherson, "The Gender Gap in Pensions and Wages," *Review of Economics and Statistics* 72 (May 1990): 259–65; Edward Montgomery, Kathryn Shaw, and Mary Ellen Benedict, "Pensions and Wages: An Hedonic Price Theory Approach," *International Economic Review* 33 (1992): 111–28; Schiller and Weiss, "Pensions and Wages," at chapter 2, note 23; and Smith, "Compensating Differentials," at chapter 2, note 23. Evidence on quits and wages is found in Allen, Clark, and McDermed, "Job Mobility," at chapter 3, note 13; Alan Gustman and Thomas Steinmeier, "Pension Portability and Labor Mobility: Evidence from the SIPP," *Journal of Public Economics* 50 (March 1993): 299–323; and Gustman and Steinmeier, *Pension Incentives and Job Mobility*, at chapter 3, note 26.

9. See Alan Kreuger and Larry Summers, "Efficiency Wages and the Wage Structure," *Econometrica* 56 (March 1988): 259–94.

10. A full discussion of these different loss patterns is found in George Akerlof and Lawrence Katz, "Workers' Trust Funds and the Logic of Wage Profiles," *Quarterly Journal of Economics* 96 (August 1989): 525–36.

11. See chapter 8, note 9.

12. The Internal Revenue Code restricts the amount of pay that can be deferred in the form of a pension. See Allen et al., *Pension Planning*, at chapter 1, note 5.

13. To show this, consider that the maximum deferred wage involves a zero period 1 wage. Thus, if the premium is set equal to expected wage increases ($p = qd$), the payoff from staying is $2 + qd$, which exceeds the alternative wage offer, $1 + d$, if condition (8.11) holds.

14. The pension only solution has no wage tilt: $w_1 = w_2$. Also, by assumption, $w_2 = w_3$. Thus $w_1 + w_2$ is two-thirds of the lifetime wage, $2 + qd$. Condition (8.8) therefore is $.67(2 + qd) > 1 + d$, which simplifies to (8.12).

15. When pensions and wage tilt are maximized, a quitter receives zero compensation for period 1 work in order to accept a job offer of $1 + d$ in period 2. Therefore the long-tenure firm must offer a period 2 wage of $1 + d$. The expected lifetime wages for these workers outside long-tenure firms is $2 + qd$. The extra indenture premium is thus $[1 + d] - [2 + qd] = d[1 - q] - 1$, which is positive when condition 8.13 is satisfied. Added to the regular indenture premium, $qd$, the total indenture premium amount is $d[1 - q] - 1 + qd = d - 1$. The lifetime wage in long-tenure firms is thus $2 + d - 1 = 1 + d$.

16. The alternative wage is $1 + d$, but the wage upon staying is $2 + p = 2 + d - 1 = 1 + d$.

17. If applicants are hired randomly, the likelihood of a better wage offer for all workers is .5. One half of these are expected to reject their offers because the value of $d$ on their lottery tickets is less than 2. Thus the net quit rate is .25.

18. The low quit rate characterization of defined contribution plans is general if the model is modified so that firms have more information. Suppose firms can see job applicants' lottery tickets. In this case the problem of erecting efficacious deferred wages is more manageable, because the firm can reject applicants

with high $d$/low $q$ combination lottery tickets. Even though it is optimal for these kinds of workers to wait for better job offers in long-tenure firms, they are not hired unless the deferred wage scheme is efficacious for them. This selection procedure makes it likely that workers with small probabilities of obtaining job offers with large increases will be employed in defined contribution firms. In this case, we again have the result that defined contribution firms are characterized by low quit probabilities.

CHAPTER NINE

1. The literature has long recognized the proposition that internal discount rates vary across individuals and may have important implications for economic behavior. Citing work done a century before, Fisher develops the basic paradigm: Unless capital markets are perfect, in the sense that borrowing against future income is unlimited and costless, individuals' choices about investment activities depend on their rates of time preference. In this sense, decision making is expected to be influenced by individuals' subjective discount rates. See Irving Fisher, *The Theory of Interest* (New York: Macmillan, 1930).

Studies consistently reveal results that suggest a large dispersion of discount rates across individuals. See Victor Fuchs, "Time Preference and Health: An Exploratory Study," in *Economic Aspects of Health,* ed. Victor Fuchs (Chicago: University of Chicago Press for National Bureau of Economic Research, 1982); Jerry Hausman, "Individual Discount Rates and the Purchase and Utilization of Energy-Using Durables," *Bell Journal of Economics* 10 (spring 1979): 33–54; Mordecai Kurz, Robert Spiegelman, and Richard West, *The Experimental Horizon and the Rate of Time Preference for the Seattle and Denver Income Maintenance Experiments,* Occasional Paper (Stanford, Calif.: Stanford Research Institute, November 1973); and Emily Lawrence, "Poverty and the Rate of Time Preference: Evidence from Panel Data," *Journal of Political Economy* 99 (February 1991): 54–77. Also, see Shlomo Maital and Sharona Maital, "Time Preference, Delay of Gratification and the Intergenerational Transmission of Economic Inequality," in *Essays in Labor Market Analysis,* ed. Orley Ashenfelter and W. Oates (New York: John Wiley, 1977).

2. The role of discount rates in decisions to pursue higher education is adequately captured in models of human capital; for example, Becker, *Human Capital,* at chapter 2, note 22.

3. As discussed in section 2.6, the bulk of the pension literature revolves around the implicit pension contract affiliated with defined benefit plans; see Dorsey, "Pension Portability," and Gustman, Mitchell, and Steinmeier, "Role of Pensions," at chapter 1, note 2.

4. For example, production might depend heavily on teamwork, where it is difficult to measure the contribution of each team member without incurring significant monitoring costs (for example, see Alchian and Demsetz, "Production," at chapter 8, note 2).

5. Past research has relied on purchases of energy-saving durables, calculations of social security present values, temporal growth in consumption patterns, and surveys eliciting subjective responses to money trade-offs now versus at some future date. See Hausman, "Individual Discount Rates," at chapter 9, note 1, and

Cornelia Reimers and Marjorie Honig, "Responses to Social Security by Men and Women: Myopic versus Farsighted Behavior," mimeographed, Hunter College, 1993. See also Lawrence, "Poverty and the Rate of Time Preference"; Fuchs, "Time Preference and Health"; and Maital and Maital, "Time Preference," all at chapter 9, note 1.

6.   This model is similar to that of Becker and Stigler, "Law Enforcement Malfeasance," at chapter 2, note 22, which characterizes the benefits of law enforcement officials' engaging in fraud (where there might be a propensity to engage in crime) and a cost of getting caught in some future period.

7.   The benefit may occur either because the worker feels ill or because he gets the chance to go fishing instead of work.

8.   I develop this model in chapter 11.

9.   For the first three years of service, annual leave is thirteen days per annum, then nineteen days until fifteen years of service, then twenty-six days.

10.   If leave is unused at retirement, workers' pension annuities are increased, creating some shadow price for taking time off. The additional pension value translates to a pay rate of about 33 percent of the wage for time unused. Given this small payoff rate and considering even modest internal discount rates, it seems reasonable to consider sick time as fully paid, at least for workers far from retirement.

11.   My samples are separated into those covered by the Federal Employee Retirement System (FERS), which covers all workers hired after 1983, and workers hired before 1 January 1984, covered by the Civil Service Retirement System (CSRS). I can replicate the results using the CSRS data. I am indebted to the Defense Manpower Data Center for providing me with these data.

12.   See note a to table 9.1.

13.   See Fuchs, "Time Preference," at chapter 9, note 1. Also see P. Farrell and V. Fuchs, "Schooling and Health: The Cigarette Connection," unpublished paper, Stanford University, May 1982.

14.   Evans and Montgomery use this relation to argue that smoking as a teenager is a good proxy for internal discount rates, which they use in the context of making decisions about education. See William Evans and Edward Montgomery, "Education and Health: Where There's Smoke There's an Instrument," unpublished paper, University of Maryland, January 1996.

15.   The household unit is chosen so that at least one member is within this age range. Spouses may have ages outside these ranges, but I restrict the analysis to those within the age range 51–61.

16.   Although the health hazards of smoking were known to some extent before 1964, the historical data clearly identify the release of this study as a landmark in smoking consumption in the United States. Consumption began a precipitous fall after its release and continued well into the 1970s. See, for example, Evans and Montgomery, "Where There's Smoke," at chapter 9, note 14.

17.   Most smoking decisions are made at young ages, particularly before 1964. See Fuchs, "Time Preference," at chapter 9, note 1.

18.   Sixty-two percent of the sample smoked for some period, but about half of these quit by the time they were 50. The relation between discount rates and smoking propensities still holds if smoking is viewed as "rational" addiction. See

Gary Becker and Kevin Murphy, "A Theory of Rational Addiction," *Journal of Political Economy* 96 (1988): 675–700.

19.   For those who report that they quit smoking, the survey records the number of years since quitting; hence, smoking status as of age 50 can be constructed for the entire sample.

20.   I also exclude a few respondents who are in postretirement jobs after retiring from their main jobs. In particular, I exclude those who report starting their job within the past five years while also reporting that they "retired" from a previous job in which they had been employed at least five years.

21.   See Evans and Montgomery, "Where There's Smoke," at chapter 9, note 14.

22.   The Health and Retirement Survey (HRS) includes a wide variety of health queries. The variables include separate dummy variables denoting that the respondent ever had cancer, a heart attack, a stroke; currently has diabetes, high blood pressure, arthritis requiring medication; reports extreme difficulty jogging a mile, walking several blocks, or climbing a flight of stairs. The variables also include the number of days spent in a hospital during the past twelve months and the number of days missed from work owing to illness during the past twelve months (with a dummy variable denoting more than ninety-five days missed). Finally, using the Metropolitan Life height and weight tables (for "medium" frames), I construct a dummy variable denoting weight 50 percent above recommended levels for reported height.

23.   In particular, the HRS asks whether the respondent would take another job that had an equal chance of doubling his salary or cutting it by one-third. I assign a value of one to answering yes to this query.

24.   For salaried workers, I derive the hourly wage by dividing their weekly salary by the usual weekly hours.

25.   A similar finding is reported for very young workers, buttressing the hypothesis that the wage-smoking connection is independent of health effects. See Philip Levine, Tara Gustafson, and Ann Velenchik, "More Bad News for Smokers? The Effects of Cigarette Smoking on Labor Market Outcomes," National Bureau of Economic Research Working Paper 5270, September 1995.

26.   The question reads: "In deciding how much of their (family) income to spend or save, people are likely to think about different financial planning periods. In planning your (family's) saving and spending, which of the time periods listed is most important to you (and your spouse)? Next few months, next year, next few years, next 5–10 years, longer than 10 years?"

27.   I set the continuous value to the mean of the range permitted within each category; for those reporting a horizon of more than ten years, I set the value to 12.5. The results are qualitatively similar if I enter the data as separate dummy variables.

28.   That is to say, the survey also asks respondents what likelihood they attach to living to age 75. The response is measured on a metric from one to ten, where ten is certainty of living to that age and zero is no chance.

29.   That is, .018 (log 10 − log .5) = .054.

30.   This finding is similar to one reported in Fuchs, except that Fuchs's proxy for discount rates is the individual's response to a money trade-off question. If I

estimate a logit model of nonsmoking at age 50 against the log of the planning horizon, *PH,* the coefficient on log *PH* is −.084($t$ = 2.73), $n$ = 4,627. The incremental effect is .4, which is large in comparison with the mean of the dependent variable (.67). A respondent who reports a ten-year horizon has a 96 percent chance of being a nonsmoker at age 50; one who reports a six-month horizon has a 46 percent probability. See Fuchs, "Time Preference," at chapter 9, note 1.

31.    The incremental effect for the horizon variable compares workers with a ten-year versus six-month horizon, other variables set to their mean values.

32.    The question asks whether workers are included in the plan. They are coded as covered if they answer yes.

33.    The survey includes IRAs and Keough accounts in the same variable. To exclude many of the Keough accounts, I evaluated accounts with less than $100,000, though the results are not altered if I include the larger accounts.

34.    Tenure is expected to be affected by defined benefit plan coverage, which introduces a causality problem.

35.    The incremental effect is the probability of savings participation for two values of the independent variable, holding all other variables at their mean levels. In the case of the nonsmoking variable, the independent variable is set at one versus zero; in the case of the horizon, it is set at ten years versus six months.

36.    Recall that the data are restricted to workers covered by the FERS retirement system (but the results are replicated if I use data describing workers covered by the CSRS retirement system). Since FERS does not permit voluntary contributions to the 401k plan during the first year of service, tenure is restricted to greater than one year in the empirical work. See chapter 9, note 11.

37.    These numbers are comparable with national estimates. See James Poterba, Steven Venti, and David Wise, "Do 401(k) Contributions Crowd out Other Personal Savings?" *Journal of Public Economics* 50 (1995): 1–32.

38.    The government contributes 1 percent unconditionally, then matches voluntary contributions on a 50 percent basis up to 5 percent of pay; workers can save an additional 5 percent of pay in the plan. The savings rate is the one in effect as of October 1993 when the sample was drawn.

39.    The incremental effect on the wage compares the change in the savings rate as a result of setting the wage to the first and third quartiles, all other variables set to their mean values.

40.    The expected savings rate for a worker with mean characteristics and with a zero sick leave balance is 3.6 percent of wages.

41.    Some low discounters may not have opportunities to pursue education; some high discounters may attain education because it is financed by parents; and so on.

42.    See Fuchs, "Time Preference," at chapter 9, note 1.

43.    See chapter 9, note 4.

44.    The firm is constrained to pay wages in the aggregate that equal workers' value of marginal product, and thus the wage rate is a function of the number of high discounters in each cohort of hires and how many survive each period. Wages paid to a cohort of workers must equal their value of marginal product in each period: $w_t[H_t + L] = [1 + d]L + [1 + d - y]H_t$, where $L$ is the number of low discounters in each cohort of hires and $H_t$ is the number of high discounters

in the cohort who have not quit by period $t$. Rearranging this expression yields (9.6).

45.   This argument is a natural extension of Salop and Salop, "Self Selection," at chapter 2, note 30, which uses wage tilt to sort for workers based on quit propensities. Some evidence has been reported implicating low discounters with defined benefit firms. Curme and Even use data describing the degree of credit constraint to identify workers with high propensities to spend. They find that credit-constrained workers are less likely to be found in firms that use defined benefit plans. See Michael Curme and William Even, "Pensions, Borrowing Constraints and Self-Selection," *Journal of Human Resources* 30 (fall 1995): 701–12.

46.   For example, the median worker in my federal worker database has used 65 percent of his accrued sick leave to date; 25 percent have 13 percent or less left; 5 percent have zero balances. Almost 30 percent of eligible workers in 1993 contribute zero to the 401k plans, despite a 50 percent match rate.

47.   By regulation, cliff vesting can be no more than five years. Whereas five-year cliff vesting is almost universal in defined benefit plans, it typically is much shorter in defined contribution plans. The firm can and sometimes does use immediate vesting. See U.S. Department of Labor, *Employee Benefits*, at chapter 2, note 3.

48.   Since the interest rate is zero, the contribution amount $s$ available in one period is valued by the firm and low discounters as $s$. High discounters attach a value of $s/(1 + r)$ for the contribution amount if it is one period away. Thus the amount of the deferred wage that is discounted is $s - s/(1 + r) = sr/(1 + r)$.

49.   I ignore the 10 percent excise tax levied against withdrawals before age $59^{1}/_{2}$. Workers who can resist the lump sum reveal their low discount rates. Thus, after investing in the sorting process, they earn the right to collect the no-monitoring premium over their career. This aspect of the model is related to quasi-rent models in the product quality literature, where high-quality products command premiums after demonstrating their quality. Firms are reluctant to erode the quality signal, because they stand to lose the right to collect the quality premiums. See Carl Shapiro, "Premiums for High Quality Products as Returns to Reputation," *Quarterly Journal of Economics* 98 (November 1983): 659–79.

50.   If $n$ is the horizon of low discounters, expected tenure of the average high discounter in a no-monitoring firm is: $n_H = q + 2q(1 - q) + 3q(1 - q)^2 + \ldots + q(1 - q)^{n-1} + (1 - q)^n$, where the last term captures the possibility of not quitting through $n$ periods. As $n$ approaches infinity, the solution approaches $1/q$. For a finite $n$, we have $n_H = [1 - (1 - q)^n]/q$, $0 < q < 1$.

51.   See Joseph Piacentini, "Preserving Portable Benefits," unpublished paper, Employee Benefit Research Institute, 1990.

52.   McCarthy reports that the average generosity factor is 1 percent; see his *Findings from Survey*, at chapter 3, note 15.

53.   More particularly, $\hat{T} = \lambda L/w_{88} + error$, where $\hat{T}$ is estimated tenure at the time the lump sum was taken, $\lambda$ is the average generosity of defined benefit pensions, $L$ is the amount of the lump sum, and $w_{88}$ is the individual's annual wage observed in May 1988. I set $\lambda$ to .15 (see McCarthy, *Findings from Survey*, at chapter 3, note 15). I include time dummy variables to control for different nominal values of the lump sums taken in different years.

54. The restriction on tenure ensures that the lump sum was not awarded by the current employer.

55. Other independent variables are set to their mean values.

56. The standard error on the coefficient is understated in this application because it does not reflect the error in the estimated variable.

57. I set all the independent variables to their mean values and calculate the participation probability, alternatively setting the IRA rollover variable to one or zero.

58. In the typical private pension plan, retirement occurs about age 61; the typical replacement rate is 30 percent of final wage for those leaving with thirty years of tenure. See McCarthy, *Findings from Survey,* at chapter 3, note 15. In the CSRS, workers who have thirty years of service can depart at age 55 with a 56 percent replacement rate.

59. Technically, federal workers contribute 7 percent of their salaries to the pension, and this money is available to those who quit. In reality, the economic value of each year of work in terms of pension benefits is closer to 30 percent, making the economics of quitting unattractive for low discounters, but perhaps quite attractive for high discounters.

60. I do not have 401k contribution data for this sample in 1986 (participants in CSRS are entitled to contribute 5 percent of pay into the 401k plan, with no matching amounts). But in the 1993 data, my CSRS sample evinces a strong correlation between high $\beta$s and 401k contributions.

61. In the 1993 data, there are no low-tenure workers with CSRS coverage.

62. I estimate the following equation:

$$1 - \beta_x = a + \varnothing(1 - \beta_0) + \gamma\log(1 + x) + \text{error}, \tag{a}$$

where $\beta_0$ is the sick leave balance (as a percentage of sick leave earned to date) on 1 January 1987, $\beta_x$ is the same calculation on the worker's quit date, and $x$ is the number of months (or fractions thereof) that elapse between January 1 and the worker's quit date during 1987. I use a semi-log formulation after confirming from plotted data that the use of sick leave escalates as workers approach their quit date. Estimating this equation using ordinary least squares for 827 workers who quit the federal government yields $\gamma = .022$ ($t = 3.47$).

To confirm this result, I reestimate (a) for 244 workers who quit the Air Force during 1987 but transferred elsewhere in the government. Since sick leave is transferable throughout the government, these quitters are not expected to use extra sick leave before their departure. In fact the data reveal some tendency for these workers to build up sick leave before leaving, though the result is not statistically different from zero: the estimated value of $\gamma$ for this group, where $x$ is months to departure from the Air Force, is $-.015$ ($t = 1.46$).

I used the value of $\gamma$ to adjust observed sick leave on 1 January 1987 for all 1987 quits to a point twelve months preceding their quit date:

$$\mathring{\beta}_0 = \beta_0 + \gamma[\log(1 + 12) - \log(1 + x)]. \tag{b}$$

63. Quits are oversampled in the data. Thus I estimate a weighted logit model where the dependent variable equals unity if the worker quit during 1987, zero otherwise, and the weights are the ratios of population to sample propor-

tions. The oversample of quits improves the efficiency of the estimates, and the weighting offsets the bias imparted by the choice-based sample.

64.    The list of independent variables is the same as shown in the notes to table 9.1. Retirement eligibility sets in at age 55, so I exclude workers over age 54.

65.    The incremental effect is the difference in the probability of quitting where the sick leave variable is set alternatively to unity and zero, setting other variables to their mean values. The quit probability when $\beta$ is one equals .12 percent, and when $\beta$ is zero, 2.2 percent.

66.    When these variables are included, the coefficient on the sick leave balance variable is $-2.60$; without these variables, the same coefficient is $-2.83$.

67.    In FERS, the "employee" contribution toward the defined benefit plan is approximately .9 percent of pay. Workers can join the 401k plan after one year of tenure. The government makes a 1 percent unconditional contribution to each worker's account, in which workers vest immediately. Beyond this contribution, workers can make voluntary contributions that are subject to a matching schedule.

68.    The predicted quit probabilities for the extreme values of $\beta$ are: $\beta = 0(.028)$ and $\beta = 1(.020)$.

69.    To test for difference in coefficients, I include both CSRS and FERS workers in the quit estimates, and I include a FERS zero-one dummy variable, $F$, the $\beta$ variable, and the interaction between $F$ and $\beta$. The coefficient on $\beta$ is $-2.43 (t = 3.88)$, and the coefficient on the interaction term is $1.46 (t = 1.79)$. Consistent with these findings, the relative impact of sick leave balance on the quit probability is also smaller for FERS workers. The estimated quit probability for a FERS worker with no sick leave available is 7.7 percent, which is only 2.75 times the quit probability for a worker with all his sick leave intact. The relative impact of sick leave for CSRS workers at the same two extremes is thirteen times.

70.    The essence of the results remains if firms have a noisy proxy for internal discount rates.

71.    See Steven Lippman and John McCall, "The Economics of Job Search: A Survey," *Economic Inquiry* 14 (June 1976): 155–89.

72.    Recall that the interest rate is assumed to be zero, and thus the deferred wage is comparable to the cash wage.

73.    The results do not depend on a zero variance, but as low discounters' information levels become lower (variance increases), sorting becomes less efficient.

74.    That is, $\tilde{w}_H - \tilde{a}_H = w_c + w_d/(1 + r)^n - 1 - \epsilon$. Adding and subtracting $w_d$ on the right hand side of the expression gives (9.11).

75.    If the quit rate induced by the lump sum is $q$, then $H_t = H_0(1 - q)^{t-1}$, where $H_0$ is the number of high discounters in the entering cohort and $H_t$ is the number remaining in period $t$. The number of low discounters is $L$ in every period. The share of high discounters in a cohort of hires in period zero is $\alpha_t$ after $t$ periods, where $\alpha_t = H_t/(H_t + L)$. Integrating $\alpha_t$, $t = [0, n]$, and dividing by $n$ gives expression (9.14).

76.    Workers invest in the attainment of a valuable and marketable signal;

namely, that they have low discount rates. In this sense the model is an application of the general theory of signaling. See Michael Spence, "Informational Aspects of Market Structures: An Introduction," *Quarterly Journal of Economics* 90 (November 1976): 591–97.

77.   These workers include those who report coverage by a defined contribution plan but have a zero balance in their account, or those who report they are not covered but admit that they are eligible to participate. In the latter case, the data do not reveal the type of plan, but I make the presumption that these are workers in 401k plans who choose not to contribute.

CHAPTER TEN

1.   Most literature on 401k plans is related to the savings function. See William Bassett, Michael Fleming, and Anthony Rodrigues, "How Workers Use 401k Plans: The Participation, Contribution and Withdrawal Decisions," mimeographed, Federal Reserve Bank of New York, 1996. See also Eric Engen, William Gale, and John Scholz, "Do Savings Incentives Work?" *Brookings Papers on Economic Activity* 1 (1994): 85–180; Poterba et al., "Do 401(k) Contributions," at chapter 9, note 37; Andrew Samwick and Jonathan Skinner, "Abandoning the Nest Egg? 401k Plans and Inadequate Pension Savings," in *Public Policy towards Pensions*, ed. Sylvester J. Scheiber and John B. Shoven (Cambridge: MIT Press, forthcoming); Andrea Kusko, James Poterba, and David Wilcox, "Employee Decisions with Respect to 401k Plans: Evidence from Individual-Level Data," National Bureau of Economic Research Working Paper 4635, 1994; and Angela Chang, "Tax Policy, Lump Sum Pension Distributions, and Household Saving," *National Tax Journal* 49 (1996): 235–58.

2.   There are many variations in these kinds of plans; some contribute a fixed percentage of pay (money purchase plans); others set the percentage contribution as a function of company performance or other criteria (profit sharing plans). Still others are stock bonus plans. But for present purposes, these nuances are not important.

3.   That is, set $m = m^*$, where $m^*v = y$.

4.   Suppose that the contribution rates for the $j$th type of worker, $c_j$, are linear in the firm's matching rate, $m$:

$$c_j = z_j + b_j m; \quad j = L, H, \quad a_L > a_H \geq 0, \tag{a}$$

where $z_j$ are desired contribution rates without matching, and $b_j$ describe the effects of matching on workers' contribution rates. I assume that firms either know or learn the functions in (a).

The firm chooses the matching rate, $m$, and the compensating differential, $x$, so as to equate wages and values of marginal product across worker types; that is:

$$w_H = 1 + d - x + mc_H = 1 + d - y; \tag{b}$$

and

$$w_L = 1 + d - x + mc_L = 1 + d. \tag{c}$$

Substituting (c) into (b) and using (a), the optimal match rate, $m^*$, satisfies the relation

$$(z_L - z_H)m^* + (b_L - b_H)m^{*2} - y = 0. \qquad \text{(d)}$$

The optimal compensating differential, $x^*$, is equal to a low discounter's matching income:

$$x^* = m^* c_L(m^*). \qquad \text{(e)}$$

5.  If the firm attaches some value to long tenure, it can set the matching rate to create an efficiency wage, $\delta$, exclusively for low discounters; that is, set $m$ so that $\delta = m\, c_L - y > 0$. In this way the firm encourages low discounters (but not high discounters) to accumulate long tenure, competing with defined benefit plans and other deferred wage schemes. The cost of increasing tenure in a 401k plan takes the form of an efficiency wage. In a deferred wage scheme, the cost takes the form of an indenture premium.

6.  In chapter 9 I showed that quit rates indeed were lower for workers who contributed to the 401k plan than for noncontributors. Also see Kusko, Poterba, and Wilcox, "Employee Decisions," at chapter 10, note 1.

7.  See Robert Lucas, "On the Size Distribution of Business Firms," *Bell Journal of Economics* 9 (1978): 508–23.

8.  Indeed, one theory of pensions is built around the idea that transactions costs in large firms require vehicles like pensions to manage the firm's workforce composition. See Donald Parsons, "Retirement Age and Retirement Income: The Role of the Firm," in *Assessing Knowledge of Retirement Behavior,* ed. Eric Hanushek and Nancy Maritato (Washington, D.C.: National Academy Press, 1996).

9.  I exclude both respondents who are not covered by a 401k plan and those who report that they do not know if they are covered.

10.  The firm-size question is asked only if the respondent reports that the firm has plants in more than one location. Information about firm sizes above these break points is not reported in the CPS. I also include dummy variables equal to one if the worker does not know plant or firm size, zero otherwise.

11.  See Richard Freeman, "Unionism and the Dispersion of Wages," *Industrial and Labor Relations Review* 34 (October 1980): 3–24.

12.  Respondents report whether the firm makes contributions to the 401k plan. The CPS does not ask respondents to differentiate between an unconditional contribution to the plan and a matching contribution, but given the predominance of matching formulas in these plans, I make the assumption that affirmative answers to the question, Does your firm make contributions to the plan? indicate the presence of matching. See U.S. Department of Labor, *Employee Benefits,* at chapter 2, note 3.

13.  The incremental effect is the difference in the probability of observing matching when the independent variable is set alternatively to one or zero and other independent variables are set to their mean values.

14.  Within grade, workers are advanced one step per annum for three steps; then one step every two years for three steps; then one step each three years, until they reach step ten (or are promoted to a higher grade).

15. See list of variables (not reported) in note b to table 10.2.

16. For example, workers already at step ten within a grade cannot receive a quality step increase.

17. Technically there are four rating categories in federal agencies: outstanding, exceeds fully satisfactory, fully satisfactory, and unsatisfactory. Virtually no workers have unsatisfactory ratings, and I exclude 6 percent of the observations with no ratings of record.

18. Generally, the rating of record pertains to the fiscal year ending 30 September 1992, but similar results are obtained if I use the ratings for the year ending 30 September 1993

19. See note b to table 10.3.

20. Technically, in exchange for offering a defined benefit pension (in addition to the 401k), the government requires workers to "contribute" nine-tenths of 1 percent of pay, which is refunded (without interest) upon quitting the federal government.

21. The sick leave balance may itself be a function of the quit decision: those who anticipate quitting are expected to use their sick leave more intensively before their departure. Other independent variables included in the estimates are reported in note c to table 10.4.

22. The rate of contributions is not expected to be influenced by upper-end restrictions in some plans on the permissible range of percentage of pay contributions. The average 401k plan permits contributions up to 14 percent of pay; over 90 percent of plans permit contributions of at least 10 percent; over half of these plans permit contributions over 15 percent. Thus, within the range of contribution rates reported in the CPS, it is reasonable to infer that the rates are not influenced by upper limits. See U.S. Department of Labor, *Employee Benefits*, at chapter 2, note 3.

23. The age and family income variables (not reported) reflect the expected patterns. The coefficient on age is .0037 ($t$-value = 3.81); the coefficient on age-squared is $-.00003$ ($t = 2.42$). Although the coefficients on each of the dummy variables are not reported, they show a steady upward progression of savings rates from the lowest to the highest family income categories.

24. The description of the incremental effect is found in the notes to table 10.6. Also, it is worth noting that the typical matching rate is 50 percent. See U.S. Department of Labor, *Employee Benefits*, at chaper 2, note 3.

CHAPTER ELEVEN

1. The literature on absenteeism is not well developed. Early papers on this subject include Steven Allen, "An Empirical Model of Work Attendance," *Review of Economics and Statistics* 63 (1981): 77–87, and J. Paul Leigh, "The Effects of Union Membership on Absence from Work Due to Illness," *Journal of Labor Research* 2 (1981): 329–36.

2. Workers with less than three years of tenure are awarded thirteen days of paid annual leave, and those with more than fifteen years of service receive twenty-six days.

3. As noted in chapter 4, sick leave in the government is paid, but for those who remain until retirement age, unused sick leave counts toward a higher pen-

sion annuity. Thus there is some shadow price for taking sick leave beyond its signal of unreliability. The payoff rate, however, is only approximately one-third of the final wage. Given the relatively small payoff, discounting for time preference, and a probability less than one of being in the government at retirement age, it seems safe to assume that, at least for workers not close to retirement age, sick leave is viewed as paid time off. To minimize the potential for the shadow price effect to contaminate the data, I exclude workers older than 45 from some of the wage estimates. I also verify and expand on the results using an instrumental approach with Current Population Survey data (see section 11.5 below).

4. The denominator is years of tenure times 104 hours, where part years of tenure are credited at the rate of two hours of sick leave earned per week. The numerator is sick leave hours unused as of 1 January 1987.

5. Wages in the federal government are set in much the same ways as in private companies. There are fifteen grades and ten steps within each grade. Moves between grades confer wage increases in the 10–15 percent range; each step within a grade confers a 3 percent increase in salary. Good workers are promoted to higher grades more often and receive step increases faster than poorer performers. Thus wage dispersions are significant for individuals with equal tenure and education.

6. See chapter 11, note 3.

7. See Allen, "Empirical Model," at chapter 11, note 1, and Mary Corcoran and Greg Duncan, "Work History, Labor Force Attachments and Earnings Differences between Races and Sexes," *Journal of Human Resources* 14 (winter 1979): 3–20.

8. Sick leave balances are available in the data as of the end of 1986.

9. The probability that a worker with mean sample characteristics has a supervisory job is 6.9 percent if the sick leave balance is zero and 41.2 percent if 100 percent of earned sick leave is still available.

10. These results are similar to those in George Borjas, "Discrimination in the HEW: Is the Doctor Sick or Are the Patients Healthy?" *Journal of Law and Economics* 21 (1978): 97–110. Borjas estimates wage differences in the federal government across sex and race using 1977 data.

11. For example, see Corcoran and Duncan, "Work History," chapter 11, note 7; Audrey Light and Manuelite Ureta, "Gender Differences in Wages and Job Turnover among Continuously Employed Workers," *Journal of Labor Economics* 10 (April 1992): 156–81; Jacob Mincer and Solomon Polachek, "Family Investments in Human Capital: Earnings from Women," *Journal of Political Economy* 82 (March 1987): S576–108; and Alison Wellington, "Changes in the Male/Female Wage Gap, 1976–85," *Journal of Human Resources* 28 (spring 1993): 383–411. For an overview, see Victor Fuchs, "Women's Quest for Economic Equality," *Journal of Economic Perspectives* 1 (winter 1989): 25–41.

12. See Gary Becker, *The Economics of Discrimination*, 2d ed. (Chicago: University of Chicago Press, 1971).

13. See Kenneth Arrow, "Some Models of Racial Discrimination," in *Racial Discrimination in Economic Life*, ed. Anthony H. Pascal (Lexington, Mass.: Lexington Books, 1972); and Edmund Phelps, "The Statistical Theory of Racism and Sexism," *American Economic Review* 69 (March 1972): 659–61.

14.   The highest rating is "outstanding" (6 percent); a high rating is "exceeds fully satisfactory" (20 percent); an average rating is "fully satisfactory" (70 percent); and finally, "unsatisfactory" (4 percent).

15.   The probability that a white male with mean sample characteristics received a high rating is 33 percent. The probability that a white female with mean sample characteristics received a high rating is 33 plus 9.4 percent, or 42.4 percent.

16.   The forced removal rate in the federal government is only 1.3 percent per annum. I add 631 removals from the oversample file to magnify this probability ten times and estimate a weighted logit model where the weights are the ratios of population-to-sample proportions. The dependent variable equals one if a worker is fired during 1987, zero otherwise.

17.   Gary Becker, "Human Capital, Effort and the Sexual Division of Labor," *Journal of Labor Economics* 3 (January 1985): S33–58.

18.   The results are not significantly affected when I include occupation dummy variables: reliability among females remains substantially below that among males even within occupations.

19.   After workers use all earned sick leave and all available annual leave, the only way to take time off is leave without pay.

20.   As discussed in chapter 4, owing to the large portion of compensation that is deferred, quitting in the federal government is advertised as one of the least desirable traits.

21.   For the estimates in table 11.3, columns 3 and 4, I use the oversample file. In these cases I use a weighted logit model to correct the bias, where the weights are the population-to-sample proportions in the choice-based sample. The independent variables included in the estimates are shown in the notes to table 11.3.

22.   See Mark Meitzam, "Differences in Male and Female Job Quitting Behavior," *Journal of Labor Economics* 4 (April 1986): 151–67, and W. Kip Viscusi, "Differences in Worker Quitting," *Review of Economics and Statistics* 62 (August 1980): 388–98.

23.   I include observations from the oversample file, and I estimate a weighted logit model where the weights are the population-to-sample proportions in the choice-based sample.

24.   This is a good example of a bonding signal, one in which workers make a demonstrable investment to convey the idea of quality. See Spence, "Informational Aspects," at chapter 9, note 76, and Pauline Ippolito, "Bonding and Nonbonding Signals of Product Quality," *Journal of Business* 63 (January 1990): 41–60.

25.   Even pursues the idea that a rapid return to work after childbearing conveys a signal that a female worker is serious about continuing her career. See William Even, "Career Interruptions Following Childbirth," *Journal of Labor Economics* 5 (April 1987): 255–77.

26.   Recall that the unreliability index equals unity if the worker quit or took LWOP during 1987, took twenty days of sick leave in 1986, or had a zero sick leave in January 1987, zero otherwise.

27.  Performance ratings are defined in chapter 11, note 14.

28.  I reestimate the wage equation in table 11.1, column 2, across all workers in the federal database with fewer than ten years of tenure, including two additional variables: a high-quality signal dummy variable equal to unity if a female worker attains a high performance rating (but not the highest rating) and holds a bachelor's degree (but not a graduate degree); and a highest-quality signal dummy variable equal to unity if a female worker either attains the highest job performance rating possible or holds a master's degree or more. The coefficients on the two high-quality signals are .03 ($t = .81$) and $-.005$ ($t = .19$).

29.  The survey asks workers who normally work thirty-five or more hours per week why they worked less than thirty-five hours the week before the survey. Four choices are offered to describe unscheduled time off for personal reasons: own illness, bad weather, too busy with home or school, and other reason. My results are based on the own illness variable, which accounts for approximately half of the personal reasons cited. The results are similar when I estimate the model using an index equal to unity if any of the personal reasons is cited.

30.  Full-time workers are those who report themselves as "full time." I exclude self-employed respondents from the sample.

31.  I exclude salaried workers earning more than $999 per week because their salary is not coded. Fifty-two percent of the sample are hourly workers; the rest are salaried workers. The results are essentially the same if only hourly wage earners are included in the analysis.

32.  Other variables are included in the estimates (see notes to table 11.6), but their incremental effects are not reported.

33.  The probability that a white male with mean characteristics calls in sick is 2 percent (the intercept term). The probabilities for white and black females equal this number, plus the incremental effects (1.1 and 1.8 percent).

34.  The probability that a white male with children takes sick leave is .020 (the intercept term). The probability that a white female with children takes sick leave is .044. A comparable number is found for black females with children. The results are consistent with the literature associating females with conflicts between home and work responsibilities. See Becker, "Human Capital, Effort," at chapter 11, note 17; Fuchs, "Women's Quest," at chapter 11, note 11; and Mincer and Polachek, "Family Investments," at chapter 11, note 11.

35.  I set the two-earner dummy variable and the white female dummy variable to unity, set the black male and black female dummy variables to zero, and set the other variables to their mean sample values. When the variables indicating higher spouse wage are set to zero, the probability of taking sick leave is .022. When the higher spouse wage dummy variable is set to unity and the percentage higher wage is set to 50 percent, the probability increases to .045.

36.  In 24 percent of two-earner households, the female earns a higher wage than her spouse, but the wage differential is only 10 percent.

37.  See, for example, Corcoran and Duncan, "Work History," at chapter 11, note 7.

38.  The standard error is not corrected to reflect the uncertainty in the predicted variable itself, and thus it is somewhat understated in this application.

39. That is, $(1 - e^{-6.45*.03} = .175)$.

40. See Salop and Salop, "Self Selection," at chapter 2, note 30, and Even and MacPherson, "Gender Gap in Pensions and Wages," at chapter 8, note 9.

41. These variables include age, service, square terms, and category variables denoting education level.

42. See Gustman and Steinmeier, *Pension Incentives*, at chapter 3, note 26.

43. To obtain information on spouses' wages, I arrange the data by household identifier. The survey queries male respondents on whether they are heads of households and asks female respondents whether they are wives of heads of households. When both questions are answered yes and both spouses report their wages, a two-earner dummy variable is set to unity and the spouse's wage and sick leave benefit are recorded in the respondent's own record. Where more than two individuals within the household answer yes to these questions, I cannot be sure to match the correct male and female in the household as a married couple, and thus I do not include them within the subset of two-earner couples.

CHAPTER TWELVE

1. Hay-Huggins Company, *Pension Plan Expense Study for the PBGC* (Washington, D.C.: Hay-Huggins, 1990).

2. An update of these cost estimates through 1996 showed that relative and absolute costs did not change importantly after 1991. See Edward Hustead, "Retirement Income Plan Administrative Expenses 1981 through 1996," unpublished paper, Hay Group, Washington, D.C., 1996.

3. Compare a differential cost of $-\$2$ in 1981 with $14 in 1991 for the plan with ten thousand participants; compare $2 in 1981 and $34 in 1991 for the plan with five hundred participants.

4. This estimate was made by the authors of the study.

5. In the comprehensive income tax treatment, earnings saved for future consumption are subject to a so-called double tax: once when the wages are received, and again in the form of taxation of interest, which effectively taxes earnings a second time. To illustrate, consider a worker who decides to save $1 of current wages to support retirement consumption twenty years hence. Suppose that the marginal tax rate, denoted by $t$, is the same in both periods, that the nominal interest rate is $i$, and the real rate of interest is zero. In twenty years, the $1 is worth $I_{20} = (1 - t)\$1\ e^{i(1-t)20}$. If $i$ is 8 percent and $t$ is 20 percent, then $I_{20} = \$2.87$. In year-zero dollars, this amount is valued at $2.87\ e^{-i20} = \$0.58$. If instead the worker saves the $1 in a pension fund, the after-tax pension in year twenty is $C_{20} = \$1\ e^{i20}\ (1 - t) = \$3.96$. The value of this amount in year zero is $C_{20}\ e^{-i20} = \$0.80$. Clearly, the worker is better off saving in a pension fund and receiving consumption tax treatment than using a regular savings vehicle.

6. The nominal cash wage in year twenty-five is $121.82 (= \$10 \times e^{(.10 \times 25\ \text{years})}$). The lump sum pension is 10 percent times twenty-five years of service times final wage, or $304.50. Discounted to year zero at the 10 percent interest rate, the pension is worth $25.

7. Recall that the example assumes that the portfolio comprises zero-risk securities yielding a zero real rate of interest.

8. If assets exceed this amount, plus one year of normal cost contributions, the firm is prevented from making contributions until assets are reduced below this level.

9. The salary growth offsets the discount rate, and thus ongoing liabilities in the example are a linear function of service level.

10. The rules have a limit on contributions. Defined contribution plans have a limit on contributions of $30,000 per person per year. Defined benefit plans have similar kinds of limits. The pensions also must satisfy so-called discrimination tests, which essentially require that high- and low-income workers be treated alike in the plan.

11. The new limit was enacted in the Omnibus Budget Reconciliation Act (OBRA) of 1987.

12. The expression is the same as in chapter 12, note 6, except that the wage-growth factor $(e^{(.10 \times 25 \text{ years})})$ is replaced by the factor 1.5.

13. That is, $1.5 e^{-.10(24)} \approx \$0.13$.

14. For example, at year fifteen, $PVT(15,0) \times 150\% = .1 \times 15 \text{ years} \times \$10 e^{-.10(10)} \times 150\% = \$8.27$.

15. The old limit still applies, however, so that contributions in excess of ongoing liabilities are not permitted.

16. This number is derived by calculating the value of the pension savings outside the trust fund and multiplying by the assumed interest rate (10 percent) times the assumed tax rate (33 percent), accumulating the tax over twenty-five years, and expressing it in real terms.

17. Liabilities for the plan are obtained by adding the liability for each of twenty-five workers in the firm, with service levels varying from zero to twenty-five years. At a 10 percent interest rate, and 10 percent wage growth, ongoing liabilities in this pension plan amount to $312. The termination value of benefits multiplied by 150 percent turns out to be $237, or $75 less than ongoing liabilities. If the tax rate is 33 percent and interest earnings are $7.50 (10 percent interest rate times $75), the effective tax levied against pension savings amounts to $2.50 per year (33 percent tax times $7.50 in interest earnings). This tax is equivalent to 9.9 percent of the annual pension benefits distributed from the trust fund, which amount to $25 per year.

18. I incorporate retirees into the model by assuming that the $25 benefit value in the multiperson firm described above is the result of an indexed annuity paid from age 65 until death at age 80. Including retirees reduces the impact of the new limit because retiree annuities, whether flat nominal amounts or contractually indexed to inflation (as in my model), are counted as ongoing and termination benefits in the Internal Revenue Code (IRC).

19. ERISA stands for the Employee Retirement Income Security Act.

20. See the American Academy of Actuaries, Committee on Pension Actuarial Principles and Practices, *Pension Cost Method Analysis, 1985* (Washington, D.C.: American Academy of Actuaries, 1985).

21. Assets equal ongoing liabilities (using the interest rate and salary projection assumptions given above), plus normal cost contributions to accommodate new accruals during the year. At the start of the simulations, there are neither

experience gains nor losses to amortize, nor is there unfunded past service liability. I assume the actuary uses market value assets.

22. The model uses the census of workers and retirees and the wages and benefit levels in the Academy plans, and it calculates contribution amounts under either ERISA ("old") funding rules or OBRA ("new") funding rules. The plans also have built-in assumptions about turnover and mortality. The model "ages" these plans to accommodate more service accumulations, turnover, retirements, and deaths.

I assume that these firms try to attain the highest funding levels permitted by either law. Toward this end, I assume that under pre-OBRA rules, these plans use an interest rate assumption equal to the average of those used by clients of Wyatt and Company during each year over the period minus .5 percent. After OBRA, I assume they use the lowest rate permitted by law (90 percent of the so-called interest rate corridor). Overall wage growth is set equal to the interest rate minus 2 percent. In addition, the Academy plans assume some progression of salary within the firm (in real terms), based on typical experiences in firms offering these types of plans. Actual wage growth in the model is set equal to changes in the Bureau of Labor Statistics nonagricultural wage index. I assume that the plans are 100 percent invested in one-year Treasury bills.

23. The code also includes all workers earning over approximately \$99,000 in the highly compensated category even if they are below the top two deciles in the wage distribution, as well as substantial owners and top officers not otherwise included in the salary guidelines; see Allen et al., *Pension Planning*, at chapter 1, note 5, and Daniel Garrett, "The Effects of Nondiscrimination Rules on 401k Contributions," mimeographed, Stanford University, 1996. The salary guidelines are indexed; the numbers cited here pertain to 1994.

24. Let the simple average contribution rate (expressed as a percentage of the cash wage) of the lower-compensation group be $c_{LC}$. The highly compensated group's contribution rate is restricted to $c_{HC} = \max\{1.25c_{LC}, \min(2c_{LC}, 2\% + c_{LC})\}$. Over the range $1\% < c_{LC} < 8\%$, then $c_{HC}^{\max} = c_{LC} + .02$. For $c_{LC} > 8\%$, then $c_{HC}^{\max} = 1.25 \times c_{LC}$, so that, for example, if $c_{LC} = 10\%$, then $c_{HC}^{\max} = 12.5\%$.

25. I implicitly assume that the highly paid group has sufficient savings in tax-exposed vehicles so that its supply curve to the 401k plan is horizontal at $m = 0$ over the relevant range.

26. Substitute expressions (12.3) and (12.6) into (12.8), differentiate with respect to $m$, and set the result equal to zero.

27. Substitute (12.3), (12.6), and (12.9) into (12.8) and divide by $W_{HC}$.

28. The value of a dollar of savings in a tax-exposed vehicle is $W = (1 - t)e^{i(1-t)n}$ over $n$ periods, where $i$ is the interest rate and $t$ is the marginal tax rate (assumed constant over the relevant range). An investment of $1 - T$ accumulated at the tax free rate yields the same end period wealth: $(1 - T)(1 - t)e^{in} = W$, which implies that the tax savings, $T$, is $1 - e^{-itn}$. When $t = .4$, $i = .08$, and $n$ = twenty years, the value of the tax savings, $T$, is .47. If the interest rate is 10 or 6 percent, then $T$ is .55 or .38; if the tax rate is .3 or .5, then $T$ is .3 or .55; if the horizon is 10 or 30, then $T$ is .27 or .62.

29. Among those not highly compensated, the average annual salary re-

ported in the CPS is $30,866 in 1994 dollars. Since the CPS truncates the wage data at approximately $66,000 in 1994 dollars, I use the HRS data to get some estimate of average wage above this level. Adjusting the 1992 HRS data to 1994 dollars, I find that the average salary in this group is approximately $90,000. Thus the ratio of $W_H/W_L$ is approximately 3.

30. The results of a tobit estimate in table 10.6 show estimates of incremental effects on the matching variable of .003 (1988 data) and .011 (1993 data). I use a number at the upper range of the estimates. The CPS does not report the amount of the matching formula, but other data suggest that a 50 percent match rate is prevalent. See U.S. Department of Labor, *Employee Benefits*, at chapter 2, note 3. Thus, if the savings rate increases by 1.1 percent for a match of 50 percent, the results suggest an estimate of $b$ in (12.11) equal to 2.2 percent, or $b = .022$.

31. I use wage data in the 1988 CPS, May supplement, for workers covered by 401k plans. Adjusting to 1988 wage levels, the CPS data reveal that among workers covered by 401k plans, approximately 8 percent are "highly compensated" (earning more than $66,000 per annum in 1993 dollars), and 92 percent are "not highly compensated."

32. In question 21 of form 5500, all 401k plans that impose some participation limit (for example, a one-year waiting period) must provide information concerning the number of highly compensated workers compared with the total eligible for participation. These fields are completed by approximately one-fourth of pensions; these plans have 9 million participants.

33. For example, suppose that with a matching amount, 50 percent of those not highly paid contribute 10 percent of their pay to the 401k, and the other 50 percent of workers in this group save nothing. Recall that the average pay in this group is about $30,000. Assuming that the firm cannot ex post reduce wages for participants selectively, it effects the compensating differential by reducing the $30,000 salary to the not highly paid by $750. After matching, half of the workers are effectively paid $30,750 and half $29,250. A 5 percent range in pay has been created even though the firm values all these workers the same.

34. I set the omitted firm-size category to 500–1,000 employees. The dependent variable is $n_{HC}/n_{LC}$. I have the following results:

| Coefficient | $t$-Value Firm-Size | Dummy Variable (number of employees) |
|---|---|---|
| .136 | 17.83 | Intercept |
| .016 | 1.12 | <500 |
| .008 | 0.65 | 1,000–1,999 |
| −.02 | 1.95 | 2,000–4,999 |
| −.02 | 1.92 | 5,000–9,999 |
| .001 | 0.10 | 10,000 or more |

$r^2 = .01$, observations = 1,631, mean of dependent variable = .13 (median = .087). The median is similar to the 8 percent estimate from the CPS (see chap. 12, n. 31).

35. These numbers are based on the 1988 CPS, May supplement.

CHAPTER THIRTEEN

1. The latest data available pertain to 1992. In that year, $78 billion in benefits was paid from defined benefit plans. Assets in defined benefit plans amounted to about $1 trillion. See U.S. Department of Labor, Pension and Welfare Benefits Administration, *Abstract of 1991 Form 5500 Annual Reports*, no. 4 winter 1996.

2. In 1992 defined contribution plans paid about $75 billion to pension beneficiaries, mostly in lump sums. See Pension and Welfare Benefits Administration,*Abstract,* at chapter 13, note 1. Also see U.S. Department of Labor, Pension and Welfare Benefits Administration, *Trends in Pensions 1992* (Washington, D.C.: GPO, 1992).

3. These plans can, and often do, offer annuity benefits as an option. Virtually no defined contribution plan requires a benefit in annuity form.

4. Individuals not covered by pensions can save up to $2,000 a year in Individual Retirement Accounts.

5. For example, see David Bradford, *Blueprints for Basic Tax Reform* (Washington, D.C.: U.S. Department of the Treasury, 1977), and Robert Hall and Alvin Rabushka, *The Flat Tax*, 2d ed., (Stanford, Calif.: Hoover Institution Press, 1995).

6. The present value of $1 in twenty-five years, given an interest rate of 10 percent, is .082; thus $7.30 × .082 = $0.60.

7. See the previous note.

8. It also is apparent why consumption tax treatment of *all* savings has been proposed. See Hall and Rabushka, *Flat Tax,* at chapter 13, note 5.

9. The restrictions are specifically addressed to discrimination in favor of highly compensated employees. The rules, which are numerous and complex, are found in IRC 401(a)(4), 410(b), and 401(a)(26). Also, see Allen et al., *Pension Planning,* at chapter 1, note 5.

10. Different plans can cover broad categories, such as blue- and white-collar workers, and different subsidiaries and divisions, but the plans cannot be arranged to give favorable treatment to higher-wage earners.

11. Exceptions are possible. For example, if one portion of the workforce is covered by a union, it may have a different plan than nonunion workers do. Also, the firm can discriminate *against* higher-income workers; that is, it can offer more benefits to lower-paid workers compared with higher-paid workers.

12. See Clark and McDermed, *Choice of Pension Plans,* at chapter 7, note 3, and Hay-Huggins Company, *Pension Plan Cost Study,* at chapter 12, note 1.

13. For example, as of 1997 actuaries are required to cap projected salary at the age 65 retirement date beyond $160,000. This cap can seriously limit plans with young workers who earn modest salaries. See Allen et al., *Pension Planning,* at chapter 1, note 5.

14. These restrictions are found in IRC 4980 A(c).

15. Workers not covered by pensions are permitted to save only $2,000 per year in an Individual Retirement Account that is afforded full pension tax treatment. Others who have coverage are entitled to only a partial tax advantage compared with firm-offered pensions.

16. Some high discounters may continue to be covered because some firms

that want to attract low discounters may require pension coverage by all workers in the firm. To the extent that these pensions pay annuities, some high discounters who inadvertently end up accumulating long tenure in these firms will have private pension income during retirement.

## CHAPTER FOURTEEN

1. Presumably, if high discounters see impoverished old people who did not save, then as they themselves approach old age they will begin to respond by saving. If they know that the government will bail them out, however, they will have no incentive to contribute to the savings pool.

2. This is not a new idea and has been used many times to provide an economic justification for government involvement in public retirement programs. See, for example, Richard A. Musgrave and Peggy B. Musgrave, *Public Finance in Theory and Practice*, 2d ed. (New York: McGraw-Hill, 1976), 687. In a broader context, other theories of social security have been suggested. See Alan Blinder, "Why Is the Government in the Pension Business?" in *Social Security and Private Pensions*, ed. Susan M. Wachter (Lexington, Mass: Lexington Books, 1988).

3. See Martin Feldstein, "Social Security, Induced Retirement and Aggregate Capital Accumulation," *Journal of Political Economy* 82 (September 1974): 905–26.

4. The problem arises because pay-as-you-go money displaces money that otherwise would be saved in the capital markets to support future consumption. See Feldstein, "Social Security," at chapter 14, note 3.

5. I refer to the social security system broadly, including Old Age, Survivors, and Disability Insurance (OASDI), Medicare including Hospital Insurance (HI) and supplemental insurance, Medicaid for the aged, and Supplemental Security Income for the aged (SSI).

6. See U.S. Social Security Administration, *Annual Statistical Supplement to the Social Security Bulletin, 1996* (Washington, D.C.: GPO, 1997), 35.

7. See, for example, Richard Burkhauser and John Turner, "When Is the Social Security Tax a Tax?" *Public Finance Quarterly* 13 (1985): 253–68, and Richard Burkhauser and Jennifer Warlick, "Disentangling the Annuity from the Redistributive Aspects of Social Security in the U.S.," *Review of Income and Wealth* 27 (December 1981): 401–21.

8. This problem is attributable to the so-called baby boom generation and to increasing expected lifetimes.

9. See Eugene Steuerle and Jon Bakija, *Retooling Social Security for the 21st Century* (Washington, D.C.: Urban Institute, 1994). The numbers I show in figure 14.1 are taken from table 5.3 in their book. The numbers exclude some mortality adjustments they make in separate tables, but the qualitative nature of the results is not changed by this omission. Other estimates can be found in Michael Boskin et al., "Social Security: A Financial Appraisal across and within Generations," *National Tax Journal* 40 (March 1987): 19–34. These calculations show that for the cohort retiring in 2025, the internal rate of return is in the vicinity of 1 percent, which suggests that on average social security is partly a tax. In addition, Boskin et al. did not account for higher taxes required to balance the funds, and they relied on midrange social security projections.

10.   Board of Trustees, Federal OASIDI Trust Funds, *The 1996 Annual Report of the Board of Trustees of the Federal OASI and DI Trust Funds* (Washington, D.C.: GPO, 5 June 1996).

11.   The authors use the following definitions: average wage is the so-called average wage index used by the Social Security Administration, high wage is the maximum wage subject to the OASI assessment, and low wage is 45 percent of the average wage. See Steuerle and Bakija, *Retooling,* at chapter 14, note 9.

12.   Using intermediate assumptions and looking at the seventy-five-year social security projection, the deficit in the OASI trust fund is approximately 1.9 percent, compared with the 10.5 tax rate now in effect. See *Trustees' Report,* 113, at chapter 14, note 10.

13.   Dean Leamer, "Cohort-Specific Measures of Lifetime Net Social Security Transfers," Office of Research and Statistics, Social Security Administration, 1994; and "A Guide to Social Security Money's Worth Issues," *Social Security Bulletin* 58 (summer 1995): 3–20.

14.   ERISA requires that the spouse benefit be at least 50 percent, but many firms offer retirees a choice of different spouse benefit levels. The retiree's annuity is reduced appropriately depending on the survivor benefit. See U.S. Department of Labor, *Employee Benefits,* at chapter 2, note 3.

15.   In the example used, the amounts are implicitly indexed to prices.

16.   Worker A's spouse could take the same "spouse benefit" of $300, but her own benefit of $600 exceeds the spouse benefit.

17.   Similarly, consider worker C, who also earns a $600 monthly social security benefit. His spouse earns her "own" benefit of say $400 in exchange for her contributions to the system. On his death, the spouse receives his benefit of $600 in place of her $400 benefit. There is no reduction in these annuities to offset the survivor benefits.

18.   This tax is in addition to the higher marginal tax rate on their labor caused by progressivity in the normal income tax schedule and by the "marriage penalty" built into the existing tax code. In effect, second earners are not treated de novo in the tax system as in a two-earner household without the benefit of marriage, but instead their income is taxed at higher marginal rates from the first hour worked.

19.   See Steurle and Bakija, *Retooling,* at chapter 14, note 9. The authors also show that the survivor benefit, even when both spouses collect their own benefits, awards a substantial windfall to married workers with different wage histories. Their numbers show that for a high-wage male and average-wage female who are both single and turn 65 in the year 2030, their combined lifetime taxes are $689,000. Present value benefits for both together are $449,000. If the same two individuals get married, their total taxes are the same, but the total present value benefits amount increases to $534,100. The incremental benefit of $85,000 is the present value of the spouse's survivor claim to the husband's higher benefit (p. 118).

20.   Life insurance is usually phased out or eliminated after retirement.

21.   Some firms offer the same absolute amount of insurance to all employees. See U.S. Department of Labor, *Employee Benefits,* at chapter 2, note 3.

22.   The life insurance benefit is 1.5 times $24,444. The survivor benefit is calculated as follows: the regular benefit the worker is entitled to is twenty

years, times 1 percent times $24,444, or $4,888 per year. The joint and survivor (J&S) benefit is 90 percent of this annuity, or $4,400. The survivor benefit is 50 percent of this amount, or $2,200. The spouse is entitled to this annuity from the date the worker would have been eligible (fifteen years hence because he was 40 years old). Assuming the spouse is female, her life expectancy from age 55 is 27.15 years (using social security mortality tables), and thus, using a 7 percent interest rate, the present value of the annuity at age 55 is $26,730. Since the spouse now is age 40, the lump sum she is entitled to is this amount, discounted for fifteen years at 7 percent per annum, or $9,355.

23.   Some plans may impart a subsidy to the J&S option.

24.   In 1995, the amount was $886. See *Statistical Supplement,* 70, at chapter 14, note 6.

25.   That is, $e^{-.02 \times 25 \text{ years}} \approx .6065 \times \$168,146 = \$101,985.$

26.   I multiply the $880 benefit by the ratio of twenty to forty-five: there are twenty years of contributions before death, and forty-five years of contributions had the worker lived through age 65.

27.   The cap differs depending on the wage level of the worker. In 1995, this cap was $1,617. See *Statistical Supplement,* 70, at chapter 14, note 6.

28.   Using continuous discounting and ignoring mortality for the children and the spouse over ages 40–54, the present value of a fourteen-year annual $1 annuity is $12.21 using a two percent interest rate. Since the annuity is $1,608 per month or $19,296 per annum, the present value is 12.21 times $19,296, or $235,604. The monthly annuity in years fifteen and sixteen is $1,320 per month or $15,840 per annum. The present value of this annuity is 1.48, and thus its present value is $15,840 times 1.48, or $23,443. Thus the total family benefits are $259,047.

29.   This annuity equals the full $880 benefit that accrues to a worker who contributes to the system until age 65 times proportional service of the deceased worker (in this case, twenty years compared with forty-five years).

30.   This value is equal to the J&S present value in table 14.1, scaled down to reflect fewer years of service accrued to date.

31.   The amount of benefits included in taxable income is the amount by which social security benefits exceed $25,000 times one-half. Thus if benefits are $12,000 and other taxable income is $32,000, the full $12,000 times 50 percent of benefits is taxed. If other taxable income is $26,000, then $6,000 times 50 percent is taxed.

32.   Under the Hall-Rabushka flat consumption tax, all social security contributions are taxable, but all benefits are exempt from taxation. The same result is derived: all money used to support retirement consumption is taxed only once. See Hall and Rabushka, *Flat Tax,* at chapter 13, note 6.

33.   *Statistical Supplement,* 19, at chapter 14, note 6.

34.   In this sense high discounters are the most likely candidates to evade the social security system, reinforcing the need to eliminate the SSI income guarantee now in place.

35.   In the context of the social security system, fair adjustments mean that the present value of benefits is expected to be the same regardless of age of retirement. The calculation assumes normal life expectancy and a discount rate equal

to the riskless interest rate. In 2005, the annuity will increase 8 percent for each year that benefits are postponed beyond normal retirement age.

36. Differential life expectancies across the population also mean that the actuarial adjustments may not be fair to all workers, which also argues for eliminating the earnings test. Also see Reimers and Honig, "Responses," at chapter 9, note 5, and A. Samwick, "Discount Rate Heterogeneity and Social Security Reform," unpublished paper, Dartmouth College, 1996.

CHAPTER FIFTEEN

1. Of new beneficiaries added to the social security rolls in 1995, 28 percent were disabled workers and their spouses and children. Of the $513 billion in benefits paid from the three social security trust funds, including part (b) Medicare supplements, in 1995, $199 billion was paid from the disability program and Medicare. Money from other public programs outside social security also is devoted to support for the aged and disabled, notably $85.1 billion by the Medicaid program and $23.5 billion from Supplemental Security Income (SSI) for the aged and disabled. See *Statistical Supplement*, 270, 181, 304, 343, at chapter 14, note 6.

2. See *Trustees' Report*, 7, 113, at chapter 14, note 10, and Board of Trustees of the Federal HI Trust Fund, *The 1996 Annual Report of the Board of Trustees of the Federal HI Trust Fund* (Washington, D.C.: GPO, 1 June 1996), 44.

3. See *Statistical Supplement*, 272, at chapter 14, note 6.

4. See *Statistical Supplement*, 19, at chapter 14, note 6.

5. In effect, older workers who have no employment opportunities commensurate with their skills are candidates for the disability program. See E. Berkowitz, "An American Perspective on Disabled Programs," unpublished paper, George Washington University, 1993.

6. See Carolyn Weaver, "Reassessing Federal Disability Insurance," *Public Interest* 106 (winter 1992): 108–21, and Berkowitz, "American Perspective," at chapter 15, note 5.

7. By this I mean that the present value of social security benefits is higher the earlier a worker can gain entry into the disability program.

8. See Weaver, "Reassessing," at chapter 15, note 6.

9. For a review of the literature, see Jonathan Leonard, "Labor Supply Incentives and Disincentives for Disabled Persons," in *Disability and the Labor Market: Economic Problems, Policies and Programs*, ed. Monroe Berkowitz and M. Anne Hill (Ithaca: ILR Press, Cornell University, 1986).

10. See, for example, Richard Burkhauser, "Accommodation in the Work Place: The Importance of ADA on Overall Disability Policy," unpublished paper, Syracuse University, 1993.

11. See Carolyn Weaver, "Incentives versus Controls in Federal Disability Policy," in *Disability and Work: Incentives, Rights and Opportunities*, ed. Carolyn Weaver (Washington, D.C.: American Enterprise Institute, 1991), 3–18.

12. See Carolyn Weaver, "Social Security Disability Policy in the 1980s and Beyond," in Berkowitz and Hill, *Disability*, at chapter 15, note 9; and Weaver, "Reassessing," at chapter 15, note 6.

13. See Weaver, "Social Security Disability Policy," at chapter 15, note 12. In effect, the rules were changed so that benefits were not eliminated merely by demonstrating a person's ability to work. Instead, it had to be shown that the disabled individual's condition had materially improved since the date of entry into the program.

14. See Weaver, "Incentives," at chapter 15, note 11.

15. See Burkhauser, "Accommodation," at chapter 15, note 10.

16. See *Annual Statistical Supplement*, 270, at chapter 14, note 6.

17. See *Annual Statistical Supplement*, 283, 285, at chapter 14, note 6.

18. That is, the number of years between age 18 and 62 is forty-four: thus $1,000 \times \exp(-.005 \times 44) = .802$.

19. See *Trustees' Report*, 34, 113, at chapter 14, note 10.

20. The present value of taxes for the disabled is obviously less than that of taxes paid by workers who remain employed until age 65: This difference in taxes is the amount of the insurance.

21. The long-term stable assessment for the DI program under current acceptance criteria is 2.2 percent under intermediate assumptions (*Trustees' Report*, at chapter 14, note 10). It follows that reducing the rolls by approximately one-half would yield an equilibrium tax rate in the range of 1 percent.

22. The budget would be allocated to each state in proportion to taxes collected there.

23. An evaluation program would have to be devised to determine if some panels were systematically scoring applicants either too high or too low. One scheme would be to pay bonuses to panels based on the standard deviation of their scores from the mean values attached to each applicant evaluated. Panels that systematically exhibited extreme scores might be eliminated from the program.

24. Exceptions could be made for those so severely and permanently disabled as to ensure a negligible denial rate on future examinations.

25. It still is not a market rate because it does not reflect different risks across occupations.

26. Medical benefits to retirees and disabled are $221 billion; Medicaid benefits to the disabled are $48.5 billion. These amounts are 43 percent of total expenditures on the aged and disabled ($622 billion). SSI amounts and states' shares of Medicaid expenditures are not included in these numbers.

27. See J. Lubitz and G. Riley, "Trends in Medicare Payments in the Last Years of Life," *New England Journal of Medicine* 328 (15 April 1993): 1092–96. The cost implications of Medicare are not necessarily restricted to the trust fund per se. Owing to restrictions on Medicare reimbursements, overhead expenses of medical care providers may have disproportionately shifted to patients covered by private insurance. See Wyatt Company, *Employer-Sponsored Health Benefits Programs: A Chronic Affliction or a Growing Malignancy?* (Washington, D.C.: Wyatt, 1992). Support for this argument is found in the finding that private insurance policy premiums have been increasing faster than medical prices. See Foster-Higgins, *Health Care Benefits Survey*, various years.

28. Sylvester Scheiber and J. Poullier, "International Health Spending: Issues and Trends," *Health Affairs* 10 (spring 1991): 113.

29.   This number represents the average monthly OASI benefit of $697 times twelve months. See *Statistical Supplement,* 19, at chapter 14, note 6.

30.   This number represents the total expenditures for old age medical care ($36.5 billion for over age 65 Medicaid and $129 billion for Medicare for the aged), divided by 26.6 million retirees in the OASI system (*Statistical Supplement,* 200, 327, 343, at chapter 14, note 6).

31.   Vouchers are a common solution for the inherent inefficiency embedded in government delivery systems of public goods. They form the basis for a recent proposal for national health care. See Stuart M. Butler and Edmund F. Haislmaier, eds., *A National Health System for America,* rev. ed. (Washington, D.C.: Heritage Foundation, 1989).

32.   See chapter 15, note 29.

33.   I do not restrict insurance firms from offering lower premiums to those who commit to policies at earlier ages.

34.   Alternatively, the market could be made entirely voluntary, in which case some workers would not be able to find insurance in the voluntary market. An assigned risk pool could then be established where poor risks are assigned to private insurers in proportion to the business they underwrite.

35.   This value could be negative for some depending on how the first-tier benefits are set; if so, some subsidy will be made by higher-wage earners. There already is a subsidy in the sense that the medical benefits are set as a proportion of social security benefits, which in turn are tilted in favor of lower-wage workers.

36.   Married workers with spouses who do not make sufficient contributions to earn their own first-tier benefit would be assessed a portion of their contributions to ensure that they and their spouses have a first-tier policy. Spouse property rights to first-tier benefits could accrue in proportion to spouse earnings during the marriage and would be accessible in the event of divorce.

37.   Under current law, the 2.9 percent Medicare tax is assessed against all labor income, regardless of limit. In effect, it is an increment to the top personal income tax bracket.

38.   The HI tax rate is fixed in the reform: the voucher amounts are set at levels that rationalize this tax rate, not vice versa.

39.   This proposal is a special case of policies that include the cost of all health insurance policies as part of taxable income. See, for example, Hall and Rabushka, *Flat Tax,* at chapter 13, note 6. Generally, the problem currently is that health insurance expenditures are exempt from taxation, thereby biasing consumption decisions in favor of too much medical expenditure.

40.   There is a good deal of variance around these estimates. For a good survey of the literature, see Ann Fisher et al., "The Value of Reducing Risks of Death: A Note on New Evidence," *Journal of Policy Analysis and Management* 8 (1989): 88–100.

41.   This calculation assumes a zero real interest rate.

42.   In reality, life expectancy is uncertain and medical providers may be risk averse. For these reasons, the policy could pay off at a rate somewhat higher than $25,000 per year and could pay something beyond actual expenses plus interest for those who outlived the payoff period. Otherwise medical procedures with clear net benefits might not be undertaken.

# SELECTED REFERENCES

## PART 1 PENSION EFFECTS ON WORKER BEHAVIOR

Allen, Steven, Robert Clark, and Ann A. McDermed. "Job Mobility, Older Workers and the Role of Pensions." *Journal of Human Resources* 28 (summer 1993): 463–81.

Berkovec, James, and Steven Stern. "Job Exit Behavior of Older Men." *Econometrica* 59 (January 1991): 189–210.

Bodie, Zvi. "Pensions as Retirement Income Insurance." *Journal of Economic Literature* 28 (March 1990): 28–49.

Burkhauser, Richard V. "The Pension Acceptance Decision of Older Workers." *Journal of Human Resources* 14 (winter 1979): 63–75.

Disney, Richard, and Edward Whitehouse. "What Are Occupational Pension Plan Entitlements Worth in Britain?" *Economica* 63 (May 1996): 213–38.

Dorsey, Stuart. "Pension Portability and Labor Market Efficiency: A Survey of the Literature." *Industrial and Labor Relations Review* 48 (January 1995): 276–92.

Fields, Gary S., and Olivia S. Mitchell. *Retirement, Pensions, and Social Security.* Cambridge: MIT Press, 1984.

Filer, Randall K., and Peter A. Petri. "A Job-Characteristics Theory of Retirement." *Review of Economics and Statistics* 70 (February 1988): 123–29.

Gustman, Alan, Olivia Mitchell, and Thomas Steinmeier. "The Role of Pensions in the Labor Market: A Survey of the Literature." *Industrial and Labor Relations Review* 47 (April 1994): 417–38.

Gustman, Alan L., and Thomas L. Steinmeier. *Pension Incentives and Job Mobility.* Kalamazoo, Mich.: Upjohn Institute, 1994.

———. "A Structural Retirement Model." *Econometrica* 54 (May 1986): 555–84.

Hanushek, Eric, and Nancy Maritato, eds. *Assessing Knowledge of Retirement Behavior.* Washington, D.C.: National Academy Press, 1996.

Hurd, Michael, and Kathleen McGarry. "The Relationship between Job Characteristics and Retirement." National Bureau of Economic Research Working Paper 4558, 1993.

Ippolito, Richard A. "The Labor Contract and True Economic Pension Liabilities." *American Economic Review* 75 (December 1985): 1031–43.

———. *Pensions, Economics, and Public Policy.* Homewood, Ill.: Dow Jones–Irwin for the Pension Research Council, 1986.

———. "Towards Explaining Earlier Retirement after 1970." *Industrial and Labor Relations Review* 43 (July 1990): 556–69.

———. "Why Federal Workers Don't Quit." *Journal of Human Resources* 22 (spring 1987): 281–99.

Johnson, Richard. "The Impact of Human Capital Investment on Pension Benefits." *Journal of Labor Economics* 3 (July 1996): 520–54.

Lazear, Edward, and Robert Moore. "Pensions and Mobility." In *Pensions in the U.S. Economy,* ed. Zvi Bodie, John B. Shoven, and David A. Wise. Chicago: University of Chicago Press, 1988.

Lumsdaine, Robin, James Stock, and David Wise. "Efficient Windows and Labor Force Reduction." *Journal of Public Economics* 43 (1990): 131–59.

Mitchell, Olivia, and R. Luzadis. "Changes in Pension Incentives through Time." *Industrial and Labor Relations Review* 42 (October 1988): 100–108.

Montgomery, Edward, Kathryn Shaw, and Mary Ellen Benedict. "Pensions and Wages: An Hedonic Price Theory Approach." *International Economic Review* 33 (1992): 111–28.

Parsons, Donald O. "The Decline in Labor Force Participation." *Journal of Political Economy* 88 (February 1980): 117–34.

Pesando, James. "The Usefulness of the Windup Measure of Pension Liabilities: A Labor Market Perspective." *Journal of Finance* 40 (1985): 927–40.

Quinn, Joseph, Richard Burkhauser, and Daniel Myers. *Passing the Torch: The Influence of Economic Incentives on Work and Retirement.* Kalamazoo, Mich.: Upjohn Institute, 1990.

Stock, James, and David Wise. "Pensions, the Option Value of Work, and Retirement." *Econometrica* 58 (September 1990): 1151–80.

PART 2 SORTING EFFECTS OF PENSIONS

Bassett, William, Michael Fleming, and Anthony Rodrigues. "How Workers Use 401k Plans: The Participation, Contribution and Withdrawal Decisions." Mimeographed. Federal Reserve Bank of New York, 1996.

Clark, Robert, and Ann McDermed. *The Choice of Pension Plans in a Changing Environment.* Washington, D.C.: American Enterprise Institute, 1990.

Curme, Michael, and William Even. "Pensions, Borrowing Constraints and Self-Selection." *Journal of Human Resources* 30 (fall 1995): 701–12.

Curme, Michael, and Lawrence Kahn. "The Impact of the Threat of Bankruptcy on the Structure of Compensation." *Journal of Labor Economics* 8 (October 1990): 419–47.

Even, William, and David MacPherson. "The Gender Gap in Pensions and Wages." *Review of Economics and Statistics* 72 (May 1990): 259–65.

Fuchs, Victor. "Time Preference and Health: An Exploratory Study." In *Eco-*

*nomic Aspects of Health,* ed. V. Fuchs. Chicago: University of Chicago Press for National Bureau of Economic Research, 1982.

Garrett, Daniel. "The Effects of Nondiscrimination Rules on 401k Contributions." Mimeographed. Stanford University, 1996.

Gustman, Alan, and Thomas Steinmeier. "The Stampede towards Defined Contribution Plans." *Industrial Relations* 31 (spring 1992): 361–69.

Hausman, Jerry. "Individual Discount Rates and the Purchase and Utilization of Energy-Using Durables." *Bell Journal of Economics* 10 (spring 1979): 33–54.

Hay-Huggins Co. "Pension Plan Expense Study for the PBGC." Final report submitted to the Pension Benefits Guaranty Corporation, June 1990.

Ippolito, Richard A. "Explaining the Growth of Defined Contribution Plans." *Industrial Relations* 34 (January 1995): 1–20.

———. "Pensions and Indenture Premia." *Journal of Human Resources* 29 (summer 1994): 795–812.

———. "A Study of Wages and Reliability." *Journal of Law and Economics* 39 (April 1996): 149–90.

Kruse, Douglas. "Pension Substitution in the 1980s: Why the Shift towards Defined Contribution Plans?" *Industrial Relations* 34 (April 1995): 218–41.

Kurz, Mordecai, Robert Spiegelman, and Richard West. *The Experimental Horizon and the Rate of Time Preference for the Seattle and Denver Income Maintenance Experiments.* Occasional Paper. Stanford, Calif.: Stanford Research Institute, November 1973.

Kusko, Andrea, James Poterba, and David Wilcox. "Employee Decisions with Respect to 401k Plans: Evidence from Individual-Level Data." National Bureau of Economic Research Working Paper 4635, 1994.

Lawrence, Emily. "Poverty and the Rate of Time Preference: Evidence from Panel Data." *Journal of Political Economy* 99 (February 1991): 54–77.

Maital, Shlomo, and Sharona Maital. "Time Preference, Delay of Gratification and the Intergenerational Transmission of Economic Inequality." In *Essays in Labor Market Analysis,* ed. O. Ashenfelter and W. Oates. New York: John Wiley, 1977.

Papke, Leslie. "Participation in and Contributions to 401k Pension Plans: Evidence from Plan Data." *Journal of Human Resources* 30 (spring 1995): 311–25.

Petersen, Mitchell. "Cash Flow Variability and Pension Plan Choice: A Role for Operating Leverage." *Journal of Financial Economics* 35 (December 1994): 361–83.

Samwick, Andrew. "Discount Rate Heterogeneity and Social Security Reform." Unpublished paper, Dartmouth College, 1996.

PART 3 INTERNAL DISCOUNT RATES AND PUBLIC POLICY

Berkowitz, Monroe, and M. Anne Hill, eds. *Disability and the Labor Market: Economic Problems, Policies and Programs.* Ithaca: ILR Press, Cornell University, 1986.

Burkhauser, Richard, and John Turner. "When Is the Social Security Tax a Tax?" *Public Finance Quarterly* 13 (July 1985): 253–68.

Burkhauser, Richard, and Jennifer Warlick. "Disentangling the Annuity from the Redistributive Aspects of Social Security in the U.S." *Review of Income and Wealth* 27 (December 1981): 401–21.

Burtless, Gary. "Social Security, Unanticipated Benefit Increases and the Timing of Retirement." *Review of Economic Studies* 53 (October 1986): 781–805.

Engen, Eric, William Gale, and John Scholz. "Do Savings Incentives Work?" *Brookings Papers on Economic Activity* 1 (1994): 85-180.

Gustman, Alan, and Thomas Steinmeier. "Changing the Social Security Work Rules after 65." *Industrial and Labor Relations Review* 44 (July 1991): 733–45.

Leamer, Dean. "Cohort-Specific Measures of Lifetime Net Social Security Transfers." Office of Research and Statistics, Social Security Administration, 1994.

———. "A Guide to Social Security Money's Worth Issues." *Social Security Bulletin* 58 (summer 1995): 3–20.

Poterba, James, Steven Venti, and David Wise. "Do 401(k) Contributions Crowd out Other Personal Savings?" *Journal of Public Economics* 50 (1995): 1–32.

Reimers, Cornelia, and Marjorie Honig. "Responses to Social Security by Men and Women: Myopic versus Far-Sighted Behavior." Mimeographed, Hunter College, 1993.

Samwick, Andrew, and Jonathan Skinner. "How Will Defined Contribution Pension Plans Affect Retirement Income?" National Bureau of Economic Research, October 1993.

Steuerle, Eugene, and Jon Bakija. *Retooling Social Security for the 21st Century.* Washington, D.C.: Urban Institute, 1994.

Weaver, Carolyn. "Reassessing Federal Disability Insurance." *Public Interest* 106 (winter 1992): 108–22.

OTHER BOOKS

Allen, E., J. Melone, J. Rosenbloom, and J. VanDerhei. *Pension Planning,* 7th ed. Homewood, Ill.: Richard D. Irwin, 1992.

Bodie, Zvi, John Shoven, and David Wise, eds. *Pensions in the U.S. Economy.* Chicago: University of Chicago Press, 1988.

Cornwell, Christopher, Stuart Dorsey, and David MacPherson. *Pensions and Productivity.* Kalamazoo, Mich.: Upjohn Institute, forthcoming.

Ghilarducci, Teresa. *Labor's Capital: The Economics and Politics of Private Pensions.* Cambridge: MIT Press, 1992.

Ippolito, Richard A. *An Economic Analysis of Pension Tax Policy in the United States.* Homewood, Ill.: Richard D. Irwin, 1990.

———. *The Economics of Pension Insurance.* Homewood, Ill.: Richard D. Irwin, 1989.

Latimar, Murray. *Industrial Pension Systems.* New York: Industrial Relations Counselors, 1932.

McGill, Dan, K. Brown, J. Haley, and Sylvester Schieber. *Fundamentals of Private Pensions,* 7th ed. Philadelphia: University of Pennsylvania for the Pension Research Council, 1996.

Turner, John. *Pension Policy for a Mobile Labor Force.* Kalamazoo, Mich.: Upjohn Institute, 1993.

Turner, John, and Noriyasu Watanabe. *Private Pension Policies in Industrialized Countries.* Kalamazoo, Mich.: Upjohn, Institute, 1995.

Wise, David A., ed. *Pensions, Labor, and Individual Choice.* Chicago: University of Chicago Press, 1985.

# INDEX